Praise for
magical journey

"This luminous memoir is a gift to any reader searching for meaning, clarity, and perhaps a bit of hard-won joy. Katrina Kenison is the best kind of guide through our life's passages: a thoughtful, fearless friend who reaches out a hand and says, *I've been here, too.*"
— Dani Shapiro, author of *Devotion*

"An extended meditation on a certain passage in life—one composed of loss and gain, deprivation and sustenance. Kenison learns the way to relinquish old pleasures and to seek out new pathways. This is a guide that we all can use— warm, intelligent and compassionate."
— Roxana Robinson, author of *Cost*

"The afternoon of life can cast long shadows, but Katrina's beautiful observations on love, loss, growth and gratitude will brighten readers' worlds considerably. You won't find a better guide or friend to accompany you through the sorrows, joys, and mysteries we are all meant to share."
— Priscilla Warner, author of *Learning to Breathe*

"No matter where you are on the journey, Kenison's own pilgrimage points the way home. She gives us permission to stop trying to improve ourselves and invites us to relax into the wonder of who we already are."

—Regina Brett, author of *Be the Miracle*

"Kenison likens the existential midlife quest to the hero's journey described by Joseph Campbell, including the death of the old self and the painful, satisfying birth of the new. With ferocious compassion, she puts words to sensations and sudden hungers that most of us dare not name."

—Carolyn Cooke, author of
Daughters of the Revolution

"Kenison, soul bared and hand extended, is right beside us as we, too, face life's next inexorable threshold: the elusive pursuit of self-acceptance."

—Margaret Roach, author of
The Backyard Parables

"Kenison's quietly courageous search for purpose in the second half of life inspires the rest of us to examine our own ordinary lives with wonder and compassion. Deeply personal and gently instructive, this poignant memoir of loss and growth affirms that we are all intimately connected, our humble human stories more alike than different."

—Stephen Cope, Director of Kripalu's Institute for Extraordinary Living and author of *The Great Work of Your Life: A Guide for the Journey to Your True Calling*

"Reading Katrina Kenison's beautifully written story helped me appreciate my own life with a new tenderness. Her book helps us realize that although our lives don't turn out perfectly, they are precious and worthy of our love."

—Hari Kirin Khalsa, author of *Art & Yoga: Kundalini Awakening in Everyday Life*

"Katrina Kenison models powerfully effective practices for cultivating presence in our everyday lives so that we can experience more compassion for ourselves and others, thereby creating more moments of love and joy."
—Libby Barnett, MSW, Reiki Master Teacher, author of *Reiki Energy Medicine, Bringing Healing Touch into Home, Hospital, and Hospice*

"In her modern re-imagining of the mythic journey, Katrina Kenison sets out to explore the interior landscape of midlife, and from the very first page her readers are eager to come along for the ride. Kenison is at once disarmingly human and courageously wise."
—Lisa Garrigues, author of *Writing Motherhood*

"Reading Katrina's comforting words is like having a heartfelt conversation with your best friend. Her experiences may not be the same but her emotions surely are. We connect with her in a surprisingly intimate way and read with pleasure what we all know to be true."
—Bonnie Harris, author of *When Your Kids Push Your Buttons*

"After the kids are gone, Kenison faces the question that haunts every mother's empty house and every woman's passage beyond midlife: What now? Deeply wise and courageous, every page of MAGICAL JOURNEY shines with beauty and pulses with truth. Read it, and you'll want to do what Kenison does: begin again."

—Karen Maezen Miller, author of *Hand Wash Cold: Care Instructions for an Ordinary Life*

magical journey

*An Apprenticeship
in Contentment*

KATRINA KENISON

GRAND CENTRAL
PUBLISHING
LARGE PRINT

Some of the events in my story have been compressed in time for the sake of narrative flow. I've changed the names and identifying characteristics of some, but not all, of the people.

The author makes grateful acknowledgment for permission to quote from the following previously published works:

"Anthem." Copyright © 1992 by Stranger Music, Inc. All rights administered by Sony/ATV Music Publishing LLC, 8 Music Square West, Nashville, TN 37203. All rights reserved. Used by permission.

"Whatever Doesn't Serve" from *Limitless*. Copyright © 2009 by Danna Faulds. Excerpt from "Breaking All the Rules" from *Go In and In*. Copyright © 2002 by Danna Faulds. Reprinted by permission of the author.

Excerpts from *Bhagavad Gita: A New Translation* by Stephen Mitchell. Copyright © 2000 by Stephen Mitchell. Used by permission of Harmony Books/Crown Publishing.

Excerpt from *Dark Nights of the Soul* by Thomas Moore. Copyright © 2004 by Thomas Moore. Used by permission of Penguin Group USA.

"We Shake with Joy" from *Evidence*. Copyright © 2010 by Mary Oliver. Reprinted by permission of Beacon Press, Boston, Massachusetts. Excerpt from "The Summer Day" from *New and Selected Poems Volume One*. Copyright © 2010 by Mary Oliver. Reprinted by permission of Beacon Press, Boston, Massachusetts.

Excerpt from *What Now?* By Ann Patchett. Copyright © 2008 by Ann Patchett. Reprinted by permission of HarperCollins Publishers.

Grand Central Publishing
Hachette Book Group
237 Park Avenue
New York, NY 10017

www.HachetteBookGroup.com

Printed in the United States of America

RRD-C

First Edition: January 2013
10 9 8 7 6 5 4 3 2 1

Grand Central Publishing is a division of Hachette Book Group, Inc.
The Grand Central Publishing name and logo is a trademark of Hachette Book Group, Inc.

The Hachette Speakers Bureau provides a wide range of authors for speaking events. To find out more, go to www.hachettespeakersbureau.com or call (866) 376-6591.

The publisher is not responsible for websites (or their content) that are not owned by the publisher.

Library of Congress Cataloging-in-Publication Data
Kenison, Katrina.
    Magical journey: an apprenticeship in contentment / Katrina Kenison.—1st ed.
        p. cm.
    ISBN 978-1-4555-0723-8 (hardcover)—ISBN 978-1-4555-2247-7 (large print trade pbk.)—
ISBN 978-1-4555-1804-3 (e-book) 1. Resilience (Personality trait) 2. Survival. 3. Hope.
4. Mothers. I. Title.
    BF698.35.R47K46 2013
    158.1085'2—dc23
                                                                                    2012025088

For Carol Cashion,
cherished friend and fellow traveler

All the arts we practice are apprenticeship. The big art is our life.

—M. C. RICHARDS

And you? When will you begin this journey into yourself?

—RUMI

contents

contents

magical journey

prologue

*M*ostly, we play Banana.

It is the last week of July, a stretch of hot, sunny, high-summer weather, and my son and I have six schools to visit in six days, strung from the Northeast Kingdom in Vermont to the southwestern corner of Massachusetts.

We've been arguing for months. Finally, here in the confines of the car, a temporary, wary truce has sprung up. I wonder if he is as tired of the battle as I am, as anxious about taking the next step, as sad about our recent past and as tentatively hopeful about the future.

Driving south on Interstate 91, the highway an empty black ribbon unspooling beneath an infinitely blue sky, we are—dare I say it—happy together, freed by travel and possibility, glad to watch the scenery rolling by.

And, as we've done all week, we keep our eyes peeled for yellow cars. The first one to call out "banana" scores a point; the first to get five wins the game. Between yellow car sightings, I tread lightly, avoiding the hot subjects—video games, failing grades, lies—that have led to this unexpected road trip, this rather desperate, last-minute decision to look into private school for our younger son.

We listen to Steely Dan's *Two Against Nature* on Jack's iPod and keep score ruthlessly, searching parking lots, driveways, the rearview mirrors. I'm grateful for this small, safe haven of a game and glad to hear him singing along to the music. I love his new, deep, rangy voice, his presence here beside me, the fact that after a year of not knowing what to do next, we are finally doing *something*. That we've set aside our hurts and misunderstandings, and lost ourselves instead in song lyrics and a car game from childhood, seems to me a good sign. I so want to believe we're doing what's best for our son at this vulnerable moment in his young life, even if it means letting go of my own cherished vision of the way our family life ought to be. Right now, the lightness between us, the singing, and this marathon game of Banana give me hope that we are.

Still, the irony of our search for a school that will admit a student a month before fall classes start is not lost on me. I've just finished writing a book about the poignance of children growing up and leaving home, about the importance of creating and protecting family time while we still can, the need to nurture our relationships with one another and to make space in our days for laughter and intimacy and ease.

I spent a year trying to prepare myself for our older son's departure for college, blinking back tears through every "last" of his senior year, anticipating how strange it would be to set just three places at the table instead of four, and wondering all the while how I could possibly bear the end of our day-in, day-out togetherness as a family. My consolation was the fact that I'd still get to be a full-time mom for three more years. I would still be needed to pack lunches, wash uniforms, and have late-night heart to hearts. Henry had had an exclusive on his parents as an infant; Jack would get to enjoy his only-child status on the back end, for his last three years of high school.

"I'm a little jealous, cuz you took a total babe to prom," Jack had written in a funny graduation sonnet for his big brother, "but, hey bro', I'll own the bathroom once you're gone." We would miss Henry terribly, but I knew what Jack meant—he was about to get a lot more space. And I was looking forward to plenty of one-on-one time with him, to family dinners, basketball games, having his friends hanging around the house, marking every milestone of his high school career by being there.

But the reality of our younger son's sophomore year in the public high school a mile from our house never aligned with any of our expectations about how things were supposed to unfold.

While I was sitting upstairs at the desk in Henry's bedroom, writing the final pages of a memoir about family togetherness, our bright, social, athletic fifteen-year-old checked out. He quit the cross country team, quit the youth group at church, quit doing homework, and descended instead to the basement and a stash of video games that became far more compelling to him than anything his real life seemed to offer. His grades fell from As and Bs to Ds and Fs. He said he didn't care, stayed up till three, and rolled out of bed at noon. For the better part of a sleepless year, we looked like a family of raccoons, our eyes ringed with dark circles, our nerves frayed. Yet no matter how much my husband and I worried, argued, talked, cajoled, and insisted that Jack pull himself together and rejoin the world of school and sports and friends and family, he refused. We tried therapy and ADHD medication, handwritten letters and midnight confrontations, carrots and sticks, holding on tight and letting go completely. Nothing worked. He would barely get off the couch.

Sometimes, straining to see beyond his sullen expression, his defenses and excuses, his aimless fury, I would catch a glimpse of the son I knew—a jokey bit of wordplay in the midst of a conversation laced with sarcasm, a sweetness in his eyes as he cuddled with the dog, or a cry of despair from some still-tender place inside. I began to suspect that behind the insolent facade was a boy who was as miserable and confused as we were. Jack's toughest battle, it seemed, was not really with us at all, but with himself. If we were going to get him back, we realized, we would first to have to let him go.

And so we pulled him out of school and sent him off into the woods, to a wilderness program in the mountains of Georgia, where he slept under a tarp for nine weeks, carried a fifty-pound pack on his back, learned to make fires with a rock and bow drill, cooked his own food, and rediscovered the joy of being alive. When it was over, he came home changed, tanned and strong, wiser, thoughtful, and full of good intentions. But his hold on those intentions was fragile at best, and it was clear there was no going back to the way things had been before. He'd lost most of a year of high school. His GPA had plummeted and his friends had moved on. None of us wanted to risk a return to the basement. So, although boarding school had never been in the plan or in the budget, we began looking for a place that felt like a fit, a school that would be willing to give him a second chance and that would challenge him as well, a new community where he might continue to thrive and grow.

By the time Jack and I make our way south to the Berkshires and our final school visit, we are both in good spirits. Hesitant at first, he's gotten on board with the idea of a fresh start in a new place and is beginning to think of himself as a student again. He's written an honest, thoughtful essay about his time in the woods, filled out half a dozen applications, and dared to imagine a better future for himself than the virtual existence he'd swapped for reality for far too long. He is serious and forthcoming in an interview, talking about the ups and downs of the last year with a forthrightness and vulnerability that surprises me and seems to impress the admissions director. Sitting down to lunch at a café near the school, Jack is as eager to share his impressions of the morning as I am to hear them. "I can picture myself there," he says tentatively, trying the idea on for size.

As soon as we get home that afternoon, Jack asks for the car keys and heads over to a friend's house, school catalogs in hand, to consider his

options. He has until five p.m. to accept the
only open spot at his first-choice school, the
one he knows will be the toughest academi-
cally, the one with a strict dress code and Saturday morning classes, and the only school,
it turns out, that is too far away for weekend
visits home. We've told him this is his choice
to make. Now I have to keep my word and let
him do it his way—at the last minute and by
his own gut instinct, not mine. At five minutes
to five, he calls me: "I'm going," he says. "Call
them quick, before I change my mind."

And so it is that four weeks later, we deliver
our son to a boarding school three hours from
where we live. Would he like some help making up his bed? I ask, as his dad lugs the last of
his belongings up the stairs to his tiny shared
dorm room on the third floor.

"No, no, I got it," he insists, hanging his new
sport coats on the rack, arranging his ties, laying claim to his new space. He is eager to get on
with it, clearly ready for us to be gone. And that's
when it finally hits me: We are about to get in
the car and drive north to an empty house. My
life as a mother of children at home is over.

～ 1 ～

called

We do not make or create our souls, we just grow them up.

—RICHARD ROHR

anuary. It is just before 5:30 a.m. when I slip out of bed, reach into my closet for a pair of socks and an old pink cardigan fleece, and tiptoe down the stairs. Yesterday's snowstorm was followed by rain, then, overnight, plummeting temperatures and clearing skies. Fully alert yet not quite ready to begin the day in earnest, I hesitate to turn on lights, pausing in the shadowed kitchen to look out upon an icebound, silent world. The landscape is so familiar, yet different every time I look out the window, changing not only with the seasons but moment to moment, depending on the light, the hour, the mood of the sky. This morning, all is still inside and out. A fat, creamy moon, just shy of full, hangs low in the west, illuminating the shiny shell of snow on the field, the bowing, ice-encrusted pine trees, the shrouded, silent mountains that are the backdrop to my days here. It is a good place to wake up in, this solid, sheltering house on a wide open New Hampshire hilltop.

Yet there's no need for me to be up at this predawn hour. There's no place I have to be by nine, no work deadline hanging over me, no lunches to prepare, no child in the house who needs to be roused, hugged, fed, and hustled out the door. After years of alarms that always seemed to go off too soon, endless exhortations to "hurry up" and my sons' predictable pleas for "just five more minutes," my schedule is no longer dictated by career demands, school hours, or children's needs.

I've poured a thousand bowls of cereal over the last twenty-odd years; these days, the only breakfast I'm expected to make is my own. I grew so accustomed to the daily stampede of feet up and down the stairs that I ceased to hear the noise; now, silence rings in my ears. I bestowed countless hasty good-bye kisses, my attention already elsewhere as I brushed lips to cheeks—only to wake up one morning and realize that all those little good-byes had led, inevitably, to big ones.

Day after day and year after year, I wrote the tardy note, packed the snack, unearthed the lost glove, hustled boys out the door, then got down to business: cleaning, shopping, cooking, writing, editing, exercising, e-mailing, driving. And, in the midst of all that doing, I found a sense of purpose. I thought I knew exactly who I was: a married woman, a mother of two, a writer and an editor, a homemaker.

Now I suspect I didn't know *who* I was, so much as where I needed to be at any given moment and what I needed to be doing— raising a family, earning a living, being a good mom, a loving wife. I tried to pay attention, to be present and grateful as I juggled kids' schedules and publishing schedules, housework and "paid" work, writing time and family time, time alone and time with friends.

And somehow—just like every other mul-
titasking mother I know—I managed it all.
Most of the time I truly loved *doing* it all, too,
loved knowing I was an essential player in this
ongoing family drama: creating a home, tending the hearth, nurturing my loved ones, raising two sons to adulthood.

If vocation can be defined, as theologian
Frederick Buechner suggests, as "the place
where your deep gladness meets the world's
deep need," then for two decades now I have
been blessed to have had a calling. Meeting
my children's needs, I found my own deep
gladness and sense of purpose. Motherhood
enlarged my view of who I was and what I was
capable of. Being with my children, watching
them grow and change and meet the world,
deepened my own relationship with the world.
In the process, I grew, too, in ways I couldn't
have begun to imagine on the day when a flush
of pink on a little white stick first told me I was
pregnant.

That moment was a turning point, as it is
for every mother. Suddenly we go from living
for one, to a profound awareness that our exis-

tence will forevermore be inextricably bound to another. Now, more than twenty years later, I find myself poised at another crossroad, uncertain of my path, yet once again sensing that powerful inner shifts are already underway.

The little boys whose lives once seemed to consume mine are young men now, their bedrooms as silent and empty as shrines. The communal rhythms of eating and sleeping and being in our household were disrupted as my sons became adolescents and then vanished altogether when, one after the other, they left home. There are no more muddy footprints to mop up, no piano recitals or big games to attend, no book reports to proofread when I'd rather go to bed (although the occasional essay does show up on my laptop late at night).

My two sons come home often. Many of our family traditions remain intact. Yet our togetherness now is not what it once was. Enormous loads of laundry are washed, favorite meals prepared, the occasional game of Balderdash still played, hours of tennis and basketball watched on TV. But always I know: They arrive to leave again, each parting a fresh reminder of a time of life that's ended. What I didn't expect and could never have anticipated was how adrift I would feel without the constant demands of family life to anchor me in place or the small, daily tasks of motherhood to give direction and shape to my days.

I can sit at my desk writing from dawn till midnight, or not at all; who cares? And is it really worth my time and effort to cook dinner anymore—a whole meal prepared, served, and cleaned up after—for just two people? I'm not sure. I'm not even sure when to go to bed, or why I still leap up in the morning to put the coffee on at six.

I tried to sneak past my fiftieth birthday without a celebration, stunned to realize I now had fewer days left on earth than I'd lived already. And, having crested the arc of life and begun to make my way down the other side, I'm a little weak-kneed, unsure of my footing on this scrabbly descent. How am I supposed to feel about aging in a world where beauty is younger than forty years old, where wrinkles mean it's time to consider "getting some work done," and where I often feel invisible when I enter a crowded room? Going down turns out to be harder than climbing up; it seems there's more to this second part of life's journey than meets the eye—and without the familiar landmarks of day-in, day-out family duty to keep me on track, I'm not at all certain of the path.

The ache I feel deep in my breast this winter is not assuaged by any of the tasks that used to add up to a life. I manage to stay busy all day, then lie awake at night, worrying about things beyond my control. I remind myself to live in the moment, yet carry a deep sadness for moments already gone. I reach out to my teenage son and feel not the old, easy intimacy I long for, but an assertion of his new independence instead; our relationship, healing slowly, is still raw and tender to the touch, like second-degree burns on my heart. Henry, busy and thriving at college in Minnesota, takes pride in his self-sufficiency. He calls to say hello, to tell me his news, but rarely to seek my counsel. Perhaps that means I've done my job well—he knows who he is, how to take care of himself, how to create a life—but it also means that, after all these years of dedicated service, I'm essentially unemployed. I answer e-mails, pay the bills, read and write, take care of the house, spend time with my husband, bring lunch to a friend. The days are full enough. And yet, the question nibbles at my edges: What now?

At times, my nostalgia for our family life as it used to be—for our own imperfect, cherished, irretrievable past—is nearly overwhelming. The life my husband and sons and I had together, cast now in the golden light of memory, seems unbearably precious; what lies ahead, darker and lonelier and less enticing. As Franciscan priest Richard Rohr has observed, our egos "prefer just about anything to falling or changing or dying." The second half of life seems to demand that we grow familiar with all three.

Yet, the phrase *midlife crisis* doesn't exactly apply; *crisis* suggests a kind of wild recklessness, an urge to overthrow, break free, and create something brand-new out of the chaos. Having spent all these years painstakingly building a life—a life that became ever more engaging and complex as our sons became teenagers—I'm hesitant to dismantle what we all worked so hard to create. At the same time, I have to face the fact that it's already come apart.

My husband and I move around the house these days like strangers, at loose ends, so unaccustomed to living alone as a couple after twenty years of family life that I sometimes wonder if there's anything left for us to say to each other. Has it really been all about the kids? And now that it's not, what will hold us together for the next twenty years?

Emotion wells up and catches me off guard at the oddest times of day, cresting and breaking like a wave. The sight of Jack's old school bus laboring up the hill gives me a pang of missing him; he won't be getting off by the mailbox as he used to do, checking to see if a new envelope from Netflix has arrived. Attending a concert at Henry's old high school, I realize that this is the last year I'll know a single student there, the last year that any other parent will know me. Driving home from the grocery store, my eyes spill brief, sudden tears at the sight of our vacant house. Turning on lamps in the living room as dusk falls, I find myself pausing, staring out the window, wondering if I will ever again experience the passionate aliveness I felt as the center of the universe for two little boys. Wiping the kitchen counter, putting the last dish away, I'm overcome with melancholy, wishing the phone would ring or, better, that the back door would fly open and the sound of teenage voices erase the quiet.

Instead, the emptiness surrounds me. I am a mother without a child. An aging woman whose arms still feel the weight of small bodies held close, whose hands recall the outlived tasks of motherhood: brushing tears from a cheek, bandaging a pinkie finger, buttering toast, testing a bath, smoothing a cowlick into place.

I wonder if there is some new calling or purpose awaiting me in the next phase of life that might begin to compare with the joys and challenges of balancing work and motherhood and family. I wonder if the best days are behind me, and whether I can find a new sense of meaning and identity in the years to come. And I wonder if other women find themselves as confused and unsettled by this stage of life as I do; whether they, too, are asking: Shall I hold tight to what I know and do what I've always done? Or do I have what it takes to create something new in my life, to discover what is important to me now, and to claim that, become that?

As the first pink streaks appear in the sky on this frozen winter morning, I take my ritual tour through the house, straightening up as I always have: ice cream bowl into the dishwasher, sofa pillows set to rights, the newspaper tidied into a pile, a book returned to the shelf. Then I turn up the heat, sit down in the silent kitchen, and allow my thoughts to drift.

So many of the things that have shaped my sense of self and filled my life over the last two decades have slipped away—my career as an editor and the steady income that went with it; the day-in-day-out responsibilities of parenthood; youthful dreams and ambitions; my bright eyes and smooth, taut skin; even the simple expectation that I would put two meals a day on the table and the family would show up to eat them.

It seems that, just as our children are coming of age as young adults, we women confront some coming-of-age rites and passages of our own. Whether we are eager and ready for change or have it thrust upon us, we find ourselves in new territory, a little lost and fumbling for direction as the years suddenly seem to pick up speed. *Thirty, forty, fifty*— how could three-quarters of my life be over? Where did it go? A few months ago, I sat at the bedside of one of my dearest friends, holding her hand as she drew her last breath. Not a day goes by without the pang of that grief and an awareness of all she's missing. Losing her, I feel even less certain of my own footing, as if ground that only recently felt firm and solid has turned into shifting sand.

Meanwhile, in my own close circle of women friends in their forties and fifties, I see a breathtaking span of challenges and possibilities— from divorce, illness, and financial crises to new careers, revived passions, and all sorts of creative endeavors; from unexpected romantic relationships to adult children struggling and in need of support; from a new ability to say

no to unwanted demands to renewed com-
mitments to community service, friendship,
and extended family. My friends are climbing mountains, passing the bar exam, learning
to live with chronic Lyme disease, recovering
from a husband's early death, taking up the
cello, selling the family home, volunteering at
a community garden, taking painting lessons,
caring for elderly parents. What amazes me
most is not the range of these experiences, but
the fact that none of our lives today resemble
the lives we took for granted just a few short
years ago. What we all have in common is a
sense of having reached a turning point. And,
as we come face-to-face with the realities of
our changing bodies, our changing roles, our
changing lives, we are aware as never before
that our time here is finite. Picking up the
pieces of lives that have been transformed by
change, rearranging them into new patterns,
we wonder how to make good use of these
remaining years, how to live now in order to
avoid regret later. And we are compelled to
meet our true selves at last.

I'm startled these days to catch sight of

myself. Can that really be my own face reflected back at me in a shop window? "Who's that?" is always my first response to this aged person, so different from the youthful, unwrinkled woman I still feel myself inside to be. And how can I possibly reconcile this outer, older, matronly version of me with the private, inner one who, confronted now with the specter of age, has a sudden, almost unseemly desire to live more passionately, to feel more intensely, to delve down beneath the surface of my life in search of something deeper?

It's as if, rounding the corner into midlife, I could see the view up ahead abruptly transforming before my eyes. There, off on the horizon, I catch glimpses of the finish line, the inexorable end of life, and suddenly everything is up for reexamination. *All* my choices seem to matter more. Knowing my steps are numbered after all, I yearn to find my own path, and then to walk forward more thoughtfully, more deliberately, than before.

As a friend from Virginia wrote me a few days ago, "I can only make so many scrapbooks and arrange so many social events and research so many colleges. I'm afraid of those do-gooder organizations where I end up in committee meetings taking an hour to decide on what color tablecloths we should use. Been there! Done that!"

I recognized the sense of urgency beneath the humor of my friend's late-night e-mail. I feel it myself. I suspect we all do. No longer indispensable, no longer assured of our old carefully crafted identities, no longer beautiful in the way we were at thirty or forty, we are hungry and searching nonetheless. Hungry, perhaps, without even knowing what it is we hunger for.

In his classic account of the hero's journey, *The Hero with a Thousand Faces*, Joseph Campbell suggests that the universal tales, or monomyths, as he calls them, that have survived for thousands of years share a common structure. The hero is given notice that, like it or not, his life is about to change. He can refuse the adventure and cling to the past (in which case there *is* no hero, nor indeed a story to tell), or he can commit to the quest—at which time a guide, or perhaps a series of magical helpers, will appear. The hero summons his courage and prepares to cross a threshold. A painful separation ensues, as the hero leaves behind what he knows and ventures into an unknown realm, beginning the process of transformation. He confronts a series of challenges, encounters both love and hardship, and undergoes a kind of death of the old self, so a new self can come into being. "It is by going down into the abyss," Campbell writes, "that we recover the treasures of life. When you stumble, there lies your treasure."

Campbell describes a number of possible stages to the journey, including acceptance of the call, rites of initiation, confusion and chaos, achievement of knowledge and understanding, a period of rest and fulfillment, and an eventual return to the starting place, where the wisdom acquired on the quest is finally integrated and shared with others.

It is a familiar, universal plot line, providing the structure for countless tales, from the stories of Odysseus and Prometheus to the life trajectories of Buddha, Moses, and Christ; even the Star Wars trilogy took its shape from

this timeless blueprint. But as Campbell himself recognized, the great mythologies and
much of the world's storytelling focuses on
the masculine journey—male rites of passage,
male spiritual development, male archetypes,
and male outcomes.

And yet there's no getting around the fact
that midlife is a time when women, too, are
called to transformation, as our old roles and
responsibilities and assumptions shift or fall
away altogether. If the first step of the hero's
journey is to accept that, like it or not, the
winds of change are already wafting through
the house, then I suspect that many of us
women find ourselves pausing at the threshold, unsure whether we're coming or going,
poised between the old, familiar territory of
hearth and home, family and children, and
the new, uncharted landscape stretching out
before us. Having found my own sense of self
and satisfaction right here in the consuming
roles of wife and mother for so long, I can feel
myself hesitating at the door, trembling at the
unknown, a little afraid to tie up my shoes,
shoulder my bag, and set forth.

And yet, I also sense that this journey is one I have to take, even if I'm not sure yet where I'm headed. As Campbell says, "We must let go of the life we've planned, so as to accept the one that's waiting for us."

And so, although I have no plane ticket in my pocket nor any itinerary pointing the way to some exotic destination, I do feel as if I'm being called to a journey of sorts, a journey that may be more spiritual in nature than physical, but one that feels as momentous and uncertain as a pilgrimage to an unknown land. Having longed for change in the past, only to resist it when it arrived, I know the feelings of restlessness and fear that are part of any major life transition. But I'm not willing to accept the idea that the hero's journey is specifically a male story, nor that growth and change are the provenance of youth, nor that the only journeys that really count require passports and an extra pair of shoes. In fact, I suspect the opposite is true—that the most significant journeys are often inner ones, those that lead not to distant realms but to the discovery of something important and deep within ourselves.

As I contemplate the silent snowfields beyond my window on this dark winter morning, I sense a stirring of intention, movement, and metamorphosis. Deep beneath the frozen earth, new life waits, patiently biding time until the blessing of sun and the benediction of rain call it forth. Sitting here alone in my slowly brightening kitchen, I wonder if my early-morning restlessness could be preparing me for an awakening of my own. And if perhaps what has felt so much like an ending might also be a beginning.

2

loss

This existence of ours is
as transient as autumn clouds.
To watch the birth and death of beings is
like looking at the movements of a dance.
A lifetime is like a flash of lightning in
  the sky,
Rushing by, like a torrent down a steep
  mountain.

—THE BUDDHA

She's been gone three months, but I'm still not used to the world without Marie in it. Missing her, I sift through memories, as if by recalling the details that made her who she was, I might somehow keep my friend close. I can almost summon her: the warmth of her voice, her quick smile and lively brown eyes, her slim, competent hands and her peony-pink pedicured toes, the way she danced with joyous abandon to "Love Shack" on New Year's Eve, drove fearlessly through Boston traffic, stretched her fingers to the sky in triangle pose.

But no matter how hard I try to conjure the essence of Marie, I can't fill in all the empty spaces. The stark, absolute absence of her—of her life, her face, her hello on the other end of the phone, her name popping up in my e-mail box, her presence here on earth—has begun to grow, as Sylvia Plath put it, "beside me like a tree." I live in the dark shadow of that loss, the shape and color of my own life changed by the too-early end of hers. And I know now, in a way I never quite did before, that time is contingent and that anything can happen.

A little over a year before Marie died, we went hiking in the White Mountains. The trip was her idea; she wanted a change of scenery and, as she said, to spend a couple of days "where the first thing I think about when I wake up in the morning isn't the fact that I have cancer." That wasn't easy anywhere, but a remote hut on the top of a mountain with four women friends for company seemed like a good place to try.

"Bruce is pissed," she told us as she adjusted her backpack in the parking lot, dismissing her husband's objection to her adventure as a bit of unnecessary fuss. "But there was no way I wasn't going to do this. He's worried about what could happen if I have some reaction to this new drug. Well, if I do, I'll turn around." Then she said, with typical matter-of-factness, as if willing it to be so, "I'll be fine." And she was.

Although we were prepared to take it slow on the way up, there was no need. Marie never did want anyone waiting around or changing a plan on her account. She'd been in the hospital that morning, had had her blood drawn for tests and received the first round of yet another experimental treatment. No longer holding out an expectation for a cure, she wasn't about to abandon all hope either, and so she'd become a willing pioneer in uncharted medical territory, game to sign on for any clinical trial willing to admit an advanced stage-four ovarian cancer patient. If some untested drug held the possibility of stalling the disease for a while longer and buying her so much as another season of life—another child's birthday, or a walk on the beach, or a trip to the farmers' market—she was there.

On this day, she'd put in her time at the doctor's office; now, she didn't want to be treated like an invalid, or to think about her husband's fears, or to consider the fact that this might be the last hike she ever took. She just wanted to climb a mountain and enjoy the scenery and laugh with her friends.

It was easy for *me* to forget Marie was as sick as she was—in part because, when she wasn't recovering from surgery or the latest round of chemo, she still seemed so much herself. So healthy. And so much more engaged with the myriad details of living than cowed by the prospect of dying. As Marie liked to point out, she never even got a cold; apart from the fact that she had stage-four cancer, she was in "damn good shape." She also had three children who still needed her and a lifetime's worth of plans. So much living yet to do. If anyone could beat the odds, if anyone could lean into her faith and call down a miracle, she could—and, well, the alternative was still too hard to picture. And indeed, with every setback, Marie had managed to brush away the tears, gather her resources, and assume her whatever-it-takes attitude—102 pounds of tenacity. Three years into the disease she wasn't expected to survive for six months, Marie had become an expert in pulling through and moving on.

This summer, she had her own hair back along with her energy, her legs were tanned and strong, her sense of humor was as sharp as ever. The years of chemo treatments and surgeries and relapses had taken their toll, but you wouldn't know it to look at her as she cheerfully clambered up through the rocks, pausing every now and then to eat a handful of trail mix and exclaim over the view. If we'd asked a stranger on the trail to guess which one of our group was sick, Marie—fit and vibrant and so obviously happy to be where she was—might well have been the last choice.

In the hut that night, the two of us had top bunks, just across from each other in the crowded dorm room. And this is what I remember: seeing her sit up in the dissolving darkness of five a.m. to swallow her new pills. She can run, I thought to myself, but she can't hide. No matter how positive and full of life she is, there aren't any mornings now, not anywhere, when cancer isn't her first thought. I gave a little wave, blew her a silent kiss across the aisle, and we snuggled back down into our sleeping bags.

In the morning, it was pouring rain, windy, and so foggy we could barely see the trail at our own feet, let alone make out the path ahead. At some point during our slippery, sloppy, painstakingly slow descent, I snapped a photo of Marie and our friend Carol, wind-whipped and drenched, rain hoods plastered to their heads, two frozen specters emerging from a swirl of mist. We all loved that picture, not only as a record of the hellish weather but even more for what it so clearly says: that our ideas of the "perfect" day, the ideal hike, the peak experience, mean next to nothing. It's the experience of being *alive*, even if you're soaked to the skin and shivering on the side of a mountain, that means everything.

*　　*　　*

Marie and I were pregnant when we met for the first time, our bellies nearly touching as we joyously discovered that we were backyard neighbors with much more than autumn due dates and a shared bit of white picket fence in common. Over the years, as our children grew, traditions were born—neighborhood cookouts and fireworks on Town Day, candlelit harvest dinners in October, annual ladies' overnights in Maine, champagne toasts, seats at the ballet, berry picking, and birthday scones. The memories accumulated as our friendship lengthened—eighteen years' worth of pristine hand-me-down clothes delivered from her house to mine in paper shopping bags, stories shared, child-rearing advice dispensed, marriages dissected, meals eaten. Eighteen years' worth of the everyday stuff of everyday life with a backyard neighbor who was supposed to be a friend forever. Circumstance might have thrown us together, but intention was going to be the glue that held us fast, through all the ups and downs of all the years to come.

When I was torn between a dream of moving to the country, in search of more space and time and quiet, and wanting to stay forever in the beloved suburban house where my husband and I had raised our sons; when I was driving myself and my family and my friends crazy with indecision, it was Marie who patiently helped me sort through my conflicting fears and desires.

Our best time for problem solving was always six a.m., no matter what the season. The makeup of our early-morning walking group changed from day to day, with various neighborhood friends appearing, rain or shine, to walk and talk our way around the hilly loop encircling a nearby golf course. If we timed it right, we could get up to the top in time to see the sun rise over the lake and still make it back down again to our own kitchens just as our children were waking up.

The men never did get it, could not comprehend why their wives would prefer a hike in the dark to a roll in the hay in the morning, but at least they could commiserate with one another. "They choose to *walk*," my husband, Steve, once said to a few of the other guys, shaking his head in mock disbelief. It became our slogan, the words we repeated to one another on all those ridiculously cold or snowy or rainy dawns when we put on our sneakers anyway, slipped out our back doors, tried in vain to shush our wildly excited dogs, and joined one another in the driveway. "We choose to walk!" And walk we did, for years, sharing the news of our lives as we made our way through the waning darkness, the dogs forming a companionable pack of their own out in front of us.

"What will you miss most of all if you move away?" Marie asked me early one morning as we huffed up the first hill. I didn't hesitate. "You. Carol. My friends," I said.

"Well, you should just go ahead and move then" was her quick reply. "Your friends aren't going anywhere. We'll always be here and we'll always be your friends, even if we don't see you every day. And besides, it's not that far. We can visit anytime."

The call came out of the blue, as such calls usually do. I was making dinner in my parents' kitchen, where we were living until our own house got built in a nearby town. My thoughts at that moment were all about getting the meal on the table, wondering whether Steve and my dad were on their way home from work, whether I should run upstairs to see if the boys were actually doing homework.

When the phone rang and I heard Carol's greeting on the line, I missed the catch in her voice and launched immediately into some inconsequential tale of my own. "I have some news," she said gently, as if apologizing in advance for being the one to interrupt my domestic doings and send me into freefall instead. "Marie is sick. And it's serious."

And with that we were all in a new place. I instantly remembered Marie's words to me when she'd urged me to follow my heart: "Your friends aren't going anywhere." And I remembered what I'd thought silently to myself that morning nearly two years earlier, as we walked on toward the sunrise: "But someday we're going to really need each other, and then what'll we do?" Of course, I'd also believed that "someday" meant the very distant future, a bridge we wouldn't have to cross for a long, long time.

As it turned out, Marie and I were both prescient. Our friendship easily survived physical separation. And, after she was diagnosed, it seemed to me that I had but one thing to offer in the face of her devastating prognosis: a willingness—no, a certainty—that I would be there for her. "Your friends aren't going anywhere," she'd told me, and I wanted more than anything to take her at her word. I might have moved away, but I wasn't going anywhere, either. I could write, I could call, I could drive the hour and a half from my house to hers. One way or another, I would figure out how to show up, just as I knew she would have done for me.

Perhaps it is human nature to train our focus upon the slightest beam of hope when darkness threatens to overwhelm, to set our sights on good outcomes even in the midst of trials and fear, to believe in a better future in order to survive the worst days. For Marie, the cultivation of a steady, clear-eyed hope became her best defense against a disease that appeared out of nowhere and for no reason and began to chip relentlessly away at everything she loved. Hope was what gave her courage to persevere against the odds, and hope was the place in which I gladly met her—for even hope with slender roots in reality seemed preferable to despair.

Marie had never taken her life for granted; she had just assumed, as we all do, that there would be a lot more of it. When she was first diagnosed, the result of a colonoscopy that turned up a suspicious-looking mass in her colon, she was shattered. The sublimity of simply being alive was brought into sudden, high relief. Less than two weeks earlier, Carol, Marie, and I had been sitting in the early-autumn sunshine having a picnic lunch for my birthday. Three longtime friends chatting about mundane, forgettable things. We had complained grievously about our wrinkles and frown marks, debated the pros and cons of eyelifts. Now one of us was fighting for her life and no one was thinking about crow's-feet anymore.

None of us knows, really, how we'd respond to a diagnosis that brings us face-to-face with our own mortality, to an illness that means that the arc of life might be bisected and our time on earth cut short. Marie struggled to get herself oriented in this new landscape, but it didn't take her long to go into action. She set herself resolutely on the path for aggressive treatment—chemotherapy, surgery, whatever else was in her doctor's arsenal. She cleared a space in an upstairs room and began a daily practice of yoga, meditation, and prayer. She gave up red meat, alcohol, sugar, and caffeine. And then she reached out and embraced her life as it already was, only more fiercely.

Not for her the overseas trip of a lifetime, fancy dinners out, or a string of intense experiences. All she wanted was her own ordinary days, the more of them the better. She wanted to read the newspaper at the breakfast table, take a walk with her friends, weed the garden, make her son's favorite chocolate cake, go to her daughter's swim meet, write a grant proposal, cook dinner, watch TV with her husband, take the dog outside, and head upstairs to bed with a book in her hand. She wanted more of what she already had.

"I'm not going to ask, 'Why me?'" Marie

said as she steeled herself for the first of her surgeries, "because I know it could just as well be anyone. So, why not me?" And that was the chilling truth of it. Life and death: two sides of the same coin, flipped at random, heads or tails, win or lose. I wished I could somehow share my friend's burden or see some scrap of meaning in this illness that seemed so meaningless. What I was coming to realize instead was that the illness was just what it was; creating a sense of meaning was up to her, and up to all of us who loved her.

I thought about how lonely she must feel— she was sick, her friends were healthy. And that constant, inescapable fact isolated her no matter how much love and support I or anyone else might try to offer. Cancer created a new, unbridgeable distance between the busy, mundane workaday world we'd all once inhabited together and her new one, a bleak medical landscape through which she had no choice but to journey alone. The healthy can travel only so far into the territory of illness. We can bear witness to a loved one's journey, walk alongside and hold a hand, offer books and pots of soup and words of encouragement, but we can't wear someone else's shoes or carry even a part of their burden. Only yesterday, my friend's life had been simple and negotiable and seemingly boundless. Now it was complicated, finite, precarious. *Precarious.* It is an old word, with its roots in the Latin *precarius*, meaning "obtained by entreaty or mere favor, hence uncertain." Suddenly, what had felt certain was not, not at all. Little wonder then that an adjective that originally meant "full of prayers" now seemed to describe everything. It seemed that if I was going to be of any help to Marie at all, I would have to renegotiate my own relationship to prayer and to make my own peace with this randomness. To confront the precarious nature of everything head on myself, just as she was being forced to do.

"The hardest thing to deal with," she admitted soon after she was diagnosed, "is the fear." And so I prayed for strength—for her and for her family and for me, too. If grief and gratitude are kindred emotions, two sides of a coin, then courage is what it takes to accommodate both at once, to stay focused on what is beautiful and abundant even as illness carves more and more of what you love away.

It is so easy to overlook the wonder of life until something threatens to snatch it from us. How willingly we sacrifice the days of our lives to trivial distractions—silly computer games, unnecessary errands, useless worry. We get caught up in our petty concerns and miss the beauty unfolding right in front of us; rushing headlong into the next thing, we fail to appreciate the blessing of the only thing we can really claim as ours to own, the present moment. We toss a few balls into the air and start juggling as fast as we can—all in an effort to do a little more, to exert a bit more control, to feel more secure or more worthy or more accomplished. But there's nothing quite like a critical diagnosis, with its ticket to the world of hospital rooms and treatment plans, to bring all the balls crashing back to earth.

Suddenly, when life hangs in the balance, we wish we could have those lost moments back, wish we could live them differently, with more love, more attention, more patience. With more gratitude for all we so blindly took for granted. Instead, we have only the truth of right here, right now: the truth of what we really want and how we really feel, the mistakes we've made and our longing for forgiveness, the love we still yearn to give and to receive. I was not thinking about any of these things when Marie first got sick. In fact, there wasn't much time for reflection at all, so caught up was I in the day-to-day diversions of getting two sons settled into new schools in a new town, shifting my work routines to a new place and still meeting my deadlines, getting plans for a house drawn up, figuring out how to play the roles of daughter, mother, and wife in my parents' house until our own was ready.

My friend's illness was like a swift, sudden slice of a blade, cutting through all of my distraction and busyness right to the bare bone of what really mattered. Witnessing Marie's determination to appreciate every ordinary moment her illness would grant her, I had no choice but to confront the fragility of my own ordinary days. It was as if something within me suddenly shifted and woke up—to a new, piercing awareness of everything.

Recognizing that life is a moment-to-moment gift meant acknowledging not only my friend's mortality, but my own as well. The realization that in fact we are all dying, all the time, to something, nearly broke my heart, but it also opened it, helped me begin to recognize the fleeting beauty of all of life. We mourn summer's passing, but winter comes nonetheless, revealing a different landscape altogether, equally lovely in its own way. The sweetest day draws to a close, night settles in, and we turn our bodies to one another for comfort and release. The moon waxes and wanes, the tides come and go to their own eternal rhythm, relationships bloom and blossom and fade, hopes rise and fall, children are born, grow up, and leave home to create lives and families of their own. Old challenges are supplanted by new ones, and somehow we must adjust and adapt, learning to ride the waves of impermanence, change, and loss with poise.

One night, soon after we'd moved into our new house in New Hampshire, I was awaiting word from Marie in the hospital. Restless, irritable, on edge with worry for her and annoyance that Jack had yet to begin a school project that was due the next day, I could barely contain my grumpiness. Holding hands with my husband and sons, saying grace—even though on this night it was a slightly congealed pizza and a hasty salad for dinner, and no one at the table was feeling particularly happy or affectionate—I had a sudden thought: "But tonight we are all here, together, and it will not always be so."

Watching Marie struggle to accept how much she was losing, I began to appreciate all I had. I would find myself sitting on the sofa in our new house, looking out the window just to watch the clouds slide across the sky. I stood stock-still in the shower, soap in hand, over-come with gratitude for my aging, intact body—sagging a bit, wrinkling, pouchy here and there, yet sturdy still. When the first frag-ile, peach-colored poppies bloomed in the garden, I sank down beside them and gazed into their black, powdery hearts, knowing that within a week the pale, papery petals would fall to the earth. I began to pay more heed to

my complicated feelings about my sons growing up, missing the little boys they had so
recently been but also marveling at the young
men they were becoming. I wanted to hold on
tight to everything and everyone I cherished
and, at the same time, saw in a way I never had
before that living on this earth, growing older,
and growing up in the true sense of the word is
really about learning how to let go.

Writing became a way to do both, to cap-
ture what was and to transform the past into
something alive in the present. Sitting in my
quiet kitchen while the boys were at school,
collecting my thoughts and feelings onto the
page, meant that after years of change and flux
and moving from one house to another, I was
finally taking time in the day to stop and pay
attention to the small moments, the smells and
sounds and textures of my own life. I couldn't
halt the flow of time, but I could remind
myself to appreciate our days together by paying closer attention and by putting words to
details I might have brushed right past before.

There was never any question about what my
book title would be, if indeed the pages I was

writing turned out to be a book: *The Gift of an Ordinary Day*. That was the phrase I found myself repeating like a mantra as I folded socks and made fish chowder and looked over college applications and washed fingerprints off the door. If Marie's ordinary days could end in an instant, then mine could, too. Anyone's could. This simple, unavoidable truth colored everything.

Day after day, my friend was grateful to see the sun come up. At night, she chose to look upon the bright side of the moon. And in between, she tried to live her life as she always had and to spare those she loved from sadness and pain. Hard as it was to be sick, even worse was knowing that she was giving her friends and family cause to worry. And so she chose instead to offer us all the gift of her strength, to attend as much as was possible to what was good in each day, and to transform grief for all she was losing into gratitude for what she still had.

When her CA125 rose, suggesting that yet another treatment was failing, Marie sank into despair, and then she pulled herself back out again and got busy making pesto for the freezer, delighted by the abundance of basil in her garden. Three months after a bowel obstruction required yet more surgery and a colostomy, she spent a summer day at the beach with her family. "My first outing in a bathing suit, in the water, out in the sun," she reported later that night. "It was glorious and the ocean was beautiful."

"I know you didn't want to be my spiritual guide," I teased her once, "but, sorry, you already are, just by being you." It was true. It went without saying that Marie would have chosen life over her new role as mentor in the art of letting go. But she was an extraordinary teacher nonetheless. She showed by her own daily example that it is possible to enfold the process of dying into the embrace of living. It was the hardest work imaginable. And she did it the way she did everything: simply, quietly, and extraordinarily well.

"You should be home," Marie said to me one day a few months ago, as we drank the last of our green tea. "I'm sure your family needs you."

"There's no one, anywhere, who needs me right now," I answered quickly. And then, for the first time since we'd delivered Jack to school in September, it occurred to me that this was actually true. And that perhaps here was one reason, at least, to be grateful for this new, wide-open space in my life. "Steve can make his own dinner," I assured her. "The dog is fine. And there's no place I'd rather be than right here, with you."

I meant it. For years our friendship had been about doing things and going places. We'd gone to ballets and movies and South End bakeries and raspberry farms. We'd practiced yoga and shopped for jeans and planned elaborate dinner parties together. Now the doing was over, and the time had come to just be. And being—with nowhere to go and nothing to do but sit and talk and listen to each other—was enough. In fact, it was more than enough. Our conversations were sometimes light and newsy, but more often now they were deep and heartfelt and unfiltered. Either way, they were intensely comforting. There was no subject that was out of bounds, nothing, in the end, we couldn't share, nothing that went unsaid.

We had our last real conversation on a Friday in October. Henry was on his way home from school for fall break, but I was reluctant to leave my friend's bedside. She was weak but, as always, focused outward, more concerned with life than with the alternative. She wanted to know what I intended to make for dinner for Henry's homecoming and what we had planned for the weekend. "Go home and enjoy every minute of Henry's visit," she insisted. I promised her I would, and that I'd be back on Tuesday. And then, as I stood at the door and turned to say good-bye, she met my eyes with a new intensity in her own. "There is so much goodness in the world," she said, as if willing me to remember that, "so much goodness."

I wish now I'd taken note of every word on that last afternoon, when she was still so completely *here* and so absolutely herself. Wish I'd had some way of knowing then that when I saw her next, just three days later, she would have to gather her resources even to smile, and make an effort just to gaze into my face and murmur a few words. "Cute sweater," she said softly, even then, as always, finding something kind to say to *me*. And then: "You are so sweet to come. So sweet. I'm so glad you're here."

It was a brilliant, sunny October morning. Marie's husband, who had been at her side when I arrived, left to do some errands. The house was still, peaceful. I pulled up a chair and took my friend's small hand in mine. She closed her eyes. And with that she began in earnest the hard, hallowed work of leaving.

"You know, when the time comes," a wise older friend had told me, "everything will be exactly as it is meant to be." I held on to those words all through Marie's last days and found them to be true. Those who were meant to be there were there. Her grown children arrived from New York and Philadelphia, her teenage daughter stayed home from school, surrounded by girls from her swim team. Food appeared on the table, friends from near and far showed up at the door, the new puppy peed on the floor, the teenagers came and went, poems were read aloud, wine was poured, music was played, tears were shed, fires were lit, sheets were changed, and dishes were washed. There was laughter, even in the midst of sadness. Above all, there was love—healing, unconditional, infinite, all-powerful.

Death and life, one inextricable from the other. What Marie taught me, taught all of us who were with her, is that a softened heart can accommodate both, a loving home can accommodate both, a family can accommodate both. With love and instinct to guide us, her family and closest friends transformed her bedroom into a sacred space, surrounding her with photos and flowers, candles and lavender, love and reassurance. And each of us who took part in her vigil found our own fears transformed as well.

None of us really knows what to expect from death, or whether we are truly up to the task we've taken on when we promise a loved one that we'll "be there." And then, having made clear our intention to be present come what may, we find that even in the most challenging circumstances, we do know what to do. Our hearts tell us how to make love visible.

Our hands know, without being taught, how to soothe a brow, change a sick bed, and tend a body. Dying in the prime of life is hard physical work. And, despite the most attentive ministrations, life's final stages are not always beautiful. To be human, it seems, is to suffer and to pray for an end to suffering. But in the end, in the ultimate moments of life, there is peace, and grace, and even, for one brief instant, a glimpse of the great mystery beyond this earthly realm.

In the months since my friend left, I've often wondered what to do with this new knowledge, how to bear it and move forward under its weight now that she's gone. Marie's passing brought me face-to-face with my own most vulnerable self and, at the same time, revealed to me an inner fortitude I had no idea I possessed. Sitting with my friend through the long days and nights of her final week on earth, I learned much about our human capacity to be present. I learned that we can be of use simply by abiding quietly with an open heart. I learned that there is courage in acceptance, and that staying settles the soul and strengthens the spirit. Death fills us up and empties us out, both at the same time. There is only so much we can do, and yet we find meaning and peace in the work of holding space for what is. The peace comes, I think, from knowing that we are exactly where we are meant to be, and offering exactly what is ours to offer: our full, undivided, devoted attention—quite a rarity in our busy, distracted everyday lives. Having made a promise to my friend long ago that, no matter what, I would stay, I found myself relieved of any impulse to go. Staying—in mind and body and spirit—was in itself a kind of journey, and traveling quietly at her side to death's door was, apart from giving birth, the single most important thing I have ever done.

Throughout the four years of her illness, I carried my friend in my heart all the time, as did everyone else who loved her. If I wasn't with her, I was thinking about her, aware of the contrast between my relatively easy life and her increasingly difficult one. Composing long e-mails, visiting, talking, listening, trying to figure out what she might need from me and how best to offer it to her, I realized that no matter how much I gave, I was receiving just as much, if not more, in return. Marie never was comfortable taking; one way or another, she always found ways to give back, to be as true and good a friend in sickness as she had been in health.

During that time, my own life changed dramatically—a move into a new house, the loss of a job and a return to writing, the departure from home of first one son and then the other, the publication of a book, the slow creation of a new life and a new community in a new place. Through it all, Marie was my cheerleader and sounding board, continually urging me to broaden my horizons, to keep growing and changing and learning right alongside her.

Now that she's gone, I'm surprised to realize how much of her lives on in me. If it is true that the summons to change comes in many different guises, then certainly the death of a loved one can be seen as a threshold, beyond which lies new territory for all those left behind. I am both immeasurably more and immeasurably less because of my friend's presence in my life— more for having known her, less for having lost her, and yet also increasingly aware as the weeks pass of all the ways she is with me still.

Joseph Campbell asserts that once the hero commits to his quest, whether consciously or unconsciously, then magical helpers arrive to point the way. And, in fact, I find consolation in the idea that I am somehow guided now by my friend's invisible hand. Pausing, tuning in to what I've come to think of as "the Marie channel," I can almost always imagine just what she would say if she were here, can even hear the tone of her voice as she urges me forward, with me in spirit if not in body, and still supporting me in this journey between who I once was and who I'm now becoming.

I think often of her parting words to me, the ones she wanted to make absolutely sure I heard: "There is so much goodness in the world." And I know she was right, there *is* so much goodness, even in the midst of sorrow. Accepting the approach of her own death at last, what Marie discovered was not darkness but goodness; surrendering, what she experienced was not loss but courage and grace. And therein lies the lesson she left with me.

Life offers each of us the opportunity to practice dying a little every day. If I can learn to accept change and loss rather than fighting against it, perhaps I can also find my way to a freer, more light-hearted existence during these years of aging and transformation. "We shake with joy," writes poet Mary Oliver, "we shake with grief. What a time they have, these two housed as they are in the same body." This is of course the challenge: learning to allow space for both our joy and our grief. Certainly that is what Marie wanted those left behind to do in her memory—not to mourn her death, but to remember and celebrate her life by embracing and fully experiencing our own.

Even in her very last days, Marie believed she had a little more time; she still wanted to finish letters she'd begun to each of her three children. But in the end, she didn't need to write her final message down, for we all knew already exactly the words she would have used: Notice. Cherish. Laugh. Love.

I think now of a gorgeous September afternoon, when the windows were open and sunlight poured into the room where Marie,

Carol, and I were sitting together, the two of us taking turns rubbing Marie's feet. "Do you remember our hike in the Whites?" Marie asked, with just a touch of wistfulness. "Do you think we really lived that enough? Did we appreciate it enough?"

"We did," Carol and I assured her, each of us easily recalling both the joy and the rain. The joy *of* the rain. "We absolutely did."

~ 3 ~

pierced

*There are barricades around the heart
asking to be breached. Sooner or later we
all run out of excuses for staying small
and safe.*

—DANNA FAULDS

I love earrings. But the idea of anything punc-
turing, piercing, or poking my body makes me
queasy. I first tried getting my ears pierced in
college, fortified by two glasses of wine and my
friends' assurance that this was "nothing." Six
months later, I was still creeped out every time
I had to work a slender stud through the soft,
fat flesh of my ear lobe. One night, preparing
to go out, I stood in the dormitory bathroom,
teeth clenched, perspiration beading out all

over my body, and began the dreaded ritual of putting on my earrings. The next thing I knew, I was down on the cold tile floor, coming out of a dead faint.

That was it for me. Fear shaped my style: I would buy funky old vintage clip-ons and stake out my own unpierced territory somewhere to the far right of fashion. (Needless to say, the thought of a tattoo has never been entertained.) Flash forward three decades. I am no longer a young woman making some sort of retro-hip statement with her clunky old-lady earrings. I'm an old lady wearing clunky old-lady earrings. Earrings, by the way, that pinch and hurt.

I'm not sure where the idea comes from, but chatting with a friend on the phone one night, I suddenly blurt out that I'd like to get my ears pierced. The words surprise me; until the moment they come out of my mouth, I hadn't known I was thinking about doing any such thing. But my friend Deb is all over it. "Tomorrow?" she asks, without missing a beat. And then, before I can change my mind, she assures me, "I'll find out where you should go. And I'll meet you and hold your hand."

Which is how I happen to find myself at four thirty on a winter afternoon at Claire's, where I have never been, in the mall, where I never go, watching a freckle-faced nine-year-old girl squinch up her eyes and hold steady while a young woman pops a couple of sterile studs into her ears. "It doesn't hurt at all," the little girl assures me when she's done.

I remind my friend that I have tried this once before, and that I didn't have the stomach for it. "Yeah," she replies, "but that was before childbirth. You can handle it now." We are giggling like two teenagers, but I also know there's no way I can back out; Deb has taken the afternoon off to be with me. Then, sealing the deal, she pulls a small white box out of her purse. "These are your inspiration," she says, and opens it to reveal a beautiful pair of dangling handmade drops fashioned of clear Lucite resin and silver and pearl. They are elegant, contemporary, light as air. Utterly unlike anything I've ever owned.

My friend approves the placement of two purple dots on my ears. She holds both my clammy hands in hers and in less than a minute it is over.

For weeks I've had a longing to *do* something, without any clear idea of what that something might be. When friends ask, "How are you?" I pause, unsure how to respond. How can I explain that though life is apparently back to "normal," nothing feels as it did before? Grief and silent bedrooms and the inexorable march of time have all conspired to subtly alter the inner landscape of my being, so that what once was familiar and solid now seems foreign and fragile; days that used to seem rich and full feel drained of life, hard and empty as the winter sky. A few mornings ago, I cleaned a closet and took two bags of old clothes to the consignment store—as if by shedding the clothes I don't wear anymore, I could also cast off the roles that no longer fit either. Then I strapped on my snowshoes and took a long hike through the woods. But the aching, restless feeling didn't go away.

I suspect I need to be more patient. Emotions

have no statute of limitations, after all, and my desire for direction and clarity won't be satisfied immediately, but over time. There are no ready answers nor any wrong turns, only this slow, halting process of feeling my way forward, discovering what's important now, finding meaning where there appears to be none. I know, too, that on the outside, I look like exactly the same person I was a month ago, six months ago, a year ago. A little older, but the same. I get up in the morning and pull on the same black yoga pants, the same T-shirt and gray sweater; I run a brush through my hair, apply the same Clinique Winter Berry lipstick, measure out four scoops of coffee from the tin on the counter.

Yet there is something going on here beneath the surface, something shifting inside that has yet to manifest anywhere else. I'm not simply an older version of who I used to be. Having become acquainted with death, I feel a little less afraid of life. Having felt my heart break open, I know just how vulnerable I really am. Having been reminded that we are all dying, that none of us can ever hold on to anything,

I want to learn how to let go with more grace. Having so recently shed one identity—that of the 24/7 brush-your-teeth-and-bring-a-jacket mom—I'm wondering what other layers of "me" might be buried beneath the familiar roles of mother, wife, daughter, employee. Invisible, dormant layers perhaps, but layers I'm finally ready to excavate and explore—if only by laying some old, worn-out fears to rest and opening myself to new possibilities.

My friend and neighbor, author Thomas Moore, has spent decades considering and writing about the complex workings of the human soul. "It is my conviction," he says, "that deep changes in life follow movements of imagination." Yet it is in our very nature as humans to be restless, eager to be anyplace other than where we are. "Not here, not this, not now," we think when things start to feel uncomfortable. "Surely, there's someplace else I'm supposed to be." Discomfort, he points out, is usually our cue to flee, to go in search of some better option, some quick and easy balm for the pain.

He's right, of course. Having made up my

mind that it's time to change course, I want to lock the door behind me, plug my final destination into the GPS, and be on my way. The moment I decide that I'm ready for something different, I want to write up my to-do list and get on with the transformation. But as Moore points out again and again, the soul doesn't thrive on grand schemes or ambitious agendas. In fact, he suggests, slight shifts in imagination can have deeper and more lasting impact on our lives than major efforts at change. Real transformation, in other words, begins with subtle, imperceptible movement deep inside.

One morning, I spend an hour rereading *Care of the Soul*, a book that altered my life long before I found myself living a mile up the street from its author. Now, passages I highlighted in yellow years ago speak to me like old friends. "How many times do we lose an occasion for soul work by leaping ahead to final solutions without pausing to savor the undertones?" Moore asks. "We are a radically bottom-line society, eager to act and to end tension, and thus we lose opportunities to know ourselves for our motives and our secrets." His words both console me and slow me down. Perhaps it's just too soon to know exactly where I'm headed, ridiculous to think I can slough off my old skin and don some new, post-child-raising persona as easily as I tossed out my old high-waisted jeans and replaced them with two new, low-rise pairs that stretch. For now, I will try to be patient but not passive, receptive to the primordial whisper but not too impulsive in my answer to its call. After all, as my wise neighbor reminds me, it is not in hasty reaction to discomfort, but in the more subtle and creative realm of response, that something new can unfold.

It's been three years since my older son left for college, five months since we dropped the younger one off at school, four months since my friend passed away. Over the summer, watching the final, relentless progression of her illness, I almost felt as if a part of me was dying as well. Every moment of joy was circumscribed by a dark rim of sadness; each glimpse of beauty undercut by its own impermanence. Optimistic by nature, grateful by practice, I felt neither contentment nor gratitude, but as if my own resilient temperament had been stolen away, replaced by a moody, melancholic surrogate version of myself.

The symptoms of diminishment were not just emotional, they were physical as well: Lugging my own heavy heart around in my chest was hard, thankless work. My menstrual periods, always regular, stopped. My skin was perceptibly thinner, more fragile, sprinkled, all of a sudden, with pale brown age spots. My hair grew brittle and fine and dry. Sleep was impossible. At night I lay spread-eagled in bed like the victim of a crime, nightgown hiked up, sheets kicked off, awaiting the inevitable rush of heat and the racing heart that signaled the onslaught of yet another hot-flash marathon. By morning, I was a husk of myself, hollowed out, exhausted, parched—as if the relentless brush fires of the night were scorching the person I'd been right out of me.

Meanwhile, my husband would awaken at my side. Well rested, ready for action, and ever hopeful, he would run a tentative hand down my thigh. It was all I could do not to swat him. The slightest trace of his finger against my skin, the briefest murmur of desire in my ear, and I released a sudden slick of sweat and a spasm of silent, unprovoked fury. I didn't care if I never had sex again, but I would have sold my soul for a decent night's sleep. Alone.

I mourned the swift, sudden loss of youth and yearning; he mourned the end of life as he knew it. For surely we had lost our way, taken some detour and wound up in an arid marital desert. Joan Anderson, author of *A Year by the Sea*, a memoir of her midlife hiatus from her marriage, suggests that women would do well to take the word *menopause* literally. "At this age," she claims, "we really do need a pause from men." I couldn't have agreed more. My husband didn't know what to make of me, sweating and tossing and turning through the night, then stumbling through my days like a sleepwalker. And I couldn't get far enough away from him. If I acquiesced to an effort at intimacy—and any contact whatsoever most certainly *did* require an effort—it was soon obvious that there was nothing left in me to arouse. The barren scrape of lovemaking was too high a price to pay for a few minutes of connection; the pleasure of being together vanished. Life felt tenuous and bleak, as if all my own bright colors had faded away. Who knew that growing old would be as difficult and emotional and confusing as growing up?

On the October afternoon after my friend died, I remember driving slowly, carefully north, back to my own house and family. Henry had gone back to school, Jack was home for a long weekend; I hadn't seen Steve for a week, or even given much thought to the world beyond my friend's hushed bedroom. Returning home, exhausted and fragile after a couple hours of restless half-sleep, I wasn't quite sure whether the world itself had changed or I had. Nothing seemed as it had been. Even my hands on the steering wheel felt odd. Just hours earlier, those hands had smoothed my friend's hair and gently closed her eyes; now, asked to resume their old everyday tasks, it was almost as if they were doing each thing for the first time.

Everything that should have been familiar and comforting appeared new and strange:

the autumn landscape rolling by, aglow in the late afternoon light; the cars zipping to and fro on the busy highway; the crowded, brightly lit market in town, where I'd bought food for hundreds of meals. All of this moving, and doing, and buying was overwhelming—too much, too fast, too pointless. And meanwhile, unnoticed and unremarked on, there was the exquisite, empty sky, the golden trees, the pure light of the sun at dusk, the sharp, transparent air. The contrast—between the hollow busyness and the luminous, heartbreaking beauty, between my own heightened awareness and everyone else's apparent obliviousness—was almost unbearable.

There is a phrase well known to yoga students and meditators: *beginner's mind*. I did not know then how death can guide us gently back toward life, nor how grief not only changes us but reveals us. I did not know that sorrow resolves, over time, into an intimate, useful sadness, that it can deepen our capacity for tenderness, for love. Yet already, weary as I was, I could tell that something was different. Zen teacher Blanche Hartman defines *beginner's mind* as a mind that "faces life like a small child, full of curiosity and wonder and amazement." It is a mind that is not already made up, but rather one that meets experience without expectation and preconception.

Perhaps there are no earthly experiences that return us more powerfully and fully to these qualities of beginner's mind than birth and death. Confronted with the greatest of mysteries—the miracle of a first breath, the unfathomable drama of a last one—we are stopped in our tracks, reminded of all that we don't know and never will. Catching a glimpse of the vast realms that exist out beyond our well-worn, ingrained habits of mind, we do become like innocent children again, amazed by infinite possibility, in awe as we ponder the big questions: What does it mean to be human? How do I live a life that is impermanent? Who am I?

Home at last, feeling as raw and defenseless as a small child myself, I set down my bags and took in the scene in my own kitchen, unchanged since I'd left a week ago, yet not the same at all. It felt almost as if I were entering a holy place, a place I was seeing for the first time, through tender new eyes that noticed everything. I kissed my husband hello and wrapped my arms around Jack's solid, six-foot-tall body. And then, right in the midst of my exhausted sadness, like sudden flares cascading through a dark night sky, hot little pricks of joy pierced my heart, as if the very presence of death was also what was drawing me back into the sweet, vehement embrace of my own life.

So much of my energy these days seems to go into managing disappointment in the way things are, staving off worry about what might be, fearing that who I am, at my core, is not really enough. I want things to be one way, and then, when they turn out differently, I struggle, as if desperate not to fail whatever test I've constructed out of the moment. I had been struggling all summer, all fall, wishing everything could be different—wishing for sleep and sex and energy and laughter, instead of exhaustion and depletion, hot flashes and despair. Wishing Jack was still at the high school a mile from our house and sitting at the dinner table with us every night, instead of living three hours away. Wishing my friend could have more good days instead of so many hard ones. Wishing I could be wiser, and with her more often, and of more use to her than I was. Wishing I could be a more graceful, more attractive, more competent version of myself.

The events of the last few months, and certainly of the last few days, had been profound reminders that, no matter how much effort I pour into trying to reshape reality, I am not really in control of much at all. At the moment, I couldn't imagine tomorrow or next week or next year. I wasn't even sure I could unpack my suitcase or make a salad for dinner. And yet for once in my life, I was okay with not knowing. I was okay with not being in charge. In fact, it was a relief to let everything fall away. To be stripped bare of my usual baggage of beliefs and wants and opinions and expectations. I was home. I was bone-tired. I was humbled and sad and grateful all at once. There was nothing to do except just stand there in the middle of my own kitchen and wait to see what happened next.

What happened next was this: My husband took my hand and walked me slowly up the stairs. He filled the bathtub with hot water, poured in a packet of lavender bath crystals, and gently, as if I might break in two, removed my clothes. He helped me into the tub and sat quietly as I slid down into the hot, silky, scented water. And then, with great care and devotion, he began to touch me: cheek, shoulder, breast, knee, thigh. To his surprise, I let him. To my surprise, my tired, depleted body lifted itself, almost imperceptibly, to meet his hand. Slowly but surely, deep inside, something clenched and hard began to soften and melt. Tears rolled down my cheeks. Small, fiery tendrils of desire spiraled up through my belly. Beginner's mind. Beginner's body. Beginner's sex.

In an ancient Zen story from China, a student preparing to set forth on a pilgrimage is approached by his teacher. Seeing the young man with his pack on his back and his walking stick in hand, the teacher asks, "What is the purpose of this pilgrimage?" The student answers, "I don't know." The wise teacher nods approvingly, saying, "Not knowing is most intimate." Such is the vulnerability—and the sweetness—of not knowing.

Perhaps the real point of life is simply to wear us down until we have no choice but to start abandoning our defenses. We learn that the way things are is simply the way they are meant to be right now, and then, suddenly, at long last, we catch a glimpse of the abundance in the moment—abundance even in the face of things falling apart. Embarking on a journey without knowing quite where we're headed, or even why we need to go, we are freed to be open and curious, ready to find out, rather than obligated to find the "right" way.

Writing here, struggling to find words for my own anxiety about loss and change and growing old, I realize that even these sentences, so slow to find their way to the page, arise not from any expertise or knowing on my part, but out of the very questions I'm wrestling with. I'm beginning to think there's something to be said for any experience that begins in a place of *not* knowing, for any pilgrimage undertaken not with a desire to pile up yet more experiences, but simply with a willingness to go forth and see what happens next.

Four months after my friend's death, I am getting a little more comfortable in this place of not knowing. Not a day goes by when I don't sense her presence or notice something that she, in particular, would appreciate, and this invisible connection is in itself a kind of not knowing, a not knowing that is most intimate. I have no idea where she is. At the same time, I'm struck by how often I feel her with me. I think of her when I wear the dark brown beaded necklace she made me for Christmas one year, when I turn the page on the calendar she gave me last fall, and each time I brew a cup of Japanese Sencha green tea, which she mail-ordered for me the last time she ordered some for herself. I suspect now that she gave me a year's supply on purpose, certain that with every cup I would be reminded of all the afternoons we spent together, all those cups of tea shared on the couch in her family room as we talked our way toward parting.

In our culture, we do not have much face-to-face experience with death; rarely are we reminded that the veil between this life and the next is gossamer thin, separated by only one breath, a current of energy, a single beat of the heart. Standing on one side and witnessing a loved one's passage to the other changes us. It changed me. Most of all, it has made me aware of my own fragile "beingness" in this world— of both my mortality and my human impulse to push that awareness away. For it turns out that mourning is complicated. I grieve the loss of my friend but also, truth be told, I mourn for myself. Myself as I was, as I am no longer, as I will never be again.

We may not know the purpose of our pilgrimage, and yet we answer the call and go anyway. We are given a diagnosis, we are handed a pink slip, we get a phone call that changes everything. Life surprises us, and suddenly the carefully crafted plan is in need of revision or has to be scrapped altogether. Instead of answers and explanation and reasons *why*, we are asked to put one foot in front of the other and to keep moving.

Already my fifties look and feel different from my thirties, or even my forties. I have yet to grow accustomed to my crepey neck, my wrinkled elbows, the small puckered lines gathering around my mouth. But I am choosing not to dwell these days on what gravity is drawing downward, and to focus instead on the heart's enduring ability to uplift. I know now to be grateful for every night of peaceful sleep, for every moment of pleasure in my husband's embrace, for every morning that I swing my two strong legs out of bed and look forward to the day.

Surely Marie meant for me to find the photo of the two of us taken in Maine on our last overnight trip. We are squinting into the camera, laughing, our hands full of flat rocks to carry home from the beach—as if by taking possession of those eternal stones we could somehow hold on to the day itself. She had tucked the picture into the book of Mary Oliver's poems I'd loaned her last fall. No doubt she imagined me retrieving my book from the basket by her bed after she was gone. And she knew, of course, that when I found the photo I would also read the poem she had marked with it, the one that ends: "Doesn't everything die at last, and too soon? Tell me, what is it you plan to do with your one wild and precious life?"

I'm pretty sure that a trip to the mall and a twenty-two-dollar ear piercing is not the kind of transcendent experience Joseph Campbell had in mind for his hero when he urged, "Move, move, get rid of the life you had planned," but no matter. To me—the same girl who passed out thirty years ago while slipping a silver wire into her earlobe and never dared try it again—saying "yes" to this humble adventure feels both significant and symbolic, a reminder that I'm ready to orient myself to something different, to be more accepting of what comes my way, to become intimate with not knowing.

Today, under harsh fluorescent lights and with Muzak wafting through the air, with a good friend at my side and a gift of lovely new earrings in my hand, I set forth. No one else can tell, but I know it. Growth begins in silence, evolution with a heartbeat, journeys from where we are: standing in one place and daring to imagine a new horizon.

~4~

stillness

Except for the point, the still
point, there would be no dance,
and there is only the dance.

— T. S. ELIOT

$\mathcal{I}$ leave my old purple yoga mat rolled out these days, on the floor between the living room and the kitchen. If I have to step over it just to walk from one room to the next, then perhaps I'll be more likely to peel off my socks and practice, if only for a few minutes. The psychology is pretty good. Once I'm actually on the yoga mat, I tend to stay for a while. And daily practice is my secret goal this winter. I'm afraid that if I make too big a deal out of this, if I tell myself (or anyone else) that I'm going to do yoga every single day for a month, I'll fail. Better to sneak up on this intention, leave the mat in place, and then simply make the choice each day to come and stretch and sit quietly for a while.

From this spot on the floor, I can look out through the unused French doors to the stone wall in our yard, where a small red squirrel has taken up residence. Usually, if I'm here, he's there, poised on the same rock day after day, tail curled into a question mark and gazing right back at me, not at all shy of my presence on the other side of the glass. I'm absurdly grateful for his company, as if we've made an unspoken pact to show up together and bear silent, companionable witness to the stillness.

For the first time in my adult life, I find myself with a multitude of empty hours to fill and a great deal of choice about how to spend my time. And yet how easily a day can go astray. There is always something somewhere that needs cleaning or mending or organizing, always a phone call I could return or an in-box full of e-mail messages awaiting my response.

I make promises to friends and family and neighbors, call my kids, edit a son's paper, agree to speaking engagements and lunch dates and writing projects, and then am surprised at how little time I actually spend doing meaningful work.

It used to be that I could derive some sense of structure and accomplishment in my life by pointing to the number of words written or annual story anthologies published, the number of royalty checks deposited, meals made and mouths fed on a daily basis, the number of loads of laundry washed and folded and put away in drawers.

But my life is no longer lived by the numbers. I can choose to shape it differently now, or I can allow myself to be pushed and pulled in countless directions. I can run around and occupy myself with endless tasks, or I can move more slowly, and to a simpler rhythm. I can while away hours in front of a computer screen, or I can refuse to allow technology and its distractions to kidnap me from my days. And yet there is a learning curve even to this new, self-generated schedule—and I am often frustrated by my own aimless, habitual busyness, by my lack of clarity and intention.

Today, the phone rings just as I am settling down on my yoga mat; I resist for a moment, then haul myself up off the floor to check the caller ID—and am delighted to see the number displayed on my phone. My friend Nancy was another regular walking partner in my former suburban life. Our children grew up together, went to school together, carpooled together, played countless games of baseball in both backyards. In the summers, our two families vacationed together. And meanwhile, for years, Nancy and I kept a standing early Monday morning walking date, never quite realizing how hard such a dedicated, rain-or-shine commitment might be to replicate elsewhere. First her family moved away, then ours did. And as our children grew up and apart so did we, life's demands eventually taking precedence over the halfway-point meetings we'd promised each other we'd make in order to preserve our friendship. Now I do a quick mental tally—has it really been nearly a year since I've seen her?

It's good to hear my old friend's voice. We talk first, as always, about our children, who's where and doing what. Nancy has two in college and one left at home, a junior in high school. It still catches me off guard sometimes, the fact that all these children of ours, the ones we used to double-buckle two at a time into seat belts in the back of the car for quick trips downtown for pizza, are grown up now and scattered all over the country. Wasn't it just yesterday that there were five of them crowded into the rear of our old green minivan, singing "Down in the Backpack" at the tops of their lungs? The last time we gathered the kids around a campfire to roast hot dogs and read out loud from *Finn Family Moomintroll*, or sat around a table long after bedtime, with a deck of cards and a pile of dented spoons, did any of us realize that such moments were already becoming memories, never to be repeated? Even now, all these years later, I wish we could re-create those times, summon our young adult children back into the fold with promises of raucous late-night games of Spoons and pans of freshly made Rice Krispies Treats. It will never happen, of course. A wedding, maybe, will bring those far-flung childhood friends back together again; I can't imagine that much else would.

"Now, tell me about you," I say, after we've completed the checklist on all the kids.

"It's been a hard time," Nancy says, surprising me. I think of her as my most enviably solid friend, always perfectly clear in her convictions and deeply committed to her passions. An intuitive organic gardener, beekeeper, artist, and teacher, as well as a devoted mother, Nancy has always struck me as someone whose life is in exquisite alignment with her beliefs. Tall and tanned and strong, as casually elegant in her straw hat, work boots, and rolled up jeans as she is at ease in her dressy evening clothes, she is the friend I always want most to emulate. Where I feel uncertain of my own gifts, I'm quite certain her only trouble must be choosing which of her many creative talents to pursue—painting, music, gardening, knitting, or teaching a group of third-graders how to plant potatoes. She's good at everything and always exploring something new, whether it's learning to play the cello or building a chicken coop in the backyard.

So I don't expect what's coming next. "I feel as if I've lost myself," she says. "All these years of taking care of everyone else, of feeling as if I always have to be right here, making sure every meal gets on the table and that everyone's needs are met. I always *wanted* to do it, but I also really believed that what was going on in everyone else's life was more important than what was going on in mine. I guess I believed that nothing very important *was* going on in mine."

Her words catch me off guard. Somehow, I'd assumed I must be the only one going through such an awkward, unsettling change of life. But even with one son still at home, my friend is wrestling with change just as I am. In the last year, after a lifetime of perfectly good health, a critical kidney condition landed her in the emergency room; she is still dealing with the aftereffects. Meanwhile, just as her first two children were leaving home, her husband's career took off in a new direction;

he'd published an important political book and become a sought-after public speaker, in demand all over the country.

"My house is emptying and my husband is on a plane almost every day, off changing the world," my friend says, her voice a mixture of admiration and gravity. "How do I face myself in light of that? How do I look at my own life without feeling *less than*?"

I am quiet for a moment, considering. How naïve I was to believe that if I just worked hard enough at arranging my life when my children were small, I would someday "get there"— that is, land in some idealized place in which I would feel settled, secure, and certain. Done with all that striving. Looking around, I used to imagine that some of my friends had already arrived, had somehow gotten a jump on achieving the harmony and balance and ease I sought for myself.

Now I'm beginning to realize that none of our lives, not even the ones that appear "perfect" from the outside looking in, are without their share of challenges, disappointments, and worries. Yet it still astonishes me that my most skillful, self-sufficient friend is suffering such pangs of doubt. But, of course, I shouldn't be surprised at all. To be human and alive, it seems, is to strive and to struggle, to learn and to grow even as we endure our losses and question our ability to transcend them. It's easy to think we should be somewhere or someone else—smarter and wiser, or further along on the path, closer to having an answer. Instead we muddle along, heads down, certain everyone else must know something we haven't figured out yet: how to be happy, how to love without getting hurt, how to let go, when to hold on, how to live with uncertainty, where to find faith.

"I guess that for me," Nancy goes on, "this time is really about coming face-to-face with my dark side. All the really ugly stuff I never wanted to see. Like shame, which I seem to have a lot of. Shame that I've been pushing away and covering up for years."

"What's different now?" I ask, trying to imagine where my enthusiastic, engaged friend has been keeping that dark side hidden. I've never seen it.

"Well," she continues, "it began with a long time of just sinking down into myself, sitting still long enough to see what's really there. It was so uncomfortable, and new for me, to stop running around doing everything for everyone else, and to just be there for myself, instead. But I think I'm finally coming to a place where I can accept that dark, heavy part of me, and work with it rather than cover it up. I'm realizing that I can use all that shit as compost."

I laugh; leave it to Nancy to see the gardening metaphor here. "Really," she says. "What is compost, after all, but a bunch of old garbage that's being put to good use in the garden—it's shit, but once it's aged enough, we think of it as gold. So it's the same with all my stuff; I'm finally ready to muck around in that pile, and I'm finding I *can* work with it, and use all that dark stuff to help me to grow."

It sounds right to me, sounds, in fact, so much like my own halting journey into myself that I feel as if my friend has been reading my mind. I wonder how many of the other women I know are engaged in the same sort of private, uncomfortable, yet urgent explorations. I wonder, too, if some have managed to sidestep these hard questions. As Nancy and I are both quick to agree, if you stay busy enough, distracted enough, it's possible to give the compost pile a wide berth. Not everyone is willing to dig in.

"I think that whole episode with my kidney was a kind of soul crisis," Nancy says. "It just made me realize that healing my body really meant healing my whole life. And what I'm learning now is to take care of myself. To be kind to myself. But figuring out what I really need, and what I want to do, isn't easy; it takes daily practice and attention. I'm still not used to it. So I get up really early, and sit, and write in my journal, and try to be patient—without judging myself too harshly for not having all the answers. Of course," she says with a laugh, "the sitting and the patience and the not judging—that's the hardest part."

I know what she means. With both of my sons gone now, I, too, am feeling a new, unfamiliar sense of responsibility to myself. And yet, asking, "What am I really here to do?" just brings me face-to-face with all of my uncertainty. I haven't a clue what I'm supposed to do next; all I know for sure is that I don't want to spend any more of my days by simply filling them up. I'm pretty sure, though, that my friend is right; that the answer to "What next?" isn't to be found in more movement, but less. Perhaps the only way to begin to answer any of these questions is to sit still long enough to hear what my own heart yearns to say. To silence the chatter in my mind so the quiet voice of my soul might be allowed to speak.

Counterintuitive it may be, but I'm coming to suspect that most important journeys begin from a place of stillness, taking shape first in the realm of intuition and imagination long before we hit the road. In order to go, I first need to learn how to stay. If I'm to step out of my comfort zone and challenge myself in new ways, I first have to be willing to be fully present right where I am. Before I can move forward in my life, I must take the time to go down into it, to deepen it.

All I can do is practice. The gray winter sky melts into the mountains. The refrigerator hums into the emptiness. The heat kicks on. I stand barefoot at the front of my mat, inhale, and sweep my arms high.

From the moment I walked into my first yoga class more than a decade ago, I had a profound and completely unanticipated sense of home-coming. It was as if, after a lifetime of avoiding gym class, being inept in my body and adrift in a sea of self-consciousness, I'd finally sailed into a friendly port and dropped anchor in a welcoming harbor. I could hardly believe my good fortune. No one was trying to avoid hav-ing to pick me for a team, no one was hurling a ball at me, no one was timing me, no one was counting on me. No one was even watch-ing me. I didn't have to run, or jump, or catch, or make a pass, or swing a racquet, or think fast. There was no one to let down and no one to impress. There was no game to win or lose, no score to keep, no spectators shouting from the sidelines, no uniform, no number on my back, nobody to compete against and nothing to prove. There were no machines to master, no Top 40 songs blaring from a sound system, no TVs hanging from the ceiling, no iron to pump.

There was only me, sweating and clumsy, playing an awkward, solitary game of Twister on a borrowed yoga mat in the back corner of a crowded room where the temperature was creeping up toward a hundred degrees and everyone else seemed to know that when the teacher called out "Adho Mukha Svanasana," it meant you were supposed to plant your palms on the ground, stick your butt up into the air, extend your legs back behind you, and try to get your heels to touch the floor. I could not begin to do this.

What was amazing, though, was that in some deep, heretofore untouched place in my consciousness, I knew it really didn't matter. Whether I could manage an approximation of downward-facing dog or not was beside the point. All I had to do was show up.

I'd had no idea that morning, when I'd double-checked the schedule, put on my cozy sweatshirt and fleece pants, and headed out in search of something that might satisfy a need I didn't even know I possessed, that "power yoga" meant "hot yoga." I was dangerously overdressed. I could not touch my toes or figure out how to get my limbs out of one pose and into the next or even keep straight which was my left foot and which was my right. I was an unathletic, uncoordinated, forty-year-old mother of two and I could barely sit cross-legged on the floor, let alone do a forward bend.

Even so, I realized right away that I was on to something here, that the nearly overwhelming rush of sensations and emotions and thoughts washing through me was not a riptide to avoid, but a life current I wanted to learn to swim in. At the end of what had seemed an interminable—and yet, paradoxically, a completely absorbing—hour and a half, as I sat watching young, tattooed, barely clad men and women spray their sweat-drenched mats with some kind of natural cleanser, the teacher approached. A hugely muscled black man with a shaved head and an enormous smile, he was clearly searching for something kind and encouraging to say, something that would acknowledge my flailing, clueless, yet determined presence there in the back row of his class.

"You have a pretty game attitude," Rolf said with a grin. "I hope you'll come back."

I went back. Yoga class made me happy. It really was that simple. I was so terrible at the poses that there was no alternative but to improve, nothing to do but begin to grow, and nothing to lose in the process. Doing something hard and physical with my body was such an unfamiliar experience that I was like a kid with a new yo-yo: eager to discover what might be possible with enough practice, and willing to spend hours and hours in search of that elusive, ever-shifting edge.

"Yoga prepares our bodies to live our dreams," Rolf said. "Keep practicing, and your habits will give you up." It was true. Much as I loved going to class, what amazed me was the way my experiences on the yoga mat kept seeping into the rest of my life. The first few weeks, I had a ritual: Driving home after yoga class, I'd stop at Starbucks and treat myself to a grande latte and a doughnut, my reward for waking up in the darkness and dragging myself to a 6:30 a.m. class. But it wasn't long before the mental clarity and increased energy that yoga brought became its own reward, and it wasn't long after that that the caffeine and sugar high lost its appeal. I didn't have to give it up; I simply didn't want it anymore.

Yoga, it seemed, wasn't just about learning how to balance on one leg; it was about bringing the disparate parts of myself into balance with one another, tapping into the wisdom of my own body, learning to tune in to what the yogis call the "inner teacher." Everything I intuitively believed about being present for my young children was reinforced by what I was learning about being present on my yoga mat.

Witnessing the frenzied activity of my mind in class, I came to see how much energy I put into unproductive thinking everywhere else. Becoming aware of the intense feelings that arose during practice, I grew more conscious of my words and actions in the other areas of my life. Having always yearned for deeper relationships, I suddenly found it easier to go deep myself. Slowly, almost imperceptibly, the challenges of my marriage, motherhood, career, and family life were transformed in my mind from obstacles I needed to overcome into blessings to be grateful for and opportunities for growth.

"Your life is your practice," Rolf reminded us again and again. With wonder and relief, I began to see that he was right, that my own everyday life with my husband and our young children was in fact a spiritual practice, worthy of my deepest care and attention and respect. Whether I was on my yoga mat or at the kitchen sink, reaching down to grab my big toes or mediating an argument in the backyard, the challenge was exactly the same: learning to be fully present in the moment-by-moment experience of being alive.

More than ten years later, I am still practicing. Still getting lost and finding my way back into the moment, still trying too hard and then remembering that yoga is less about doing than about being, still learning how to show up and pay attention on the mat and in my life. But something has shifted, too. Yoga is no longer just something I do; it has become part of who I am, as inextricable from my sense of self and well-being as eating and walking and reading and writing.

When we moved from the suburbs to the

country, the first thing I did for myself was search out a yoga class. I didn't know a soul in the dusty, drafty church hall—so different from the hip urban studio I'd left behind, packed with bodies and heated till the windows dripped with condensation. I was unaccustomed to my new teacher's emphasis on alignment, had never practiced in a room that wasn't hot and crowded, wasn't used to moving so slowly or holding poses for so long. Everything about this new class was different and yet, at the end of ninety minutes, I felt stitched back together, more comfortable in my body, more at ease in my life.

Practice is practice, no matter where it is or what form it takes. And home, I was beginning to realize, was not just the new house we had built, the address on the mailbox, the view from the front door, or the clatter of dishes at the breakfast table. Home was also the invisible, inviolable place deep within me, a still point to which I could always return, simply by bringing myself back to the present moment, quieting my busy mind, and coming to rest on the wave of my own breath.

*   *   *

Now I find myself called even more power-fully to that inner hearth of my soul. Day after day, I try to remember to be grateful for all I have—for my family and our good health, for love and laughter, for the roof over our heads and enough money in the bank to pay the bills. Yet there's no escaping the fact that many of the changes of these last years, even those changes we sought, have been accompanied by sorrow. It was both exciting and heartbreaking to leave a home and a way of life we loved and start fresh elsewhere. It was both challenging and demoralizing to lose a well-paid job and a professional identity, and have to figure out a new way to earn a living. It was both won-derful and wrenching to watch a shy firstborn come of age and choose a college halfway across the country. It was both inspiring and painful to see our younger son gather his cour-age and depart for boarding school.

And it has been both sad and deeply hum-bling to become an empty-nester so soon, to watch a dear friend die too young, to outgrow so many old dreams and then find myself at a loss to identify new ones. I may have gained some ground, but I've certainly lost some, too.

My impulse, always, is to push away sadness by being productive. By focusing outward, on other people and their problems, other loved ones and their needs, I can sidestep my own. But the process of growing into this new self seems to demand a period of descent, a willingness to dig into my own depths, to a deeper, darker place than I'm accustomed to inhabiting. A willingness, too, to pay attention to the silence inside. To stop, be quiet, and just listen—strange and self-indulgent as that feels. Just as yoga class first offered me a way to become more present in my life as a wife and mother, I am trusting yoga to help me see the way forward now, even if "forward," for the moment, appears to mean "down."

I do know, after more than a decade of practice, that the unnamed need that led me to my first yoga class all those years ago was really a yearning for internal quiet. A yearning that grew out of weariness and effort and fear that no matter how hard I worked at the all-consuming tasks of grown-up life, I would never be quite good enough. There was so much at stake—children to raise, a living to earn, a home to create, a marriage to uphold. How could I become the person I aspired to be, the mother my children deserved, the wife my husband wanted, the editor worthy of her title? Yoga seemed to suggest that I could stop trying so hard. That I didn't have to keep searching for ways to improve myself; I could just be who I was instead.

"Allow your awareness to rest in the sensations of the breath," Alexandra, my new teacher in New Hampshire, says. Her voice is quiet, her manner unhurried. And in this stillness, in these brief, fleeting moments in which my mind and body come to rest, the tight knots of sadness and anxiety begin to loosen. Maybe I am enough after all. Maybe things will all work out. Maybe they already have. And maybe it is enough for now to place a bit of faith in both the beauty and the darkness of my life as it is.

In the midst of these long, cold, winter days in a house that feels emptied of life, I do at least know this: With my sons away at school, with my husband at work all day, with my friend gone and no one expecting me to show up anywhere, I can either run away from my loneliness, or I can practice tolerating myself as I am. For once in my life, there is nowhere I need to be. I can be just as still and just as solitary as my own restless mind will permit. But I wonder: Do I have the courage to be "home alone" with myself, to enter into the deeper rhythm of my own being?

The question leads me back, again and again, to the yoga mat. The days are piling up. The red squirrel presides from his perch on the rock, our old dog Gracie lies by the door, her eyes half open, watching me. Silence fills the house, melting snow drips from the roof like a stream of clear pebbles falling to earth, and my body moves slowly through the familiar sequences. I am like a swimmer doing laps, steady, in flow, outside of time. The moving and doing is the easy part; what's harder for me is the sitting and the stillness, the moment when I come to a stop and then have to stay right where I am.

The clock ticks relentlessly now, and I hear it, feel life passing me by. I wonder what I'm missing and whether I can bear one more moment of this futile attempt to empty my mind of worries and regrets and plans. *Tick, tock.* The light is dim in the interior world. I want nothing more than to flee. To escape from myself. To get up and go *do* something.

I think about the Buddhist nun Pema Chö-drön's suggestion that we try exchanging our intense desire to be comfortable for a willing-ness to be curious instead, opening ourselves to both the bitter and the sweet experiences in life, the light and the shadow.

"To lead a more passionate, full, and delight-ful life," she writes, "we must realize that we can endure a lot of pain and pleasure for the sake of finding out who we are and what this world is." How odd, to realize that my biggest challenge right now is just to stay right here, to be still, to find out who I am and where I'm meant to go by sitting in one place and seeing what comes to me.

Each day, at the end of my practice, I lie on my back in a pose I think of as "heart on a block." With a yoga block resting beneath my shoulder blades, my chest wide open and arched up to the sky, it feels as if my lifted heart is fully exposed, beating and vulnerable, a kind of physical sacrifice to the present moment. And this is when I cry.

I started doing this pose to counteract the middle-aged slump of my shoulders, but it turns out to bring forth something other than improved posture. I need only to lie back, place my heart on the block, and take one long, deep breath before the tears start leaking from the corners of my eyes. Quiet, sneaky tears that surprise me every time, tears that seem to well up of their own accord and to flow from the very depths of my being. There is no intensity, no great emotion behind them, just a gentle, apparently necessary release, an overflow, it seems, of all the sadness I've ever known. All the sadness I've not had a place for, or any idea what to do with.

My first inclination always, when the tears start, is to jump up and get on with things. I am not a weeper! But some deeper instinct is telling me to stay, that tears, too, are part of this practice, necessary to this work of releasing what was in order to accept what is. "If we're committed to comfort at any cost," Pema says, "as soon as we come up against the least edge of pain, we're going to run; we'll never know what's beyond that particular barrier or wall or fearful thing."

In stillness and solitude, comfort is hardly a given. Being alone, and confronting all the emotions and feelings that come bubbling up, turns out to be much more difficult than filling my days with activities and errands and good deeds for others. Waiting for the world to offer itself up at my feet, I meet instead a weepy, vulnerable self who wouldn't be caught dead in the busy, well-lighted universe I normally inhabit. I do want to run, to get away from this person who is so not the "me" I'm in the business of being. I could be strong and steadfast at a deathbed. I can sit for hours consoling a friend or rubbing a sick child's back. I am good at listening to a loved one's troubles, at holding a quiet space for another's suffering.

But making the choice to just hang in there with my own rather pathetic self for a while demands a different kind of perseverance altogether, a kind of strength that lays bare all of my weakness. And so I try, day after day, not to scorn this raw, sorrowful soul, not to dry my eyes and bolt, but to settle into the darkness instead, heart open, experiencing the humiliating truth of my own silent, barren place.

When we lose anything we cherish—a way of life, a loved one, a dream, a belief, even the day-in-day-out presence of a child at home—a space that was filled in our lives, and in our hearts, is suddenly empty. Sorrow, then, is surely a human, natural response. And yet how reluctant we are in this noisy, busy, get-over-it-and-move-on culture to give grief its due.

Lying with my heart up in the air and my tears dripping down into my ears, I have to surrender all over again to the truth that being alive means letting go. I have to trust that being right where I am really is some kind of progress, and that there is a reason I've been called to visit this lonely darkness. For months I have been sensing it, avoiding it, scared of it. And now I'm here. Perhaps something is germinating in this place. Perhaps it's not the words I might one day write about it, or even what I end up doing next, that will make me who I am, but rather the time I spend right here, allowing my eyes to grow accustomed to the shadows. If I am quiet and patient and brave, maybe I'll begin to sense a stirring within the stillness. But for now, staying put and allowing myself some time and space at last to fully experience all these feelings of loss and pain and separation seems to be the only way I know to both grieve and honor all that's over—a necessary step, it seems, on this fumbling journey toward what is yet to be.

～ 5 ～

going

*When a great moment knocks on the
door of your life, it is often no louder
than the beating of your heart,
and it is very easy to miss it.*

—BORIS PASTERNAK

$\mathcal{I}$ don't notice Margaret has been gone until
she returns. But there she is in yoga class one
night, looking the same as always and yet, in
some subtle way, different. Has she lost weight?
I wonder. Done something with her hair? Or
maybe she just had a really good day. Whatever it is, I can't take my eyes off her. There's
a steadiness in her gaze when she says hello, a
slow deliberation in her movements, an aura of
calm I've never seen in her before.

"Welcome back!" someone calls out as we head toward the coat hooks at the end of class. "Was it great?"

"Amazing," Margaret replies in a low, earnest voice. "Really hard. And really wonderful."

"What was hard and wonderful?" I ask, eager to hear what's brought about this change. Margaret turns toward me. "I just finished a yoga teacher training," she explains. "I spent a month at Kripalu and got certified." She hesitates a moment, then adds, "But now I'm having a little trouble readjusting to my old life. I'm so eager for things to change, and every-thing's just the same as before. They told us to be patient, that things would begin to happen, but I'm finding patience almost impossible. Coming home has been a bit of a letdown."

"Well, I noticed a change in you right away!" I say. "So things are already happening. Maybe *you* just can't see it yet."

I think about Margaret all the way home. A few years older than me, she is neither very thin, nor very young, nor rich, nor particularly self-assured. I suspect she has her struggles in yoga class and in life, just like me. She recently lost a job she needed but had never loved; she has a son in the service, far from home, another away at college, and a husband who likes to come home at night to find his dinner on the table. So how, I wonder, had she found the courage, the time, the money, the *permission* to drop out of her life for an entire month to go do yoga? I really want to know.

Because I think I want to do it, too.

Ever since I breathed and sweated through my first yoga class more than ten years ago, I've longed for more. But what I really wanted seemed, well, unseemly for a middle-aged, nonathletic, stoop-shouldered, wide-hipped, not very bendy yoga student such as me: full immersion. For years I've dreamed of doing a teacher training. And for years that dream has been effectively and repeatedly popped by a voice inside that tells me to forget it. I am too old, the voice points out. And besides, I would never be good enough at yoga, or flexible enough, or knowledgeable enough to teach. The truth is, I'm not even sure I want to *be* a teacher; maybe I just wish I could be more *like* a yoga teacher, more graceful and grounded and poised. More supple on the mat, but also more supple in my life, more supple in the world.

I wish I'd discovered yoga at twenty instead of forty, wish I had a body that lent itself to forward and backward bending, and that I didn't break out in a sweat at the mere thought of turning upside down. Teacher material I am probably not. The question is, What am I? How can I be in this place of change, so ready for movement and progress, and at the same time feel so uncertain about where to plant my foot?

It feels as if my daily practice at home, my quiet sitting time, even my heart-on-a-block tears, are giving me a new foundation to build upon, a touchstone I can keep returning to. I still don't know where I'm going, and yet as the days go by, I'm beginning to feel just a little less lost. I can feel my body growing stronger and more flexible, my sadness slowly transforming into something more bearable and tender, my discomfort at going inward easing at last toward something approaching relief at the opportunity to stop doing so much and to simply *be* instead. I am learning how to stay.

And yoga is turning out to be my bridge over this chasm between what's over and what's next, as if my practice has been preparing my mind and body and spirit for...what?

One day an old publishing friend calls. "I'm thinking about going on a yoga retreat," she says, "and it's just your kind of thing. I'd love you to come with me."

"Sounds fabulous," I say. "Let me think about it." I hang up and scan through the link she sends: luxurious thatched-roof ocean-side cabanas, yoga mornings, afternoons on the beach, sunset meditations, rum cocktails for dinner. It looks beautiful, relaxing, fun.

And I have not the slightest bit of interest in any of it. Fortunately, the price alone, nearly five thousand dollars for four days, makes it easy to decline—there's no way I could spend that kind of money on myself, let alone try to justify it on our budget. And yet, my old colleague's decision to treat herself to some sun salutations in the sand is not lost on me—I love that she is doing this for herself, that she is willing to say, "I want this now." In the midst of an unexpected, wrenching divorce, she's confronting circumstances at midlife she never could have anticipated. Her only child left for college. And then her esteemed cardiologist husband up and left home, too. Some doors close gently, others slam shut, shaking the house to its foundation. Some stories unfold predictably and others careen toward surprise endings. But as I think of the women I know, I realize that we are all confronting endings in our lives. We are all on journeys of one kind or another, trying to figure out where we're supposed to be going and what we're meant to be doing. I'm certainly not the only one asking, Now what?

Kripalu. I can't get the name out of my head. I watch Margaret sitting cross-legged, eyes closed, on her yoga mat one night, waiting for class to start, the picture of stillness. And then, as soon as I get home, I go online and look up teacher training. There's one beginning in just over a month. The cost for twenty-eight days in the cheapest dorm room available is a little less than the four-day tropical yoga vacation. A whole month of living and breathing yoga for less than it would cost for a long weekend.

Suddenly, in this context, teacher training looks like a bargain. For once the mocking, predictable voice inside my head that says "No way" is silent. In fact, I think I can just barely make out some other, quieter voice, whispering, "Maybe."

I pencil the dates on my calendar, print out the application, labor over the questions as if I'm applying to college ("Why do you want to be certified as a yoga instructor at this time in your life?," "How do you plan to apply your yoga teaching skills in your life and your work?," "What teaching/leadership skills do you currently embody that would support your future work as a yoga teacher?"), and then I tuck the form into a folder and put it away.

I can predict how Steve will respond to the idea, and I'm not ready, or confident enough, to defend it to him or to anyone else for that matter. But the next step, unavoidable and essential, is to come clean about what I want to do. One night I ask my yoga teacher if she'd like to join me in the morning for a dawn hike. "There's something I'd like to talk over with you," I say.

We meet just before sunrise, in the parking lot at the bottom of Pack Monadnock, my favorite winter trek. With our trusty MICRO-spikes pulled on over our boots, we can generally climb up the icy trail to the summit in about forty-five minutes—time enough for me to confess my unlikely dream. I can't go off and do a teacher training without letting Alexandra know; at the same time, I'm bashful about revealing my secret aspirations to my own extraordinarily gifted teacher, a woman with decades of experience and dedication and in whose footsteps I could never presume to follow. It's a bit, I think to myself, like telling Meryl Streep that I admire her work so much that, now that the kids are grown, I'm thinking of taking up acting myself.

"This sounds like a perfect plan," Alexandra says, as we pause halfway up the mountain to catch our breath and admire the dawn light sparkling through the ice-encrusted trees. "You don't have to figure out the next step, just go do the training and see what happens. I think it'll be great for you."

In her mid-fifties, with a grown son recently

settled into his first apartment and permanent job, she herself is preparing for a two-month trip to India, to practice yoga and study meditation with a master. "I couldn't have done a trip like this even a year ago," my teacher says. "But my son's life is really his own now. Which means that I can live mine in a very different way, too. I figured if I was ever going to take my backpack and travel around India for a few months by myself, I better go do it now."

Her ready, generous support shouldn't surprise me, but by the time we get to the top of the mountain, I'm almost giddy with relief, finally willing to admit to myself how much it means to me to go with my teacher's blessing and encouragement. I may be doing basic training just a few hours away from home, while my teacher is heading for an ashram halfway around the world, and yet surely the impulse behind both our midlife odysseys is similar—a desire to respond to the newfound freedom of these later years by pursuing our passions and stretching ourselves, in the belief that what strengthens our bodies will also fuel our spirits, and that in taking seriously this work of caring more creatively for ourselves we will discover as well some new, more skillful ways of bringing that caring into the world.

We linger at the top of the mountain for a while, surveying the views of sky and mountains in all directions, the horizonless spectacle of a perfectly clear winter morning, and the minuscule outline of Boston shimmering in the distance at the farthest edge of sight. On a rare, crystalline morning such as this one, it's possible to catch a glimpse of flashing gold in the sunlight, the State House roof—less than a hundred miles from where we stand, yet a world away from this silent, snow-covered mountain in New Hampshire.

Thirty years ago, I sat in editorial meetings just steps down the hill from that building, desperately trying to fake it till I made it as an editor and wishing I could be older and savvier, rather than the neophyte, eager-to-please college graduate I so clearly was. Funny, I think to myself now, squinting to bring the distant city skyline into focus—thrilled as I was with my blossoming career, there is no way I would trade my confusing midlife "now" for that relentlessly ambitious "then," with its attendant anxiety and pressure to perform.

Alexandra rummages in her coat pocket for a moment, and pulls out a necklace of colored stones on a strand of twisted sterling links.

"I'm kind of a random gift giver," she says, smiling, placing the necklace over my hat and around my neck. "This was brought to me from an ashram in Rishikesh, by a friend who was doing yoga there. The stones represent the seven chakras, the spiritual energy centers in your body. Funny, but somehow, I knew it was meant to go to you this morning."

I don't expect my husband to be quite so sympathetic to my proposition, but time is running out. And so, with the application deadline approaching, I do something I'm not at all proud of. I set him up.

It's easy to choose the moment: Both boys are home at the same time, overlapping for a few days of their winter breaks. We are squeezed into a booth at Chili's, settling in for our traditional Friday-night dinner there. Henry, newly legal, orders a frozen margarita and, feigning nonchalance, hands the waitress his ID. Jack takes a long drink of his Coke and slides the glass over to me—still his way of making sure he won't drink it all before the food arrives. While we wait for our nachos, I summon my resolve and launch into my speech: "So, how would you guys feel about me going away for a month to do a yoga teacher training?"

I can feel Steve stiffen beside me and begin to open his mouth, but I look right at him and keep talking. "I'd have to miss part of Jack's spring vacation in March, which means that you two would have to go do some college visits alone. But I'd finish in time to meet the three of you in Florida, at the beginning of Henry's spring break, and we'd all have a few days at my folks' house together. It actually starts next month; I'd have to apply this week, and I don't know if it's full, or if they will even take me, but it's actually something I've always wanted to do and suddenly, well, it feels as if the time might be right."

The boys leap in first, as I knew they would, to say, "Go for it. You should do this, Mom!" Of course, they aren't paying the tuition, and they aren't living at home, and they aren't depending on me for food and folded laundry and love and company. In fact, they'd probably prefer to have me locked up somewhere for a while, too busy with my own stuff to worry about theirs.

"Dad and I can do the college visits," Jack adds. "No problem." Henry, too, is full of encouragement. "You'd be a really good yoga teacher," he says, always my biggest fan. Steve is silent, outnumbered, not willing to protest too much over dinner.

But later, alone in our bedroom, he lets me know: He's furious. Angry because I didn't discuss this privately with him first, angry that I want to leave home for four weeks, angry at the thought of being alone for so long, even angry, I think, to realize that his first response to his wife's heartfelt desire is anger. But he has his reasons. A month *is* a long time. It *is* a lot of money. Most of all, the whole scheme seems to him like a whim—pointless, indulgent, out of character. "Maybe I'll take a trip to Paris," he says, tossing his T-shirt into the hamper. "I could use a treat myself."

*   *   *

Nineteen eighty-seven. My dad buys the video camera so he can record his only daughter's wedding. It is heavy and cumbersome and no one in the family has ever filmed anything before, but various relatives dutifully heft the camera, take their turns behind the lens, and an hour or so of random, candid moments from the weekend are captured. A few days later, back home in our Cambridge condo, my new husband and I pop the VHS cassette into our tape player, have some laughs at the shots of people's feet and the sight of my uncle Chet tearing up the dance floor with my college roommate, and then we consign the movie to a drawer.

As newlyweds the two of us have a secret metaphor for our marriage: a field of pure, untrammeled snow, unsullied by the footprints of betrayal, harsh words, pettiness, or resentment. We've witnessed our parents' mistakes, watched friends' relationships die, seen seemingly solid marriages fall apart. Ours, we are certain, will be different. We will talk things over. We'll be kind, give each other lots of space, never go to bed angry.

There are things about me that drive him nuts. I don't balance my checkbook, replace the butter in the dish, iron his shirts, want sex often enough. I sweep the kitchen floor every day but never vacuum the sand out of the car. He isn't perfect either. He frets about money, doesn't rinse the kitchen sponge, leaves the toilet seat up, wants sex all the time. He won't take his shoes off in the house but is compulsive about keeping the car clean. Slowly, deliberately, we learn to surrender bits of ourselves in order to please each other. "Clean snow," we say often, surveying the modest territory of our untested, spic-and-span marriage. Shorthand for, "I love you, I trust you, we're doing fine."

We have a baby, and then another. We leave our snug urban condo for a rambling old house in the suburbs with a leaky roof and a yard and gardens to tend. We work hard, nurture friendships, care for our children, attend Little League games and school plays and piano recitals, decorate Christmas trees, plant hydrangeas on Mother's Day, and celebrate every birthday with chocolate cake. The years roll by, disappointments are absorbed, jobs lost, new careers begun. We worry about our sons, toss and turn through countless sleepless nights, and reassure each other as dawn breaks that they'll be okay. We move from the suburbs to the country, build a house, send one child off to college, begin to prepare ourselves for the departure of the second.

Along the way, we learn some of the hard, inexorable lessons of love. Human beings fail each other. Even good relationships are complicated by misunderstandings and hurt feelings, bruised and healed by acts of betrayal and tenderness. Seasons change. Young love grows old. Hearts develop calluses. Marriages endure the vicissitudes of weather and time, mistakes made and forgiven, dreams realized and relinquished.

Not long ago, I came across a box of old family movies and had a few of them transferred onto DVDs. Now, with both boys home at the same time, I slip a disk into the TV. We all sit down to watch the wedding, a glimpse of our "before" world, the world as it was before two children arrived and took up residence at the center of our lives. The shock of seeing long-ago versions of our loved ones gathered on the eve of our marriage, glasses raised for a rehearsal dinner toast, is funny and wrenching all at once. I catch my breath as my heart swells. So many of these people have died. And yet, miraculously, here they are, alive and well, smiling and cracking jokes and wishing us everlasting happiness. As if "everlasting" was a wish that really could come true.

The real surprise to me, however, is not the resurrection of the dead but of our own young, innocent, head-over-heels-in-love selves, poised on the threshold of our life together. I'm stunned by the intense, exclusionary, passionately absorbed "us-ness" of us. We could barely take our hands off each other, or tear our eyes away. While our sons laugh at the adoring way I once gazed up at their dad, as if there were no one else in the room, I am brushing away tears. When did our rapturous love affair turn into a relationship requiring so much compromise and negotiation and hard work? How could we not have noticed the snow melting?

What I didn't know twenty-four years ago,

on the day I donned an ivory lace dress and became a wife, was that every marriage is a gamble and the stakes are always high. Love, after all, is not synonymous with permanence; we offer our hearts into each other's safe-keeping on faith alone. Our relationship has survived, adapted, deepened, but it is hardly immaculate. In fact, the landscape of our lives together is a muddy crisscross of mishaps and memories, exultation and grief, hallowed land-marks and forgotten detours made along the way as we each learned, one day at a time, what it means to love another person for the long haul.

At twenty-seven, I didn't realize how arro-gant we were, to assume we could somehow do a better job of being married than anyone else. Perhaps it was that hubris that allowed us to speak our vows in the first place, to make those promises without hesitation, to believe in something as flimsy as the capacity of com-mitted love to sustain a marriage for better and for worse, in sickness and in health, till death do us part. If we're lucky, we may be just over halfway through this journey together, but here on the backside it's easy to foresee the challenges ahead—old age, infirmity, illness, loss. I wonder where the joy will come from now, and what will sustain us through the pain.

Already this life we spent so many years building and inhabiting is shrinking, like a house in which the unused rooms are closed down one by one, the lights flicked off, the doors shut. We have gone from being a lively, bustling, fully engaged family of four living and working and eating and sleeping together under one roof, all the way back to two again. But neither of us is the same person we used to be, nor can we ever again view our marriage as a pristine expanse of pure white snow. The years have tarnished us, exposed the dark side of our togetherness as well as the light, the ways we wound each other as well as the ways we help each other to heal.

And yet now that our biological purpose as a couple has ended, now that the job of giving birth to and raising children is nearly finished, we need to envision new possibilities for this second act of our married life, new ways to enrich and nourish our relationship. New ways, I think to myself, to recognize our love for each other—not as something pure and simple and inviolate, but as the mysterious alchemy it is, the enduring product of some darker miracle.

The boys go back to school. And Steve and I go to see Victor. By the night of our appointment, I'm so unsure of what I really want, and of what this argument is really about, that I'm tempted to cancel. It's embarrassing, asking for help. Twenty-four years of married life, and we suddenly need a therapist for *this*? Other couples confront and work through challenges so much bigger—addiction, infidelity, illness, impotence, financial ruin, death. Do we really need to haul our petty problems out in front of a paid professional? Maybe I *am* being selfish. Shouldn't we just make a deal we can each live with, as we've done so many times before, and move on? And yet, the anger that flared up in Steve on the night I first suggested going away for a month is still there, smoldering beneath the surface of every conversation. It scares me.

What scares me even more is having to admit that I'm angry, too.

During the year of Jack's struggles at school and with video games, I'd gone in search of a therapist who might help us understand what was happening to our son, or who might help Jack begin to help himself. Victor's name came up again and again—everyone from my hairdresser to the guidance counselor at school seemed to know him, to think that if I was going to call anyone, I should call Victor—yet when I finally reached him on the phone, he told me his practice was full to overflowing. There simply was not room for one more miserable family or struggling soul.

Nevertheless, hearing the despair in my voice, he spoke to me with such kindness and concern that, for the first time in months, I felt a glimmer of hope. Victor generously gave me an hour of his time right then and there. His willingness to listen to a complete stranger's story, and his calm, validating counsel in response, was a gesture of pure compassion at a moment when it felt as if we'd run out of options. This wise, insightful man might not have had room for us in his appointment book, but he made space for us in his heart right away.

Many months later, after Jack had returned from the wilderness, I called Victor again. He remembered me. We were no longer in crisis, I explained, but our reunited family felt fragile, our memories of the abyss all too fresh. We wanted to make sure our son had the support he needed to keep moving forward. If we could be flexible, Victor said, he would be, too. And so it was that Jack found his way to Victor after all, as I'd hoped he would from the moment we'd first spoken. The first solo trips Jack took in the car after getting his driver's license that summer of his difficult sixteenth year were to Victor's office a half hour away. And an important part of his growing up was his willingness to assume responsibility for his meetings with this skillful, forthright man he quickly came to trust.

Now, it seems, it's our turn. As has so often happened in life, my children, simply by being their own uniquely complex selves, have led me down paths I never expected to travel. Watching Jack wrestle with growing pains beyond our experience and understanding, I learned that sometimes the best thing we can do for our children is to acknowledge our own need for help, to make room for their vulnerability by sharing our own. Jack learned a lot, in the safe and sacred space of Victor's office, about how to navigate the tumultuous landscape of his feelings and emotions. And I learned something, too, from watching Jack: that sharing our innermost struggles is a first step out of the confusion that holds us back and into the understanding that can set us free.

A New Hampshire Yankee by birth, I come from a line of folk who would never dream of discussing a personal problem with anyone outside the immediate family, let alone a therapist. Problems that couldn't be resolved in a few words behind a closed door were boxed up, taped shut, and put away out of sight. And just as in my grandparents' household the hard liquor was kept locked up in a cupboard out in the garage, so, too, were dreams and fears placed under lock and key, stowed away in silent, hidden hearts.

Vulnerability was a synonym for weakness; you didn't ask for help, you simply sealed up the cracks in the facade, shut your mouth, and got back to your housework. Goodness was equated with kindness to be sure, but it was also defined by strength and forbearance—by rising early, staying busy, and, once all basic physical needs were met, by not wanting and not wasting.

For some reason, I find myself thinking of my parents, and their parents before them, as Steve and I climb the steep back stairs to Victor's office in a run-down, converted Victorian house on a city side street. My parents' fiery, complicated relationship was volatile for decades after, as their contemporary, John Updike, once observed, "the 1960s arrived and wrecked all our 1950s marriages." My parents' marriage floundered but survived and grew stronger, mysteriously flourishing after more than fifty years, the two of them having finally, privately, arrived at a committed, lasting peace with each other. I am grateful for all they've lived through and forgiven in each other, but can't imagine enduring such steep ups and downs myself or suffering so in the hot crucible of love.

For all the years I knew them, both sets of my grandparents slept in separate bedrooms, went about their separate, stoic lives, sharing an address, a dinner table, a routine, and yet in so many essential ways, apart, keeping their own counsel. I spent much time in both of those homes as a child and adored my grandparents, yet have little sense of what bound them together or what their marriages were made of, other than a sense of duty, habit, history, social mores and expectations. I remember their bickering; I often observed their resigned tolerance toward each other, but felt little tenderness between them. Love might have been part of the picture, but I don't recall ever hearing it spoken or seeing it expressed. Life, like a hand of cards, was played close to the chest. Who knew what went on within the clandestine negotiations of those Depression-era unions, or what arguments and agreements led to those austere beds in separate rooms? And what, I wonder, would my taciturn New England grandparents think of their impassioned,

menopausal granddaughter lifting the curtain on her family's business, exposing the
entangled intimacy of her marriage to a near
stranger instead of quietly capitulating to the
defeats and disappointments of old age?

"How can I help?" Victor asks as we settle
into our seats, me on the worn green sofa,
Steve—deliberately, I think—lowering himself into a separate chair, instead of right next
to me. My heart is racing; the very fact that we
have agreed to come here and talk about our
troubles makes them feel more serious than I
want to believe they are. I take a deep breath,
remind myself to listen well, and decide to let
my husband speak first.

It feels like a safe place, this shabby, cozy,
overheated room with its mismatched furniture and colorless carpet, its ancient, brown
macramé wall-hanging, and strategically placed
tissue boxes and squeeze toys. Maybe, I tell
myself, this is the right first step into something
new. And maybe the pain we're both feeling
will, in the end, make us stronger, wiser, better
suited to the next phase of our life together.

Victor, slight as an elf and cheerfully benevolent as a Buddha, sits across from us, propping his small foot in its plaster cast on a pillow on the floor. "A little surgery," he says, gesturing, "and a slow recovery."

I glance at Steve; I know him so well, know that he would much prefer to sit and chat about sports injuries and broken ankle bones than the invisible hurt that's brought us through the door. And yet he leans forward and plunges in. "I think we've had a really good marriage; no, we *have* a really good marriage," he says, correcting himself. "But now that our boys are gone, it feels as if we're going our separate ways, too. And all of a sudden Katrina has this idea that she wants to leave home for a month, and go do yoga, which seems to me like, well, an extravagance that we don't need. I think of all the things we could be doing together that she doesn't seem to have any interest in. Of how else we could be spending all that money. And I guess the fact that she'd rather go off by herself and do her own thing makes me wonder how much she really cares about being with me."

And that's when I realize that my hard-working, solid, emotionally self-sufficient husband may be as scared and confused about what's next as I am. I've been so focused on all the ways my own life is changing that I haven't really considered the fact that his is changing, too. He may still get up and go to the office every day, work out at the gym, come home, eat dinner, sleep, and get up in the morning to do it all again. But I'm not the only one who's lost a job here. I'm not the only one who's feeling bereft, who's mourned the departure of our children, felt the quiet of our empty house, and wondered what will fill up the space that not so long ago was occupied by two boys. In his case, two boys asking for help with math problems or challenging their dad to Ping-Pong in the basement or dishing out huge bowls of ice cream to eat while cheering for the Celtics on TV. There's a hole at the center of his life, too.

"In the fall, Katrina lost a really close friend," Steve continues, "and for months before that she was completely focused on being with her, helping her. So even when my wife *was* home, it was almost as if she was only half there, because she'd be writing an e-mail to her friend, or thinking about her. That was a hard time for her. For us. And she certainly wasn't focused on me. But I understood. I never said a word about that. But now, it feels as if she's leaving again. And it makes me think I've fallen pretty low on her list of priorities."

Whoa. So *this* is what the argument is really about. How could I not have realized that my husband had his own story of loss here, or that he was seeing a very different movie playing in his mind (abandonment!) than I was seeing in mine (growth!)? And now what? I reach for one of Victor's tissues, and try to gather my own thoughts.

I recall all the years when our boys were young, years that I stayed behind while my publishing-executive husband traveled the world for work: Singapore, Nepal, Germany, England, New York. There was never a question; his job as a vice president of a company took him elsewhere, my job as a mother and editor kept me home. I envied him those adventures a little, but not too much; home was where I wanted to be anyway. In more recent years, as

Steve slowly built his own business from scratch and I tried to offset the loss of my annual editing income by writing, our finances and circumstances dictated that we both stay home. There were college tuitions to think about, no money—or time—to spare, and the needs of our two teenage sons took clear precedence over ours. It was absolutely clear where we needed to be and what we needed to be doing: working, parenting, paying bills, making meals, getting kids from point A to point B.

But that chapter is over. My husband, it turns out, was expecting that our sons' departure would mean more time for the two of us. And I was assuming, once they'd left the house, that I would be free to toss down my dishtowel and get out of there myself. No wonder we're both feeling hurt and angry. And what a relief it is, finally, to understand why.

The problem is, I still want to go.

Much as I love my husband, and uncertain as I am of my path, I also have a feeling that if I don't figure out a way to leave home for a while and challenge myself in some new way, a part of me I haven't even met yet might just dry up and die. I don't know if my dear, long-gone, cookie-baking, girdle-wearing, church-going grandmothers ever yearned for adventures of their own; they never let on. I do know my mother's midlife journey into herself was begun in heartbreak and exacted a high price, but that surviving it also made her strong, both clearer about who she was and more understanding of a marriage she returned to on her own terms.

I wonder, though, if there is another way. A way to answer a soul's call without doing harm to those left behind, a way of deepening love and confidence and cooperation in a marriage even while allowing for more space and distance within the relationship. A way for me to, as Joseph Campbell advises, "say a hearty 'yes' to my adventure," without risking the love and trust of the man who signed on all those years ago to share and bear witness to the entire narrative—and who is still at the center of my story.

"I feel like you heard me," Steve says later as we drive home through the winter darkness beneath a sky pricked with stars. There is no one on the road but us, the empty snowfields on both sides glittering under a knife-edged sliver of moon. And I am suddenly overcome with gratitude for his steady, familiar presence beside me, his hands on the wheel guiding us home.

"And I think that's what I really needed most, for you to know how I feel," he continues. "I wasn't part of your special friendship with Marie, or part of her death. That was a very intense experience you went through that we didn't share.

"And now, I guess I worry about you going off to do this other thing that's important to you, but that I'm not part of either. I worry that this will change you, and that as time goes by we'll have even less to share. But," he adds, reaching over to find my hand, "I think I'm starting to understand why you want to go. I think you should. I'm going to figure out how to use that time myself, to do a few things I've been putting off. Maybe a separation will be good for both of us."

To grow without growing apart, to allow the one you love to be different today than he or

she was yesterday and to love him or her anyway, even as you struggle to figure out what's
changed: Perhaps this is the challenge that must
ultimately be surmounted in every long-term
relationship if it's to remain fresh and resilient,
rather than growing stale and stiff with age, too
brittle to bend and stretch with time. I know
my husband and I love each other. But it seems
we're both coming to see that love alone isn't
enough to keep a commitment alive; we need
imagination, too. And enough creativity and
courage to create a new form for our marriage,
a marriage that's growing old and being forced
to adapt, just as we are.

What I see now is that although the invisible, inner part of this journey began months
ago within the recesses of my own heart, as I
adjusted to Jack's absence and said good-bye
to my friend and saw the life I'd known vanishing before my eyes, it's suddenly taken on
a whole new dimension. Now that I actually
want to pack a bag and walk out the door, this
symbolic voyage becomes a physical one. No
wonder it seems a little threatening to my husband. He's the one being left behind.

Is the way opening at my feet? To my relief, it seems to be. I don't even realize it until this moment: Not only is it important for me to stretch my wings, it matters tremendously that I do so with Steve's approval and consent. Growth happens, after all, not only in the solitary darkness, but in the light as well; not only in private excavations of the soul, but in our evolving relationships with those we love. My life is in his hands, just as his rests in mine—this, after all, is what we agreed to, the deal we made all those years ago: to be responsible for each other, responsible *to* each other, as much as to ourselves. And yet it is for our own sake, as well as the sake of the marriage, that we must each find ways to stretch as well, to allow room within the boundaries of our togetherness for change and flux and recalibration.

"Go," he says at last, meaning it. And I love him the more for that.

The day after my acceptance letter arrives from Kripalu, I meet Margaret for tea and a briefing. "It's intense," she says.

"Intense, as in physically demanding?" I ask.

"Intense, as in emotionally intense? Intense how, exactly? What else is there, besides yoga?"

I notice that my friend isn't really answering my questions. Instead, she's giving me practical advice, like, "Dress in layers for class. Bring flip-flops for the shower and a separate notebook for anatomy. And don't make any plans for the so-called 'day off'—you'll need every bit of that time to study and catch up on the reading, and to do your laundry, and to work on your practice teaching plans."

I write all this down carefully, in the innocent hope that with the right packing list and a few words of wisdom from a recent graduate, I will be well prepared. Margaret loans me her textbook and some trail maps, and I jot down a few more items she suggests: shower caddy, mug, soap, earplugs—exactly what I would need if I were eighteen and heading off to college.

Despite various friends' advice (I can even hear Marie's voice in there: "Treat yourself to a private room, for God's sake!"), I sign on to live in a dorm with a bathroom down the hall; it's cheaper, for one, but it also seems to me part of what I'm going in search of—not an escape from my life but the experience of a larger one; not just a teaching certificate, but, well, a liberal education in the art of living. All that, and something I can't even name. Some deeper sense of my own purpose, I suppose. Surely, I'll learn more from spending a month living with strangers than I would by escaping to a room of my own.

I've been practicing every day at home, trying to prepare myself for the demands of four to six hours of yoga a day. And I've gotten myself convinced that if I can't go up into a headstand in the middle of the room without fear, then I must be some kind of yoga imposter who shouldn't even be going at all. Margaret puts a stop to all that. "This isn't about what you can do," she reminds me gently, "it's about who you are."

And there it is: my first lesson of yoga teacher training. I am so used to doubting my worthiness that the minute I decide to do something, I start convincing myself that I'm not up to the job.

"Don't overdo it," she continues, "or you'll

show up injured, like I did. Take it easy. Forget the headstand. You won't even *do* headstand till the last day. The yoga is intense, but this training is about so much more than yoga.

"I'm a little envious," she confesses. And then she smiles, a deliberately mischievous twinkle in her eye. "You can't even begin to imagine how much will happen in a month."

My cell phone rings before I've pulled my car out of the parking lot. "I forgot to tell you the most important thing," Margaret says in a low voice, as if what she has to say is top-secret information. "Just remember: It's all about love."

On a bright, bitterly cold February morning, I am driving south to the Berkshires, the car piled with yoga mats and hiking gear and a couple of coffee-stained L.L.Bean tote bags full of stretch pants and T-shirts and books. I've put a vacation message on my e-mail and decided I won't commit to writing anything while I'm away. I've left a freezer full of spaghetti sauce and chicken soup for Steve. I've also worried about every single thing there is to

worry about: my age, my failing memory (all
those poses and their Sanskrit names to memorize!), constipation, catching a cold, whether
there will be coffee, my yoga ability or lack of
it, whether I have the right clothes, sleeping in
a room with people I don't know, the dog, the
kids, my husband, you name it.

But my husband has given me the one gift I
longed for—encouragement to go, and a willingness on his part to look at this month of
solitude as an opportunity to do some growing and thinking of his own. Having revealed
what he was most afraid of—that in the process of exploring my own limits I would somehow also expose the limits in our relationship
with each other—he has come full circle.

"Forget your perfect offering," as Leonard
Cohen sings. "There is a crack in everything,
that's how the light gets in." Our marriage
may not be perfect, but it is proving to be resilient. And, most important of all, we're both
trying to do a better job of hearing each other,
of being kind, of allowing for each other's different needs. Already, I sense a new tolerance
between us, as if in revealing the flaws and fis-

sures that have sprung up in our relationship and acknowledging them, we've also allowed in a little more light, and found a little more faith in the imperfect, enduring beauty of *us*.

What a long way we've come from our smug naïveté and that long-ago field of pure white snow. And the years ahead will be nothing if not challenging. But by acknowledging that we no longer need to walk side by side in lockstep, that our paths may diverge at times and then reunite us, it seems we're also making space for each other to change in ways that are essential to our separate souls. As we find our way through this more complicated landscape of loss and age and revised expectation, perhaps we can also learn new ways to be together, even when we're apart.

I slip a yoga chant CD into the car stereo and settle in to enjoy the drive. The highway is empty on this Sunday morning, the sun is shining, the world unveiled, open and exposed. And for a few hours, I am suspended in space, traveling at seventy miles an hour between all that I know and my own unwritten future.

I am wearing Marie's pale ice-blue Athleta

jacket—a winter jacket unlike any I would buy for myself. It is, in fact, utterly, impeccably *her*, and yet it fits me so perfectly that, wearing it, I almost feel as if she's here with me, or as if, in some inexplicable way, she's *in* me. I have her flip-flops in my bag, the ones she bought to wear when she went to Kripalu herself two years ago, for a weekend workshop with fellow cancer patients that filled her with hope and purpose. And even better, I am tuned right in to "the Marie channel"; I know this is exactly what my friend would want for me—the journey she didn't get to take, a full embrace of the life she didn't get to live.

"What is the purpose of this pilgrimage?" the Zen master asks the student as he stands on the path with his pack.

"I don't know."

"Not knowing is most intimate," says the master.

Not knowing, I'm finally on my way.

~6~

compassion

One's destination is never a
place, but rather a new way of
looking at things.

—HENRY MILLER

To arrive at Kripalu Center for Yoga &
Health for the first time is, perhaps inevitably,
to be disappointed. Ever since I first heard the
name years ago, I've felt pulled to this place,
drawn to its promise of transformation and
tranquility. When my friend was lost in the
grim landscape of treatments and prognoses, a
weekend workshop at Kripalu with cancer sur-
vivor and green juice goddess Kris Carr gave
her a sense of connection, empowerment, and
hope—the realization that others, too, shared

her difficult path, and that although there were many things in her life she couldn't control, there was still much she could.

"You *have* to go there," she insisted more than once. "You will love it." We talked many times of returning to Kripalu together, perusing the catalog, considering the pros and cons of different workshops, comparing our calendars. And then, instead of seizing the moment when it was actually still possible to go, we always put off the trip, in the unspoken hope that someday she'd be stronger, able to enjoy herself more.

Now, all these months later, it feels as if I've traveled more than just the three hours from home to get here, to finally fulfill my friend's wish for me and to realize this vague, unruly dream of my own. "It may be when we no longer know what to do," writes poet Wendell Berry, "that we have come to our real work, and that when we no longer know which way to go, we have begun our real journey."

For so many years, I actually *did* know what to do. How strange, to think that all the busyness of work and family life, necessary and fulfilling as it was, also allowed me to postpone this disconcerting, midlife confrontation with myself. If not knowing which way to go is the beginning of what Wendell Berry calls the "real journey," then I have most definitely been wandering around on an overgrown, inscrutable path for a while now.

By the time I get to Lenox, I am on edge, nervous and excited, and weary after getting almost no sleep on my final night at home. For some reason, my GPS does not have Kripalu's address as a possible destination, and so I drive back and forth on the same country road for nearly half an hour, my skin prickling with frustration, before I finally pull over, find my information packet, call Kripalu's main number, and listen to the recorded options. On the second try, relieved that my telephone safari has actually brought me voice to voice with a real person, I find out that I'm already there. I need only look out the window and notice where I am. Hmmm. A message from the universe about waking up? Right in front of me is a small black sign with gold letters: KRIPALU. How did I miss it?

What I finally see, as I emerge at the top of a long, winding, wooded drive, is a homely brick edifice that looks like a cross between a hospital and a low-income housing complex. There is nothing beautiful about this utilitarian building, erected in 1957 as a Jesuit seminary on a spacious knoll in the heart of the Berkshire Hills. And, despite the determinedly cheerful squadron of volunteer greeters stationed at the threshold, there is nothing Zen-like about the process of getting officially registered within. The place means business, as well it should given that thirty thousand people a year carry their dreams and desires through these doors. The staff is nothing if not efficient. I am welcomed, given a form to fill out, reminded that I will have to move my car, asked to come up with my license plate number and to sign a letter of release; should I have a heart attack on the premises, the management is not responsible. There is a line of new guests forming behind me, an assortment of duffel bags and backpacks at my feet, luggage carts and a crowd of young women in Lululemon jackets blocking the way into the lobby.

In exchange for my completed paperwork, I'm presented at the front desk with a plastic room key and a name tag on a clip, along with maps of the building and grounds, a fact sheet about the teacher training, and directions to the single elevator around the corner. And then, committing my room number to memory, I make my way through the throng of people and luggage and amiable volunteers crowding the lobby to go in search of my new home away from home: a small, bright, linoleum-tiled room on the fourth floor, as institutional and utilitarian as the novitiate's dorm it was originally designed to be. There is just space for two pairs of metal bunk beds, a single twin (already taken) in the middle, a sink, two metal chairs, a wastebasket, and three small dressers to be shared for a month with four other women.

I choose a bottom bunk, make up the bed, unpack my things, and sit, the letdown and commotion of arriving giving way, finally, to a glimmer of relief at having arrived. The view out the window settles me: the unruffled sheet of sky; the imperturbable, snow-covered fields;

the blue, embracing mountains beyond. I will come to know that landscape well in the weeks to come, will memorize the shapely silhouettes of those undulating hills. But what, I wonder, have I really come here to learn?

She is twenty, perhaps. A tall, willow wand of a girl in stretchy white capris, midriff-baring halter, and snug, fringy black sweater. Dark hair scrunched into a loose ponytail, pale latte-colored freckles scattered across high, lovely cheekbones; enormous, long-lashed, espresso eyes. With the easy grace of a dancer she flows through a series of postures and then comes to rest, standing on one foot. I watch as she lifts her arms high, sweeps her leg up behind her, arches back, and effortlessly grabs her toes in the most perfect expression of dancer pose I've ever seen.

It is dark outside, just after 6:30 a.m. on this first full day of teacher training, and in silence we have arrived, unrolled our mats, and begun our individual practices, sixty-five aspiring yoga teachers of all ages and from all walks of life, gathered together here to answer calls that seem as varied as our backgrounds. For the next twenty-eight days, we will get to know ourselves and one another in this room. Our attendance will be required at four to five sessions a day, beginning in the morning with mandatory six-thirty silent practice and ending on many nights at nine. Two hundred required hours of class time with every hour carefully counted and accounted for, six days a week packed full of lectures, posture clinics, anatomy lessons, yoga practice, meditation, practice teaching, quizzes, and experiential exercises that have already, within the first twelve hours, made me squirm with discomfort. (No, my trusty guide Margaret did not forewarn me that we would be given crayons and paper the very first night and asked to illustrate our intentions and write down our innermost aspirations, or that we would introduce ourselves to one another by coming up with imaginary book titles, or sit knee to knee with strangers and be expected to share the jumbled fears lurking in our hearts.)

To say I'm feeling overwhelmed would be an understatement. I've already failed to live up to my first commitment to myself: that, no matter what, I would have "a good attitude." What I'm experiencing on my yoga mat at this moment is a mixture of despair and defeat. What was I thinking, imagining I could do this?

The practice I've been feeling pretty good about in the privacy of my kitchen seems woefully feeble out here in the "real" yoga world. Compared to the beauty in action of the young yogini next to me, my poses feel awkward and embarrassing. I try to come back to my own center, to coordinate my breath with my movements, but it's hopeless. I'm not really present on my mat; I'm just going through the motions and watching her, in awe of this girl's serene beauty, her flexibility, the infinite potential of her young life, like a bud asserting its moment to blossom.

At the same time, I'm engaged in a merciless critique of my own unyielding hamstrings, my unwilling hips, my various other shortcomings. The girl spirals her limbs into a few more impossible positions and concludes her practice, extending her elegant toes into the air in headstand, as still and steadfast as a column.

And I give up, kneel down, and surrender my forehead to the floor in child's pose. It is going to be a long month.

Devarshi and Jurian, our two main teachers, are yin and yang, masculine and feminine, a model of friendship and a study in contrasts, bound by their evident longstanding affection for one another and their joy in a shared calling—teaching and bearing witness, again and again, to the transformation of bodies and souls. On the first full day of class, following our early-morning practice and a silent breakfast, they sit side by side on the dais to lead us, as they will each day for the next month, through the shanti mantra, our morning prayers for peace. Devarshi plays the harmonium with his eyes closed, his head tilted back, rapturously singing from the depths of his being these words he knows so well, this prayer he has offered thousands of times before in this building, in this very room, ever since he was himself a young man: *"Om Saha navavatu, Saha Nau Bhunaktu, Saha viryam karavavhai…"*

Jurian, swaying, joins her voice to his: *"Tejas-vi na-vadhi-tam astu."* And we students bow our heads to our books to read along, to form the strange Sanskrit words and to try, tentatively, to thread our own voices into this haunting, heart-piercing chant.

I don't know what the words mean yet; I don't even care. They are beautiful and passionate and sacred, and they are working their magic on me.

I am a middle-aged woman sitting on the floor in a crowded room, here on some vague, indescribable quest for a more passionate aliveness. I'm still not sure what it was that led me to try yoga teacher training rather than to climb mountains as my friend Joni is doing, or to jump back into the workforce as my friend Ellen has done, or to start a nonprofit social service agency like my friend Louise.

I know only that, for the first time since adolescence, I have been lonely and adrift, as if some current is tugging me down, pulling me beneath the surface of my life to go in search of something I have no words for. And that having allowed myself to be carried by that current, I've ended up here—instead of on the top of a four-thousand-foot peak or at a desk in an office or hosting a fund-raiser. It strikes me, however, that although my friends and I are choosing different paths through the second half of our lives, we are all probably in search of the same things: expanded horizons, a renewed sense of adventure and direction. But I suspect there's also a deeper yearning—a shared desire to come more fully into ourselves, to consecrate the inevitable processes of aging and loss into something meaningful.

The paradox of being in my fifties seems to be that even as I hunger for some new challenge, my spirit is also calling out for more quiet time, more reflection, an immersion in the hushed mystery of just being. I don't want to retreat from the world so much as experience it more fully. There are many ways to stretch, and not all of them are physical; I've enrolled for this month of training not only in the hope of finding a new edge in my yoga practice but, even more, to find out if my own heart is capable of more than I've asked of it so far.

Now it occurs to me how lucky I am to have

been given these two particular teachers, two perfectly normal middle-aged adults, fellow travelers who have been knocking around on the planet for just as long as I have, whose backgrounds could not have been more different from mine, but with whom I feel an instant, grateful kinship. Surely they, too, know something of second acts and further journeys, of loss and transformation, of looking at the road ahead and realizing that it is shorter than the distance already traveled.

As we sing together to the reedy strains of the harmonium, I begin to relax, to release some of the doubt and tension and sadness I've carried for months. Some benevolent force larger than me has brought me to this moment, to this prayer for peace and wholeness. There are important lessons for me here, of that I have no doubt. Perhaps all I need to do is open my hands and receive them.

Devarshi tells us he has been a part of Kripalu, off and on, since its ashram days, arriving as an idealistic youthful seeker and staying to become part of this spiritual community in its earliest incarnation. "Back in those days," he

recalls, "there were no yoga mats, we just practiced on the floor." He laughs. "Yoga mats!" he
says. "We thought they were a fad."

He left for a time, married, became a healing arts practitioner, a bodyworker, retreat
leader, teacher, and father. And then, having
raised a family and divorced, he came full
circle back to Kripalu, bringing a rare, long-
distance view to his current role as dean of the
Kripalu School of Yoga. Like a compassionate
spouse in an enduring, complicated marriage,
Devarshi is possessed of an affectionate, well-
seasoned perspective on Kripalu's bumpy history, from the quixotic vows of chastity and
poverty required in the seventies, when he and
his fellow ashram residents pledged obedi-
ence to a guru, through the upheavals of the
early eighties, when their leader was forced out
under a cloud of sexual scandal, to Kripalu's
reorganization and blossoming in the nineties
into a smoothly run, full-scale retreat center
and educational institution.

"Kripalu," we read in our textbooks, means
"compassion." Devarshi personifies it. At once
irreverent and kind, scholarly and funny, a

father of teenagers yet fully in touch with his own inner child, this man has absorbed the wisdom of his decades of meditation, yoga, and deep study, but I sense he's been mellowed by life's hard knocks, too. Both learned master and joyful, eternal student, he embodies confidence tempered by humility. Yoga, he takes seriously; himself, not so much. And simply by being so thoroughly comfortable in his own skin, he puts us at ease in ours. He makes us laugh. He listens with his whole being. By the end of the first day, he knows our names, all sixty-five of them. He's glad we're here. And that's enough to make us glad, too.

"The first time I ever came to take a class at Kripalu," Jurian tells us, "I thought to myself, 'I want to live here!' Well, you know the saying, 'Be careful what you wish for.'" After nearly twenty years in New York, acting on and off-Broadway, in film and on TV, Jurian followed her heart to the Berkshires, bringing to her new midlife career as a yoga teacher a lifetime's worth of experience in voice, dance, and theater arts. Slight in build, playful and ebullient as a pixie, she is also deeply grounded in the authentic language of the soul. And, although neither married nor herself a mother, she is a powerful maternal presence, easily enfolding young and old, male and female, into her nurturing embrace. Devarshi, I suspect, may push and cajole me to my yoga-warrior edge. And Jurian, through her own willingness to entrust a group of strangers with her unguarded, vulnerable self, reminds me of the strength in surrender, the grace in letting go.

"So," Devarshi says fourteen hours later, smiling as we wrap up our first full day of teacher training, "have you noticed that a single day at Kripalu can feel like a lifetime?"

It is exactly what I'm thinking. "A lot happens," he continues. "Things can change fast. And isn't it amazing how time seems to expand when you're fully present?"

He's right. Was it really just this morning that I turned off my alarm at 5:45, slipped my feet into Marie's bronze-colored flip-flops, and padded down the hall to the shower with my yoga clothes under my arm? Was it really just this morning that I convinced myself I had nothing in common with the lithe young woman practicing next to me? It *has* been a long day, and my head is spinning. But as we chant our final "omm" of the night, put away our blocks and blankets, and head for the door, what I'm actually thinking is that the month will be over all too soon. Can tomorrow possibly be as intense as today? Can I really get up in the dark nine hours from now and do all this—*feel* all this—again, and the morning after that?

Home, my family, my "real" life, feels further away than I could have thought possible, as if my own mooring has been snipped, releasing me out into open water. With no familiar landmarks in sight, surrounded by strangers who know nothing of me or my life, I can ease up, relax, and allow myself to be both lost and found. The challenge here, as Margaret tried to tell me, isn't going to be about perfecting yoga poses at all.

"You are not here to remake yourself," Devarshi suggests by way of saying good night, "but to remember yourself. Whatever you came to teacher training in search of is already inside you, just waiting to be unearthed and acknowledged." He smiles, drops his voice, and somehow includes every one of us in his gaze. "Whatever you need, you have."

Already I'm coming to suspect that, different as the details of our lives most certainly are, and varied as our experiences on this earth have been, the sixty-five men and women whom fate and circumstance have gathered together in this room are more alike than different. We are all here in response to some urge to change and grow, ready to do what it takes to become more fully who we are and, at the same time, part of something greater than ourselves. I am exhausted and inspired, grateful and relieved. I might not ever teach a single person how to do a downward-facing dog, but maybe it doesn't even matter; this, I am certain, is exactly where I'm meant to be.

"Should we go to the hot tub?" Barbara asks when we get up to our room. We have just an hour left till "lights out"; according to dorm rules, overhead lights are supposed to be switched off at nine thirty, individual reading lamps by ten. But after a long day of sitting on the floor and hours of yoga, a soak before bed sounds like good therapy—and an opportunity for us five roommates to begin to get to know one another. I'm not the only emptynester mom in the room; Barbara, single and fifty-four, an art teacher and runner, tells us she has a son back on Nantucket. I sense in her quiet voice and sad brown eyes a sensitivity that endears her to me right away. My upper bunkmate, Sierra, thirty, is a witch. A good witch, she assures us, twining a curly lock of long brown hair around her finger, but a serious practitioner of the pagan arts. She has arrived with a wand and a stash of ingredients for spells; the braided white and gold ribbons draped around her neck, she explains, aren't for show, they are a talisman for a spell—white magic to manifest her secret desires. Leah, twenty-seven, a PhD candidate in psychology, has practically grown up at Kripalu; having come here with her yogi mom for as long as she can remember, she hopes that teaching yoga will help her bridge the income gap between being a doctoral student and finding a job. Zsuzsi, a tall, quiet young woman from Germany, tells us she has grave doubts about the spiritual side of yoga but is attracted to the discipline, the stillness; and, although she and her boyfriend have chosen spartan lives of voluntary simplicity and minimal impact, she still needs to earn a living. "I am an atheist," she says shyly, "so this talk of God, and higher powers, it is not for me. I am uncomfortable saying 'omm.' And with my accent, I am not sure if I can teach. But, well"—she shrugs—"here I am. We shall see."

Diverse in age and background and intention we may be, but we are happy with one another, eager to get along and to accommodate one another's idiosyncrasies. And our first decision as a group is what, exactly, to wear to walk from our fourth-floor room down to the basement, where the sauna and hot tubs are located. Do we want to be seen wearing bathrobes in these coed hallways? Bathing suits and sweats? We arrive at a unanimous consensus— bathing suits!—discreetly turn our backs to change clothes, and troop downstairs into the bowels of the building.

There are only three other women in the communal hot tub at this late hour. Enormously fat women. Naked women. Women, clearly, with nothing to hide, nothing to prove, and no one to impress. They are older, in their sixties, talking animatedly about the day they've spent in some other program. Three ample pairs of breasts float in the roiling water. The women pause in their conversation and glance up as the five of us emerge from the steam and step gingerly into the scalding water, feeling suddenly self-conscious and ridiculously overdressed in our demure tank suits. Happy to make room for us, they glide one by one, glistening like porpoises, over to the stairs. There is no way to avert the eyes, nowhere else to look, no way to avoid noticing, as the first bather hoists herself up and out of the tub: the vast mural of horticultural tattoos blossoming across her belly and snaking up and over her pendulous, dripping bosom. She is well over two hundred pounds, and as gloriously ornate in her decor as a stained-glass window. The other two, somewhat less elaborately etched but equally nonchalant in

their nudity, follow suit, their mighty but-
tocks gleaming like moons as they climb up
the stairs. The women retrieve their towels,
give us friendly waves, and disappear into the
night. The five of us look at one another and
burst out laughing—at ourselves, at those wild
tattoos, at our own silly, pointless modesty.
"Guess we can get over it," I say. And right
then and there, we do. We've bonded. And we
are done with bathing suits.

"Yoga," says the quote from the Bhagavad
Gita posted in the stairwell to the fourth floor,
"is the practice of tolerating the consequences
of being yourself." I can't help but smile as I
pass by it on my way up to bed. This, I suspect,
is the practice of a lifetime. Oddly enough, it's
already feeling easier.

There is, it turns out, a "wheel of transformation," and a poster of it is hanging on the wall
in our classroom. I copy the diagram into my
notebook, but it feels as if I've seen it all before.
And then I realize: The words here are different, but the stages are exactly the same—they
align almost perfectly with Joseph Campbell's

vision of the hero's journey: the call to change or adventure; the hesitation at the door, or threshold; the road of trials and temptations; the abyss, or what Campbell calls "the belly of the beast" and what Devarshi has labeled "the fertile void"; followed by revelation, transformation, atonement, and the hero's eventual return to what he left behind, bearing new wisdom to share and possessed of a deeper equilibrium.

"You may think you came here to learn how to teach triangle pose to a beginner yoga student," Devarshi suggests, walking over to the poster, "but there's probably a bit more going on." Gesturing at the words *fertile void* at the bottom of the circle, he asks, "So how many of you would say you're right about here?" Nearly every hand in the room goes up.

I look around at my classmates and, for the first time, notice how neatly we cleave into two separate groups. There are the fledglings, who make up most of the class—young men and women in their late teens, twenties, and early thirties; they are either still in school or recently out and embarking on their adult lives, sorting out careers and relationships, separating from families of origin and thinking about starting families of their own, giving shape to their dreams and beginning to find their way in the world. There's no doubt that this is a time of searching and questioning for them, that they are asking themselves, "Who am I?" and "What next?"

And then there is a smaller group, those of us in our late forties and fifties. On the back side of all that building and becoming, easily old enough to be the parents of our younger classmates, we're in that phase of life some sociologists now call "second adulthood." Our children are grown, we've weathered the ups and downs of shifting careers and finances, failed marriages and reinvented relationships, illness and recovery, change and loss. But we, too, are asking, "Who am I?" and "What next?"

What's missing in the room, it occurs to me, is a group in the middle; there aren't very many here in their thirties and forties. But little wonder. Just two years ago, even six months ago, I couldn't have considered taking a chunk of time off from my life. If you have kids at home, a family to care for, a job that requires your time and energy, you might manage to slip away for a weekend now and then, but you aren't exactly free to pack your bags and walk out the door to go practice yoga for a month while you consider the big picture. You need to be home, taking the casserole out of the oven, writing the midyear report, making a costume for the school play, keeping all those balls in the air.

The fertile void may be uncomfortable, the emptiness disconcerting, but all of a sudden, looking around the room, I do suddenly appreciate what a privilege it is to be here. How lucky I am that life has afforded me this time to actually confront my own struggles and questions and doubts. You can't be in survival mode and in the fertile void at the same time. And our fast-paced, twenty-first-century lives don't offer up too many fallow seasons, or enough time, ever, to truly pause, be quiet, and turn inward.

Even now, all it would take is one child in crisis, one friend in need, an unexpected illness, or even a parent asking for help, and this hiatus would abruptly end. The fertile void would give way to a to-do list and a return to my own normal, overscheduled, outer-directed busyness.

And so, with this new perspective, I decide simply to turn my attention from what's missing in my life to what's present: a rare, unprecedented opportunity to be still and to go deep. Certainly the fertile void appears to be an essential, unavoidable part of most major life transitions, an uncomfortable, in-between place in which old layers are shed, old defenses dropped, old demons confronted. The only way out is through. But, as my friend Thomas Moore points out in his book *Dark Nights of the Soul*, being stuck is part of being human, and a dark night of the soul can be a profoundly good thing, for it allows a life that once made sense but needs reviving to break apart and then come together in a new shape.

"If the dark night is indeed a rite of passage," he writes, "your job is to let the transformation take place. Be sculpted, renewed, changed. You are the caterpillar becoming the butterfly.

Your task is to let the change happen. Do what you can to participate in and cautiously and artfully further the process. Discover the very point of personhood: the process of constant renewal."

What a comfort it is, to know that this, too, is growth and that I am not the only one floundering. Surrounded by strangers who are quickly becoming friends, practicing and learning and sharing even the most intimate details of our lives with one another, I am already feeling lighter, uplifted. Everything, it seems, is grist for the mill; every challenging moment an invitation to practice. And it is a little easier to let go when everyone around me is softening and yielding as well. What I see, as all of the carefully composed public masks we arrived here wearing begin to fall away, are tender, unguarded human faces. It's impossible not to notice how beautiful they are. How beautiful *we* are.

Although some of the questions I'm asking myself these days are the same ones I was pondering in my early twenties, the fertile void of the fifties is quite different from that youthful time of ambition and awakening, when life felt wide open, vast, and durable. In her book *Inventing the Rest of Our Lives: Women in Second Adulthood*, Suzanne Braun Levine, the first editor of *Ms.* magazine, includes an entire chapter on the fertile void, a phrase coined by Gestalt therapist Ilana Rubenfeld to describe an inevitable stage in any journey of transformation. "Every woman I spoke to got the phrase 'fertile void' the moment the words were out of my mouth," Levine reports. Soul-searching, it seems, goes with the territory of midlife endings and beginnings. Whether we are quitting jobs or bearing down even harder, ending relationships or embarking on them, ushering grown children out the door or caring for elderly parents, the fifties in particular seem to be a decade in which life as we knew it gets all shaken up. There is no escaping the downside of growing older; no way to begin the descent without letting go of some of our youthful assumptions and entering this disorienting "gravity-free zone" in which old ways of doing and being no longer work, new ones have yet to take shape, and nothing feels stable or assured.

How ironic, to realize that maturity brings not more conviction, but less. At twenty-two, I still believed I could make a life plan and then set about executing it; that there were answers to all my questions, and if I just worked hard enough, I would find them. What I feel now is both a greater sense of fragility, knowing that life is both unpredictable and finite, and at the same time, an awareness that, no matter how long I live, I'll never get things all figured out. Uncertainty is part of the human condition; perhaps contentment comes as we learn to get comfortable with it.

And so, as the days go by, I am even more grateful for my brief sabbatical, for the time and space to move slowly and deliberately into this new phase. Life, as I'm finally coming to see, isn't all onward and upward after all; it's also wide-open plateaus and shadowy thresholds, the lonely liminal spaces between what's ended and what has yet to begin. It is here that the darkness can feel most acute, our anxiety most intolerable. But perhaps it is also here, in the wild borderlands of our soul journeys, that we begin to trust our own inner compass to guide us onward. I wonder if I have the stamina to endure this silence, to allow what's next to reveal itself, rather than to grasp too quickly at some new thing just because it's there.

I'm not alone. As my classmates share their experiences of the fertile void, it becomes clear that, young or old, everyone in the room has experienced both the ache of loss and the quickening pulse of new potential. We share a sense of being on a mission without a map. There is restlessness and fear, impatience to get a move on, and doubt about where to go, a sense of urgency and, at the same time, confusion about just what it is that's so important.

Not surprisingly, Devarshi suggests, the best antidote to anxiety about the future is to be fully present in the here and now. The fertile void may feel like a long, dark, sleepless night, but it is also a sacred space and time, a place in which pain is transmuted into growth. Here, compassion takes root and is watered by tears of humility. Faith, once shaken, is gradually restored, tempered now by patience. There is no rushing the process. And yet once we begin to observe the busy workings of our minds, we can choose where to place our attention. Instead of continually wondering, "What's next?" we can bring a spirit of inquiry into the present moment. We can be still, and more considerate toward ourselves. When it is too dark to see, we can listen instead. We can ask, "What is my experience of *this* moment?"

Yoga, he reminds us, brings what is unconscious and habitual to consciousness. And then, moment by moment, breath by breath, we are free to choose: How shall I respond? Can I stay right here, right now, with what is? Can I feel my own feelings? How shall I act on this thought, this emotion?

I've known all this for years, have experienced that quiet focus on my yoga mat and, intermittently, in my life. Writing in the silence of an empty room, lying on the floor with my heart elevated and tears sliding down my cheeks, sitting in my garden and watching the mountains turn purple at sunset, standing at the bedside of a sleeping child, lying in my husband's arms after making love, I've experienced deep stillness, a sense of quiet connection, spaciousness. But suddenly, here, I glimpse another possibility: the idea that this limitless awareness, this consciousness, this equanimity, is not random. In fact, it's something I can practice and cultivate, even in dark, uncomfortable moments. It is itself a path. And walking that path is a way toward becoming it.

I may not be able to create a to-do *or* a how-to list for happiness in the next chapter of my life, or come up with tidy answers to my questions. I may not even discover that clear sense of purpose I came in search of. But I can do this. Here, with hours a day to practice and two extraordinary teachers to illuminate the way, I can begin to change my relationship with myself. I can stop striving and judging and doubting, and experience the peace of being present to whatever is actually happening. I can cultivate the wide-open, limitless gifts of attention and acceptance.

"*Yoga citta vritti nirodhah*," we chant in unison, our arms lifted overhead as we sing out the last word. "Yoga is the intentional stopping of the spontaneous activity of the mind."

What's left? Pure consciousness. A calm, compassionate witness to all the ups and downs, sorrows and joys, nagging self-doubts and constant judgments with which we fill our minds and in which we lose our days.

A line from Joseph Campbell comes back to me: "The purpose of the journey is compassion." I dismissed these words when I first encountered them last summer, as I began reading Campbell's work on the hero's journey in the hope of finding a road map for my own. Then, they seemed too obvious, too glib to be of use. Now, I'm struck by their brilliance.

~7~

love

*Love is not far away. It is as close as
your own heart. You can find it there
without walking a single step.*

—SWAMI KRIPALU

$\mathcal{I}$n a way, teacher training is like kindergarten. We begin the day singing. We have circle
time and sharing time. Our teachers tell us stories. They talk about big ideas like "alignment"
and "integration" and "consciousness," but
keep it interesting by relating these concepts to
our ordinary, everyday experiences. We memorize ten simple precepts known as the *yamas*
and the *niyamas*, the first two limbs of yoga's
eight-fold path—including truth, nonviolence,
moderation, self-discipline, surrender—ethical
guidelines, like the ten commandments, to

help us negotiate our messy, human lives more skillfully. We discuss the ancient aphorisms of Patanjali, the cryptic, compelling *yoga sutras*, and we practice saying them out loud all together, with special hand movements to help us remember the words. We get up and move our bodies and do poses with names like "cobra" and "crane" and "tree." Sometimes we put music on and dance. Then we sit quietly with our hands in our laps. We close our eyes and breathe and pay attention to our own inhalations and exhalations. And after that, we lie down on our mats, cover up with blankets, and have a rest.

Every day, I have to stop and pinch myself. *I get to do this?*

All that's required is that I show up and be present. There is no one to cook for or clean up after or take care of. My cell phone sits untouched in a drawer in my room, off. Even my e-mail is set to automatic response. As Devarshi reminds us as we settle into *shavasana*, our deep rest at the end of yoga practice, "There is nothing to do. There is nowhere to go."

After a few decades of doing and going, planning and executing, buying things and making things and fixing things, it feels strange to stop. Radical, in fact. Take away all the busyness and obligations that normally fill my days, and what remains? Or, maybe, *who* remains? Being here, coming face-to-face with myself day after day, is a bit like dumping out the junk drawer in the kitchen.

In our house, that drawer is the place where everything that doesn't have a proper home ends up: rubber bands, chip clips, a screwdriver, loose AAA batteries, old pens, a bread recipe scribbled on a pink file card, a broken necklace, leftover packets of salt and pepper, half a bag of candied ginger, a pair of tweezers, a key on a string. Not long ago, tired of rummaging around in there, I pulled the drawer out and emptied it onto the counter. What to put back in? Very little, as it turned out. There wasn't much of note in the contents of that drawer except the mess it represented. I hung the screwdriver above Steve's workbench in the basement, slid the recipe into a file folder, stored the chip clips in a cup, and threw everything else away. Suddenly, there was more breathing room in the kitchen: one perfectly empty drawer that, an hour before, had been full to bursting with stuff I didn't need.

This time away from home is a chance to empty out my own inner junk drawer, to do a psychic housecleaning. But what will be left, once my heap of old assumptions about myself and the world, my hodgepodge of judgments and insecurities, are swept away? What will go back into my empty drawer? I'm not sure yet. Transformation, it seems, is as much about unlearning as learning, as much about letting go of what's outlived as taking hold of what's new.

Ever since childhood, I've felt a tension between who I think I *should* be—smarter, more confident, more creative, more adventurous, more outgoing—and who I am: quiet, introspective, sensitive, and solitary. If I could only be *better*, I think—a better wife, a better mother, a better writer, a better *human*—then I would feel more sure of myself and more worthy. More deserving of my life. Even writing those words I realize, of course, how self-defeating they are. (No wonder emptying the junk drawer and sifting through the contents has never been very high on my list of priorities!)

Here, though, tackling the junk drawer is an unavoidable part of the curriculum. Growth and transformation occur not by changing who we are, Devarshi suggests, but as we summon the courage to *be* who we are. And that means bringing our own true, vulnerable, imperfect selves out of hiding and into the world.

One afternoon, we are asked to walk slowly around the room, making eye contact as we go. When two pairs of eyes meet and a connection is felt, we come to a stop, stand face-to-face with another person, and look right at him or her, waiting patiently to see what's there. I am standing in front of my roommate, Barbara. We both stifle an impulse to laugh. And then we each take a deep breath and look calmly, steadily, directly at each other. I try to send her a silent message with my gaze: I care about you. Then, following the instructions we've been given, she says quietly, "I'm Barbara and I want to be seen."

I allow some space around those words, giving them time to settle. And then I respond, "I see you."

We wait a beat. "I'm Katrina," I say. "And I want to be seen." We look deeply into each other's eyes, seeing, accepting, appreciating. When the moment feels complete, we nod our farewells and I move on, till my eyes meet those of another partner, another flawed, uncertain, worthy human being who wants exactly what I want, what we all want: to be seen and to be loved exactly as we really are.

It is not long before tears start to flow in the room. Allowing ourselves to be seen, releasing long-held shame or fear, and meeting another's gaze head-on is scary stuff. As we stand in the warm glow of truth and acceptance, the bastions crumble. Beneath all the layers of self-protection, beneath the facades of our carefully constructed personas, we are all vulnerable. We are all tender.

I understand now, of course, why my magical guide Margaret didn't happen to mention that our training would include 1970s-style encounter group exercises. Who on earth would want to do this? Just trying to describe it in words I find myself hesitating. It sounds so corny. So hot-tubby and est-ish and weird. "Seems kind of off-task," a friend says later when I tell him about it. Well, actually, no.

I think back to why I came to Kripalu in the first place: not because I longed to teach yoga, but because I wanted to *be* more like a yoga teacher. It wasn't really about learning to stand on my head, it was about learning to stand with more ease in my life. And yes, as our teacher Jurian said, "Be careful what you wish for." Because here I am, enrolled in a rigorous, 24/7 course in personal transformation. And what it all comes down to, of course, is finding the courage to reveal my own vulnerability and the compassion to accept things just as they are: myself as I am, my life as it is, the present moment, the joys and the sorrows, the ups and the downs, the whole ball of wax.

Day by day, my classmates and I are learning not only to lengthen our spines and open our hips, but to quiet our garrulous inner critics, to acknowledge our fears, and to open our hearts as well. Of course, I should have known:

This change, this new sense of self and direction I've been searching for, wasn't ever going to be found "out there" somewhere; it would unfold in its own time, within me. But there's no denying that I've put myself into the crucible now, a place devoted to and designed to support the dynamics of change.

In this room, there are no expectations to meet nor any identities to uphold. I'm not the mother of Henry and Jack, or the wife of Steve, or the writer of books, or the former literary editor. I'm just another work-in-progress in bare feet and yoga pants. And that is how my classmates and I come to know and to care about one another, not through our job titles or possessions or accomplishments, or lack thereof; not by our past successes and failures, but simply through the qualities we embody as we learn to live and work and practice together—generosity, humor, empathy, tolerance, kindness.

Yoga practice, studying, meditation, silence, long solitary walks at noon, early rising—it feels as if this simple, structured routine is giving "me" back to myself, the part of me who isn't longing for love or acceptance or approval, but who just *is*. The me who doesn't need to be improved or changed or concealed. I can't help but wonder if the inner calm I'm feeling, this sense of effortless being—even in the face of hard work and daily challenges—is what our teachers call the "true self" that has been there all along, a being who is, as Devarshi keeps reminding us, "infinite, eternal, and whole." This "me" seems to be someone I can befriend after all, someone both resilient and hopeful, quiet and kind, someone who is fine just as she is.

In his book *Yoga and the Quest for the True Self*, Kripalu yoga teacher and psychotherapist Stephen Cope writes about the importance of transformational space—sacred shelters in which we can safely shed old layers and ways of coping in order to undertake the hard, holy work of becoming ourselves. A transformational space could be a church retreat, a friend's isolated wilderness cabin, or a therapist's office. What's essential is the sense of protection and embrace it affords during a raw and tender time of molting and new growth. And this, I now realize, is what our wise teachers are providing for us here: a safe place in which to experiment, to make our own breaks with whatever has been outlived or isn't working in our lives, and to awaken new energies. Being here is an invitation to experience both the joy and the pain of living fully and feeling everything. The real work, it turns out, is about learning how to say "yes" to that invitation.

I will graduate in a couple of weeks having memorized the Sanskrit names for ninety poses and knowing how to lead a class through an hour and a half of yoga practice. But the most important learning and becoming is going on deep beneath the surface, as I discover that I can endure my own imperfections after all, and that I can choose to be happy with my life as is, rather than struggling against it or expecting something more. The journey, not surprisingly, isn't about getting from someplace lacking to someplace better. It is about learning how to travel well, how to negotiate the inevitable bumps in the road more skillfully.

One morning before practice, Jurian reads us

a poem called "Whatever Doesn't Serve." I'm pretty certain I'm not the only one in the room thinking, "How amazing, someone wrote this just for me."

What weight can you
put down right now,
willingly relinquishing
the pointed quills of guilt or judgment?

What burden of the heart
can lift, what dark corner
can be lit, the candle
flickering at first, then
burning bright?

With the next breath
let it go, that old story
you've told yourself
a million times.

Whatever doesn't serve
you on this path of truth,
leave it behind. Offer

this one gift: the simple
sacrifice that in the giving
sets you free to fully live.
          —DANNA FAULDS

The great hall is dark, illuminated only by candlelight. In silence, we file in and take seats on cushions arranged in a large circle on the floor. It's an important night in teacher training, the presentation of our mala beads. But first, Devarshi and Jurian are going to share with us a glimpse of the intimate practice known at Kripalu as meditation-in-motion. In Kripalu yoga, stage one of practice is simply about learning to be present on your mat, executing the poses, and paying attention to all the sensations in the mind, body, and breath as you move from one posture to the next. As your practice deepens and you progress into stage two, you begin to turn inward, sustaining postures for longer periods and coordinating your movements with a powerful flow of breath. You develop a witness consciousness, compassionately observing, rather than reacting to, the waves of sensations and emotions that arise on your mat. The third and final stage is a release into nondoing, in which you surrender the mind to the flow of energy, or "prana," moving through the body. It's no longer about doing poses, our teachers explain, but rather about allowing the poses to do you; you become your yoga, freeing your body to move in whatever way spirit and the flow of energy takes it.

I have my doubts. What I love about yoga is the structure, the fact that I have something to work toward: poses to learn and practice, better alignment to strive for, one posture following the next, a sequence of proscribed movements, a way to measure my progress. And what I don't like about dance—or this nerve-wracking concept of meditation-in-motion—is the fact that the very part of me that holds things together would have to let go. I'm not a let-it-all-hang-out sort of person. In fact, the very idea of abandoning form and structure and allowing my body to flail aimlessly around in space—in front of other people!—gives me a stomachache. Stage three is a place I'm not eager to go, a level of release and self-exposure I can't even begin to imagine.

And yet, one by one tonight, our teachers reveal themselves to us. Jurian goes first, stepping to the center of the circle. She sits, closes her eyes, breathes deeply, and waits, dropping down into the slow beat of the music reverberating through the sound system. Slowly, almost imperceptibly, she begins to sway, rising effortlessly up from the floor. Her gestures are soft, fluid, a kind of waking dream in which her body becomes a pliant vehicle for breath and movement, each lift of an arm or arch of the back arising from some place deep within. It is, I think, almost like watching someone make love—it seems that intimate, that unguarded and unscripted. She may be fully clothed, but her soul is dancing naked. And somehow she trusts herself enough to be before us like this—and us enough to be her witnesses. Such trust feels profoundly moving, holy and powerful at once.

Devarshi is next. He lies on his stomach in the center of the circle, waiting for some beat or signal in the music to inspire movement. An invisible string draws his shoulders and then his chest upward, as he arches into a powerful backbend. Yet even in him, there is gentleness. His eyes closed, he moves as if discovering his own body for the first time, with a child's innocence and utter lack of self-consciousness. It could be the performance of a pro, an act, a show he's put on over the years for hundreds of students. And yet I'm sure the opposite is true—that in fact what keeps Devarshi teaching year after year is this continual challenge to be real, to show up, to peel back the layers and confront whatever's waiting underneath. Anyone can give a lecture on how to modify yoga poses or create a posture flow. But here, in the center of this hallowed circle, our teachers are offering us something else, the gift of their own unadorned, unguarded selves.

I look around the room at my fellow classmates, silent, spellbound, as if we are indeed one breath, one beating heart, one reverent consciousness. As the chant comes to an end, Devarshi rolls over onto his side and curls into a ball, surrendering fully to some deep, invisible current. Gone for the moment is our jocular, quick-witted class teacher. Here instead, fully exposed, is an ordinary human being—simple, mortal.

It is a long time before anyone speaks. And then all most of us can manage is "thank you." We are grateful, certainly, but also humbled by what we've witnessed: humanity anchored in spirit. Our teachers have entrusted us with a sacred offering—the deepest expressions of who they are. And in receiving that trust we, too, soften and grow.

Om namo bhagavate vesudevaya. Loosely translated, the phrase means "thy will be done" in Sanskrit, or, more precisely, "I bow to you, O Lord, who are the very essence of divinity." So far in our meditation practice, we've been learning to return our wandering attention, again and again, to the inflow and outflow of the breath. Tonight, with the presentation of our mala beads, we move into mantra japa, one of the oldest forms of meditation, in which the repetition of a phrase—either spoken, whispered, or silently evoked—serves to concentrate the mind.

According to Kripalu teacher Stephen Cope, the more one practices, and the more often one works with a particular mantra, the more deeply that sound vibration settles into the synapses, neurons, and dendrites of the nervous system. It creates a groove. And the next time, that groove is easier to access, until, over months and years, it becomes a part of your consciousness. The words matter less than the practice itself. As the familiar phrase is repeated over and over again, audibly or silently, the mind grows quiet; thoughts give way to absorption in the inner vibration, and consciousness descends into stillness. Eventually, whether the mantra is "Hail Mary, full of grace," a Sansrkit phrase, or a secret word, the effect on the mind is the same: concentrated equanimity. Devoted practitioners, Cope says, find that even a couple of rounds of practice are enough to cue the mind to settle.

Our malas, consisting of 108 small rosewood beads strung and knotted on a loop of red cotton string, are the yogis' version of a rosary. They have been blessed for us and tonight we are to receive them in a simple ceremony. I sit on my cushion waiting with open hands as our teachers make their way around the circle, passing out the beads to one student at a time. When Devarshi comes to me, he crouches low and gazes right into my eyes. *"Om namo baghavade vesudevaya,"* he says, gently placing the beads into my outstretched palm.

And in that moment, under his unwavering, direct, and purely loving gaze, a door deep inside me swings open and a delicious, golden warmth pours through. There are no words between us but the whispered mantra, nothing for me to do but silently close my fingers around the coiled beads, and yet what passes from my teacher's eyes into mine in that second is indeed transformational: an invitation to behold what he already sees in me, my own divine nature.

How to find words to describe a shift so subtle and internal, yet so profound that it seems to change everything? One sacred second, so brief yet seismic? A movement from a dark, inchoate place of confusion into a space of clarity and light?

I've read lots of accounts over the years of "aha! moments." Moments when people report feeling as if they've been touched by God, or as if they are suddenly at one with the universe or finally understand just what it is they've been put on earth to do. It seems that every celebrity Oprah's ever interviewed, from hockey stars to writers to Broadway actresses, can call up an aha! moment at the drop of a hat. Every spiritual memoir contains at least one: The lightbulb flashes on, the impossible problem suddenly offers up its own solution, inspiration strikes, enlightenment occurs. I've never had such a moment myself. I certainly am not expecting one now.

And yet in this instant it feels as if everything I think I know falls away, and everything I'll ever need to know is offered to me. And that "everything," as it turns out, is just one thing: love. It sounds so mundane, so obvious. I know that. But as Devarshi moves on to meet the eyes of the next student, my own eyes fill with tears and my heart overflows with gratitude. This, I am certain, is the lesson I came here to learn: love. Love without boundaries, love without conditions, love without explanations or expectations. And this, I am also certain, is my way forward.

What would it mean if my purpose, my path, from this moment on were really this simple: to be able to look into the eyes of another human being with such compassion, such acceptance, such unconditional tenderness and devotion? To offer as much love to others as my teacher just gave to me? I already know the answer. It would mean seeing the vastness of my own soul and finally embracing it fully, without fear or judgment. It would mean standing in the world in all my vulnerability, wide open, and knowing that even when I have no idea what to do next, I can choose to do the loving thing, and it will be enough. It would mean letting go of the notion that I can make people love me by doing things for them or by acting a certain way, and believing that I am lovable just as I am. It would mean loving others that way, too, just as they are and simply for being human. It would mean abandoning the idea that life owes me anything, and accepting that the way things are right now is the way they are meant to be—and loving that. It would mean meeting each and every person along the way just as I have been met by my teacher tonight—with eyes that recognize their magnificence and a heart that is open, unafraid, and whole.

"Love is what we are born with," Marianne Williamson has written. "Fear is what we have learned here. The spiritual journey is the unlearning of fear and the acceptance of love back into our hearts." This, of course, is the elementary truth that resides at the center of every religion, every spiritual practice, every faith and wisdom tradition. It is not news. It's what Margaret tried to tell me on the phone that day: "Remember, it's all about love." I didn't get it then, brushing off her advice as if it were a line of type on a Hallmark card. And yet the concept of divine, unconditional love hits me now with the power of revelation. Suddenly, these are not just words, but a kind of calling, fuel for my life, a light in the darkness, the truth.

I enrolled in teacher training because I wasn't sure what else to do. Longing for a challenge, some new sense of purpose, I followed the faint trail of an old dream and it led me here, to this moment in this darkened hall and a circle of fellow seekers sitting on cushions, fingering strands of beads, and learning to be kinder to themselves in the hope of bringing a bit more kindness into the world. I still have no idea what form my actual work will take when I leave this place. But I do know this: No matter what I do, from now on there will always be a task within the task, and that's what will matter most—learning to meet fear with love. I want to become a conduit for love, a healing presence. I want to live fully by loving fully. And somehow, I want to offer others the simple, profound gift I received tonight: recognition of their beauty, of that divine spark that resides in each one of us.

Om namo bhagavate vasudevaya. "Thy will be done." I join my voice to the others as we chant the mantra in unison, using my thumb to move one bead across my right forefinger with each repetition. Time slows. One hundred and eight beads, one hundred and eight repetitions. The words embody a sense of calm abiding. Just here, just now, I am at peace, as if a curtain has parted and I've stepped through, arriving back in a place I never really left. Home.

Enlightenment, it turns out, is fleeting. Apparently, I've had what's known as a "yoga experience"—profound, illuminating, a quantum leap into new territory. Of course, real, lasting growth occurs slowly, over time, not overnight. And yet there is no doubt in my mind that the epiphany I experienced as my teacher's eyes met mine, random and serendipitous as it seemed, was also a kind of turning point.

Having been cracked open like a nut, there is no way I can seek refuge again in my old broken shell. Nor would I want to. What changed deep within me in that moment has not changed back. Ever since that night, it feels as if I'm looking out through new eyes, eyes that are wide open and that see beauty at every turn. It is almost as if the walls between me and everyone else are dissolving, which is both exhilarating and a little eerie, an expansion of consciousness that takes some getting used to. Suddenly, I feel a new tenderness, not only toward my classmates, but toward the cooks in the kitchen, the guy vacuuming the stairwell, the lady selling coffee in the morning, the chatty women who sit down to eat at my lunch table. It's not that I didn't notice them before, or wasn't kind; it's just that now there seems to be less space between us, almost as if I've put on a pair of 3-D glasses and the whole world, instead of being out at arm's length, is right in my face: intense, complex, exquisitely beautiful.

Obviously, there's more than yoga going on here. But I'm also coming to think: Maybe it's all yoga. Certainly this month of intense daily practice on my mat is teaching me a few things about how I want to live in the world.

It is Marie's birthday. I wake up thinking of my friend, and as I do every morning, I send her a silent "hello" as I slide my feet into her flip-flops, grateful that the fact our feet were the same size has given us this small, special connection still. I slip out of the dark room, trying not to disturb my sleeping roommates, and head for the shower, where I linger under the hot water and recall this day a year ago.

We celebrated at a party her husband arranged, inviting all her friends to show up at her favorite restaurant in Boston and then surprising her when she walked through the door expecting a dinner for two. It was a perfect night that defied sadness. We had champagne toasts and candlelight and wonderful food and lots of laughter. Marie felt good and looked radiant, her eyes sparkling, her smile as quick and easy as always. She was embarrassed by all the attention and fuss, a little put out that her husband had orchestrated this event behind her back and rounded us all up just for her sake, yet she finally allowed herself to relax into the warm glow of the moment. She cracked up at the card I gave her, one with a picture of a pert, ponytailed woman pointing a toe in the air and the line "Yoga: It's the new cocktail hour." Having given up her few vices and embraced yoga wholeheartedly since her diagnosis, Marie could appreciate the humor. For her, cat-cow and cobra pose had been taking the place of Cabernet for quite a while now.

Steve and I had driven down from New Hampshire and were spending the night; later, back at her house, Marie and I sat with mugs of tea in the family room after our husbands had gone upstairs. I knew she wanted to make the day last as long as possible, and neither of us was in any hurry to go to bed. "If I could go on just like this for a while," she said, "I would be so grateful. But I also know," she added, "that it could end at any time."

"Just like this" meant no hair and weekly chemo, but for the moment the regimen seemed to be working well enough. A plateau was a good thing, a wig a small inconvenience she'd long since gotten used to, and every day of life a gift. She had just turned fifty-five, and she was hoping for another year, hoping she just might make it to see her daughter graduate from high school.

For most of us, birthdays are about pausing to look backward and forward, taking stock of lives lived as we assess the changes wrought by time, and dreaming about what's next. But illness revises our relationship to time. My friend was thinking less about the future that night than about the legacy she would leave behind.

"I wonder what my life has meant," she mused. "What will people remember me for? I've never done anything important."

It seemed too pat and simplistic to assure her that her three extraordinary children were her legacy. She was struggling with a bigger question, one that couldn't be answered by pointing to her years of dedicated work at her church and in town affairs, her long tenure as president of the PTA at the high school, her strong marriage, gracious home, and wide circle of devoted friends. To me, it seemed obvious that her life itself was creation and legacy enough—the world was a better place because of her presence in it. But in the months since she died, I've come to see that Marie also left me a spiritual inheritance.

I am a more loving human being for having been her friend, and a wiser and braver one for having had the privilege of being her student in the demanding art of endings and partings. Marie taught all of us who loved her a powerful lesson about the beauty of ordinary life and its brevity. And her legacy lives on in those she left behind—a deeper appreciation of life in all its polarity and ambiguity, sorrow and suffering, wonder and joy.

Perhaps such appreciation, such specific and focused gratitude, is our most useful response to the death of someone we love. For within our mourning lies not only grief, but also inspiration—a summons to continue living and loving as boldly and as beautifully as we can. There was no way I could put this into words for my friend as we sat together on her last birthday; I didn't know it then. But I do know it now. Our best, most human answer to loss is love: love that we carry forward with every act of kindness, generosity, and worship. Love that dismantles barriers. Love that heals. Love that is not something we do but that is revealed instead as who we really are.

Two weeks after her birthday, Marie was hospitalized with an intestinal blockage; by the time she returned home from what would turn out to be her final surgery, with a colostomy bag and much weakened, that magical dinner party seemed like a distant memory. But I've not forgotten our late-night conversation, and

I know this for sure: I would not be standing in this shower at five thirty this morning, or meeting myself head-on here day after day, if not for her.

An important part of our training, not surprisingly, is learning to be comfortable speaking in front of the group, never my strong suit. Although becoming an author has meant I've also had to become a public speaker, it is the part of being a writer that I fear and dread the most. For weeks before even a small talk or event, I am anxious, laboring over what to say, knowing certain people will come expecting to meet some wise authority I cannot possibly ever be. I am not an expert on anything, just an ordinary wife and mother who often flounders and who has shared some of her floundering on the page. "I'm a private person," I recently said to my neighbor, who couldn't understand why I didn't leap at every invitation that came my way. This made no sense to her. "But you write about your *life*!" she said in exasperation. "There's nothing private about it!"

What she didn't understand is that there is

a vast difference between sitting alone in my silent kitchen, discovering what I feel and what I know through the slow, hesitant process of writing it down, and standing at a podium facing a crowd of people who expect me to have a few things figured out. Both are hard. But one I can do in solitude, without my knees shaking, and the other brings up all my fears and insecurities.

So far this month, I have managed to get by without ever once holding the microphone in my hand. Much as I've appreciated hearing people's stories and insights, I've held back—as I usually do—from adding my voice to the discussion. But today, it almost feels as if my friend is whispering in my ear, so close is her presence.

And it seems more than a coincidence that, instead of posture clinic, Devarshi chooses to spend the entire morning talking about life and death, and about what it is that endures when our physical journey on this earth comes to an end.

It is his way of introducing us to the Bhaga-vad Gita, the ancient Hindu scriptures considered to be both the backbone of yoga theology and a concise, practical guide to the spiritual life. "Never was there a time when I did not exist, or you," he reads aloud. "Nor will there come a time when we will cease to be. Just as in this body, the Self passes through childhood, youth, and old age, so after death it passes to another body. Physical sensations—cold and heat, pleasure and pain—are transient: they come and go, so bear them patiently."

The words land in my heart, comforting and solid, with the weight of truth. All spiritual paths it seems, whether Christian or Buddhist or Hindu or Jewish, converge here, as we contemplate the immeasurable mystery through which we spin and choose to honor that which is eternal—our oneness with all creation, the faith that we are not separate from God but that he lives in us, and we in him, forever.

Devarshi reads the entire last chapter aloud to us, each stanza gathering force: "It is better to do your own duty badly than to perfectly do another's; when you do your duty, you are naturally free from sin. No one should relinquish his duty, even though it is flawed; all actions are enveloped by flaws as fire is enveloped in smoke."

The idea that I must simply do my own work, whatever it may be, is certainly one I've been grappling with. I keep waiting for the new job description to appear, the clear signal; just as the arrival of babies compelled me to begin the work of motherhood, I've been hoping for some new "calling" to make me feel whole again, to make me feel needed in the world. But the Gita suggests that as we yield to our own true nature, our real work is revealed to us. We don't have to do it perfectly; indeed, it is the quest for perfection that holds us back. In fact, I think now, maybe I haven't even been asking myself the right questions. Instead of "What am I meant to do?" the real question may be as simple, and as endlessly challenging, as "How do I become a more loving human being?"

By the time our teacher gets to the final lines, he is reading through his own tears. "And as often as I remember the Lord's vast, wondrous form, each time I am astonished; each time I shudder with joy." We've gone way over time, but no one stirs in the room. "The end gets me every time," he says, shaking his head and wiping his eyes. It gets me, too. Grace has most certainly brought me here—to this teaching and to this moment of deep reassurance, the quiet certainty that nothing is lost, that each of us truly is infinite, eternal, and whole. Grace and, I am also certain, the spirit of my friend—a spirit no less powerful, no less present, for being invisible.

Instead of eating lunch, I race upstairs, grab Marie's pale blue jacket, and head outside for a walk. It was winter when we arrived, the landscape buried under ice and snow. Now, just a few weeks later, I smell spring in the air. There is a route I've grown to love, a quiet road that winds alongside the lake, past fields and vacant summer houses. Walking this same road, alone, nearly every day at noon has been almost like studying a new language: The quickening brook means snow is melting; a hawk inscribing circles over a meadow suggests life and movement below; opened curtains in the stone house hint that someone has arrived for the weekend. Today the lake, frozen solid a week ago, is patched with gray ice and rimmed with black water. The season is changing, and I am changing with it.

I think about all the people I love, how each one of us is somewhere right now, thinking and breathing, engaged in our own separate lives in separate places—Steve at work in his office in New Hampshire, Henry far away at college in Minnesota, Jack at his own school just thirty minutes from where I'm walking at this moment. I could take my phone out of my pocket, call my husband or text my boys, as I often do at lunchtime, but instead, for today, I listen to the silence, and tune my senses to our unspoken connection. Soon we four will be together again, sitting at the dinner table, comparing stories, reconnecting the dots of our lives into the big picture of our family. And that, I realize, is enough. There is no need now for me to reach out, to call, or to strive to make things happen. We are on our paths, each doing our own separate work of grow-ing and becoming, even as we are bound, now and always, by love. Instead of phoning, I picture each of them in my mind, send my love through the ether, and continue on my way.

Thomas Moore says that the dark night of the soul often comes just before revelation. I'm not sure the events of my last year qualify as a dark night of the soul, but certainly they have both tested me and awakened new longings. Losing one part of my life, the time of mothering children at home, felt like a small kind of death, the first of more to come. Aging, change, and the loss of a friend have taken a toll. But even heartache can bring gifts of unexpected depth and magnitude. Surely there will be more challenges to face, but perhaps I will know better now how to meet them. Softly, and with less fear.

I stop walking and stand still for a moment, allowing the noonday calm of this country road to claim me. It is as if someone has placed firm hands on my shoulders and is turning me toward the open fields, the dappled mountains, the clean seamless sky. Everywhere, invincible life is hidden, biding its time, germinating, waiting to be quickened by warmth and rain. I can't see my friend as she was, but

I sense something akin to her presence in this luminous landscape, in the unseasonably mild air, the hawk's silent flight. "Happy birthday, my dear friend," I say, my face tipped up to the sunshine. "Happy birthday, and thank you."

An hour later, I make my way to the front of our classroom, sit down on the platform, and take the microphone. I'm not sure I can trust my voice. But when Devarshi asked, after lunch, for someone to connect the morning's teachings with their own personal experience, I found my hand in the air. I reach up now, give the silver stud in my ear a little twist, and remember the day, months ago now, that I sat in the mall with my eyes squinched shut and got my ears pierced—how I promised myself at that moment that fear was not going to be my prison anymore.

And then I flick the switch to "on," take a deep breath, and begin to speak.

We end the day in pairs and down on the floor, assisting one another in deep spinal twists. It is dusk, the lights in the room are low, the mood quiet. My partner, a young girl named Anna, places a hand on my hip bone and another on my shoulder, pressing and lengthening, creating space in the rib cage.

When it's my turn, I perform the same lengthening and stretching assist on her. She is twenty-one perhaps, petite and supple, loose-limbed as a dancer. As I match my own breath to hers and ease her shoulder toward the floor with my palm, I can feel her body relaxing and releasing with each exhalation, moving deeper and deeper into the twist. It is a lovely, gentle way to bring this long afternoon of discussion and practice to a close, slowly wringing out whatever emotions and feelings are still stored up inside and awaiting release. When we're finished, I draw her legs out long on her mat, give them a little pull, and set her feet down side by side. I cover her up with a blanket, cradle her head in my palms for a moment, and place it gently back down. Then I put a hand on her forehead and sit there for a while as darkness falls.

"You're a mom, aren't you?" Anna asks, after we've said our final "omm" and are rolling up our mats. "Yes," I say, surprised by the question. Her eyes fill with sudden tears. "I could feel your motherliness," she says. "And it was so nice. I've been struggling a lot this week, and feeling overwhelmed by everything. I guess I just really needed the love of a mom. Thank you."

I give Anna a hug and a kiss on the forehead. And I thank her, too. How easy it is to miss the gift of who we are, because we're so busy trying to become somebody else. Maybe all I really need to do—all anyone needs to do—is to trust in what we love and continue to do that. The path, as I'm learning here, reveals itself as we change the way we look for it, determined in part by what we build our lives around, by what we devote ourselves to. And love, as Swami Kripalu reminds us, is never far away. It is always as close as my own heart. I can find it there without walking a single step.

practice

The everyday practice is simply to develop complete acceptance of all situations, emotions, and people.

—PEMA CHÖDRÖN

*I*t's a long way in both miles and mind-set from the silent morning sadhana at Kripalu to the house in Florida where my parents spend part of the winter and where we all convene each year for our sons' spring break.

By the time I arrive, straight from my month of yoga immersion, Steve and Jack are already here and in full vacation mode. Henry's plane from Minnesota lands an hour after mine, and then, for a couple of perfect, packed, too-short days, we are all together for the first time in months, catching up with one another, reading our books, swimming, playing Scrabble, watching March Madness college basketball and movies, making meals, and crowding around the kitchen table with my mom and dad.

For twelve straight years we've made this annual pilgrimage, but I suspect this is yet one more tradition that will soon slip away, as my parents get older, as Henry graduates from college and Jack from high school, as their adult lives take them elsewhere and vacations can no longer be expected to fall so neatly into the same end-of-March week.

As usual on our final night together, the four us of have a farewell dinner at Chili's. My sons wonder whether, in a place with no brown rice or kale on the menu, I'll be able to find something to eat. They've been watching me carefully to see if I'm "different," as if they half expect me to burst into spontaneous chant or levitate out of my seat. And they're relieved, I think, to see that I'm still just their mom, not any weirder than before. Still, in deference to me, they agree to vegetarian nachos, and then we begin to wax nostalgic, recalling the days when this late-winter trip to Florida also included time with Steve's parents, both gone now.

The boys remember begging for stops at every mom-and-pop variety store in search of the newest packs of baseball cards, thrilling trips to the Red Sox spring training grounds, shell collecting at the beach, *Little Rascals* video marathons, mini-golf, and Peanut Buster Parfaits at the DQ. One memory gives rise to another, and amid the laughter I feel myself already missing them, regretting that our time now is so brief and those innocent days so far behind us.

I say how wonderful it is, how special, to have us all here together.

"Mom," Jack says, rolling his eyes, "you say that exact same thing *every* time we're together. It's not that special."

I suppose I do say it, but he's wrong about it not being special. What my sons take for granted—home, family life, our memories and traditions—is treasured by me. And perhaps that is just as it should be. Our children, even if they are nearly all grown up, need the space and freedom to break away from what's familiar, secure in the knowledge we're holding home base for them and that there's something solid to which they can return whenever they need to regroup and reconnect. Poised between the childhoods they haven't yet begun to cherish and futures that are at once enticing and a little scary, my guess is that both our sons appreciate the haven of home more than they let on. And perhaps it's having a firm footing in the past—even if it's just this annual visit to the grandparents, the embrace of family, and a brief return to what's always been—that allows them to step boldly forth into new territory.

So, I will say what they can't possibly express: These days, when the four of us actually land in the same place at the same time, it *does* feel like an occasion—always too short, always bittersweet, always special. And then it's over.

Early the next morning we drive Jack across the state to meet up with his school tennis team for a few days of preseason training; he will fly back to school with his classmates. And a day later we drive Henry back to the airport at 6:30 a.m. for his return flight to college. It is still dark when we pull up to the curb, the heat of a Florida day just beginning to thicken the air. We hug by the car, and I repeat the same motherly things I always say at airports: that I love him and to call when he gets back to campus. I don't say anything about the bit of straggly soul patch on his chin that I wish he'd shave off, and I resist the urge to buckle up the straps flapping from his suitcase. I remind myself how lucky we are that, at twenty-one, our son is still content to spend his spring break hanging out with us. Our intimacy now is a choice he can make or not; more than any-thing, I want him to keep coming home—not out of obligation, but because he wants to.

Henry gives his dad a hug, brushes my cheek with a quick kiss, and then our older son slings his backpack onto his shoulder, pushes through the revolving door, and disappears into the bright terminal. I feel a similar revolving effect in my own stomach, as the easy togetherness of these last few days is suddenly displaced by a wave of sadness. It still gets me, just how *alone* alone feels every time we say good-bye to our children.

With one more day to spend here before
our own flight home, Steve and I drive down
the empty highway and up and over the long
bridge to Sanibel, where we used to take the
boys to the beach when they were little. It's
been years since we've been back, but as we
walk along the familiar stretch of shoreline and
watch a new generation of young sand-castle-
builders hard at work, it feels as if I need only
look over my shoulder to catch a glimpse of my
own small children splashing in the waves.

I've just spent a month practicing being fully
present, and yet strolling along the water's edge
this morning I am incapable of simply being in
the moment. Sanderlings scurry along at our
feet. The sun rises higher in the sky, the water is
perfect, the beach filling with families and sun-
bathers and shell collectors, all intent on milk-
ing their varied, carefree pleasures from the day.

And I find myself blinking back tears, trying
way too hard to savor this lovely walk with
my husband while, at the same time, fighting
to swim against a riptide of other emotions—
missing my sons, missing the life we all used
to lead together, missing their vanished child-

hoods and our own younger, more innocent parenting selves. How clearly I remember every bathing suit they ever owned; the big, cheap beach towels with hoods in the corners that could completely envelop a small, shivering boy; the bright, indestructible toys we stored at my mom's house and hauled out year after year; the small, irresistible plastic shark Jack once "borrowed" from another little boy and failed to return, and his tearful confession at the end of the day when his guilty conscience got the better of him; the smell of suntan lotion slathered onto a small bony back; the taste of gritty cheese crackers and warm iced tea; the scrim of sand in the rental car; the bags of prized shells ripening and stinking in the backseat as we headed back down the causeway, windows open wide.

Steve and I walk side by side, mostly in silence, for a mile or so, waves lapping at our feet, erasing our footprints in the sand. He's missed me this month, the longest we've ever been apart in our nearly twenty-five years together. And this is the first time we've been alone since I arrived here. I try to describe for him what my experience has been like, how much I've learned and how momentous the days before graduation had been. I tell him that I finally managed to overcome my self-consciousness and participated in a meditation-in-motion practice by candlelight, surrounded by a group of fellow students, on our final night of class.

"I never thought I could expose myself like that," I say. "Or trust other people to just accept me as I am. But by the end, we were all able to do it."

He listens, quiet, as I tell him that the graduation ceremony felt even more meaningful to me, more significant, than my graduation from college thirty years ago.

"It actually seemed like more of an achievement," I say, recalling the candles and flowers and music, the ringing bells, the tossed handfuls of rice and rose petals, the whispered words of encouragement and recognition as I made my way through the processional, the orange smear of blessed oil placed reverently on my forehead and a certificate of completion pressed into my hands. But it is as if my words only separate us further; there is no way for him to share this experience, no way for me to adequately convey it. He may be at my side, but it feels as if we are still hundreds of miles apart.

At last, the sun hot on our backs, we turn around and make our way toward the car. I stoop and pick up a broken clam shell, grayed by time, nothing special, yet worn smooth as satin to the touch. A vessel it was, but not one that would ever hold very much. Somehow it seems like the right memento to slip into my pocket at the end of this less-than-wonderful morning, a battered fragment, far from perfect, but lovely enough for me—if only as a reminder that what is truly beautiful in my life is never what I grasp at, but that which is found accidentally. Discovered, not sought after.

There is an abbreviation known to everyone at Kripalu: BRFWA. It stands for Breathe. Relax. Feel. Watch. Allow. This is how I've been learning to move into and out of poses for a month now, slowly and with awareness and compassion—a pretty effective strategy for negotiating the inevitable ups and downs of everyday experience as well.

I had assumed—naïvely, I see now—that I'd pack up all my newfound knowledge and bring it home with me. And that, having braved the rigors of teacher training, and having learned to tolerate discomfort on my yoga mat, I would also finally, maybe, become the unflappable, wise, middle-aged woman I aspire to be.

Now I realize it's not quite that simple. I'm not exactly the same person who left home more than a month ago, but it turns out this journey isn't quite as straightforward as I thought, either. It was pretty easy to stay calm and centered in "the bubble" of Kripalu, surrounded by supportive strangers. I could stay with my feelings when my feelings were mostly nerves about performing in front of the group, or being overtired and having to get up in the dark and practice anyway, or even twinges of regret about Jack and Steve heading off on college visits without me. It wasn't hard to allow myself to be vulnerable with people I would never see again.

But I can see it's going to be more challenging to keep bringing myself back to "right here" when right here means the messy, unpredictable encounters between me and the people I love most of all. Being present means showing up not only for the good times, but allowing space for the inevitable discomfort and disappointment of my own everyday life as well. It means fully embracing even the unlovable parts of those people I live with, the unlovable parts of all my relationships, the unlovable parts of *me*. It means learning to go with the flow, rather than struggling against it.

Breathe. Relax. Feel. Watch. Allow. I forgot that this simple practice was available to me as I sent my sons back into their lives. I forgot that all I really needed to do was be aware of my own feelings as I walked along the beach this morning with my husband. I forgot that when sadness arises, I can simply notice its presence—and even welcome it as a sign that I'm alive, that my heart is open, that I'm human. I forgot that my feelings just need to be felt.

The Buddhists claim that most human suffering can be traced back to a desire for things to be different than they are. What amazes me is that so much pain can be reduced to one simple fact, and that this fact is pretty much unassailable. What I needed to do this morning was say good-bye to my kids and reconnect with my husband after a few weeks apart—not exactly a tall order, nor a cause for misery. And yet there I was, falling into my same old patterns. Not wanting myself to be the way I am. Not wanting the day to be the way it was. Not wanting my husband to be the way he is. Fighting my own silent little battle with reality and missing the beauty of sea and sand and sky, the glorious abundance of the day.

BRFWA. Had I remembered my own practice, I might have taken one tiny step back and paid attention to my churning emotions, without so much distress and self-judgment. I might have allowed the poignant memories to wash through me, rather than wishing for what can't be. I might have allowed my tears to fall and then drawn a few deep breaths and let the sea air dry my cheeks. I might have held my husband's hand and shared my thoughts with him, and then turned to him for comfort, instead of trudging along in miserable silence, convinced I should somehow be doing

a "better" job of walking on the beach. I might
have relaxed into the fact that our way of being
together is in flux right now along with everything else, for certainly I can't expect to change
without our marriage shifting and changing as
well—and that, too, is okay.

For years Steve and I have been engaged in
the shared, all-consuming project of raising
children. But just as we are now finding our
way into new, more adult relationships with
our sons, we must also be willing to acknowledge the subtle metamorphosis in our relationship with each other, recommitting to what
binds us even as we acknowledge our differ-
ences and grant each other some new space in
which to grow. We don't need to renegotiate
the details of our marriage this very minute,
nor do we need to nail it all into place. It's
enough for us just to meet each other where
we are, with faith that our love is adaptable,
dynamic, lasting. I want to lean into that love,
confident in our ability to go the distance
together. And that means allowing for this
new, unfamiliar guardedness between us to
evaporate in its own time, as we find our way

back to each other, back to a more seasoned, perhaps even enlivened, intimacy.

In the meantime, though, I am chastened by the lessons of this day. Reunions can be difficult. Good-byes are always hard. And, clearly, I am going to need a lot more practice— practice in being present, practice in feeling my feelings and in letting them go, practice in loving, in accepting, and especially practice in holding those most dear to me with a lighter touch. At least I have learned this: It all *is* a practice. I just have to show up and keep on practicing. Breathe. Relax. Feel. Watch. Allow.

By the time Steve and I arrive back at our own house late the next night, our morning on the beach feels like a distant memory. We began this day in shorts and T-shirts, drinking coffee in the sunshine with my parents, padding about and gathering up our scattered things— books and laptops and sunglasses. And now, many hours and two flights later, we are home, just the two of us, back to our "real" life together. It is the same life I left behind just a month and a half ago, of course, and yet as I walk through the chilly, silent rooms, turning on lights and turning up thermostats, I sense that I will inhabit it now a little differently.

Compassion, it turns out, creates space for more compassion. And the compassion I am still learning to offer myself expands outward, into compassion for others as well. For my husband, with his private fears and hopes and feelings. And for our two very different sons, each of whom will surely make their own painful, humbling mistakes as they find their way in the world. To love them well now means to let them go, again and again. It means trusting that they will learn, as they suffer the consequences of their missteps, how to be stronger, more resilient, more thoughtful human beings.

I can't hand them each a road atlas or a list of foolproof instructions on how to avoid heartache; but I can offer the one thing I have to give, perhaps the very thing they most need from me as young adults: faith in their ability to negotiate the necessary, inevitable detours and distractions on the long, winding path called growing up.

I may be home, but the journey will clearly

be ongoing; a journey that turns out to be more about accepting the person I am now than striving to become someone else. More about embracing imperfection than about fixing things, more about staying with what is than about trying to get to some other, better place. And more about loving well than doing well. Maybe I don't need a road map, either. For it seems that the greatest gift of practice is a more open-hearted willingness to be right where I am, the ability to say a quiet, unqualified "yes" to my own life, not as I wish it could be, but as it is.

I take the seashell from my jeans pocket and rub my fingers across its silken, indented surface, shallow as my own open hand. This chalice, subtly shaped by some divine intelligence to allow water to flow in and out with ease, is what I aspire to become: a vessel through which feelings can pour in and spill right out again, without all the grasping and holding that obstructs the flow. Can I be as serene and simple as this bleached shell, rubbed smooth by wind and water, receiving and releasing, filling and emptying and filling again, eternally receptive to the currents of life?

The thought fills me with hope. I've spent a month shedding my own extra, unnecessary layers. A month discovering that, moment to moment, I can choose love over fear, letting go over gripping tight, acceptance over struggle. It's all a process and all a practice, and to live it is to learn it—albeit imperfectly, and only by making mistakes along the way. I place my broken shell next to the candlesticks on the kitchen table, where I'll see it in the morning and every day from now on, this humble reminder that time-worn and damaged is still beautiful, and that change isn't something I can will upon myself, but rather a continuous, intuitive process of flux and flow, measured in movement and progress, not perfection.

Upstairs, Steve is putting clothes away in drawers, running the water in the sink, opening and closing the closet door. I listen for a moment to the familiar sounds of our house, of my husband's footsteps overhead, of the furnace thrumming in the basement. And then, for the first time in six weeks, I switch off the kitchen lights and climb up the stairs to join my husband in our own bed.

~9~

connection

*When one tugs on a single thing
in nature, he finds it attached to
the rest of the world.*

—John Muir

$\mathcal{I}$ sit on the sofa, alone in my house on this gray spring morning, watching a pair of chickadees trade places at the birdfeeder. And then I type these words by John Muir. Is it so? Is everything really part of everything else? Am I really a single strand of thread, inextricably woven into some billowing celestial tapestry?

Just as I found solace in the Bhagavad Gita's timeless assurance that there is a part of me that will never die, that each of us is infinite, eternal, and whole, I also love this image of cosmic connection. In fact, it seems as if the ancient Hindu text and the nineteenth-century American naturalist are saying exactly the same thing: We are all one. We need only look more deeply into the nature of who we really are to see that our sense of isolation is an illusion and to have our separateness ameliorated by union. I may be but one slight thread in a vast fabric, but there's comfort in imagining the eternal interplay between my own small, temporal life and all there is.

Here in the temporal life, however, the bewildering threshold between what's over and what's next can feel like a lonely place to be, no matter how crowded it is. I was relieved to discover, as I got to know my fellow classmates at Kripalu, that almost every single one of them had felt pulled to come because they, too, were at some kind of crossroads, not sure where they were meant to be or what they were meant to be doing. But knowing I was stuck in a place that actually had a label, and that I was just one of many uncertain wanderers wondering "what's next?," didn't make it any more comfortable. The fertile void may be an unavoidable psychological stage in the process of change, but it's not a place where anyone wants to linger. What I'm finding, though, is that acknowledging my anxieties and uncertainties, even bringing them out into the bright light of day and writing about them, has made it easier to release them. Or, perhaps, it's working the other way: Slowly, as I make time to sit quietly each day and listen for the subtle voice within, my self-doubts are releasing me.

Joseph Campbell asserts that "the privilege of a lifetime is being who you are," suggesting there comes a time when we must finally recognize and lay claim to our own true selves— which means being willing to undertake the long, and often circuitous process of growing up our souls, becoming mature not only physically but spiritually as well.

For those of us who have been fully engaged in first-half-of-life journeys, raising children and earning a living and tending to the demands of hearth and home and after-school sports schedules, such inner work isn't exactly at the top of the to-do list. We've been moving too fast, and have been too engaged with the process of *building* a life, to think much about learning how to surrender to life. Too busy running around and taking care of essential real-world business to attend to the inner work of the soul. And, with all its emphasis on youth and achievement, competition and speed and material success, it could even be said that our entire culture is geared to first-half-of-life pursuits. We are a country of movers and shakers, goers and doers.

But second-half-of-life journeys seem to demand a willingness to shift gears. We begin to hit some potholes in the road; unexpected obstacles throw us off course; paths that seemed clear just yesterday are suddenly obscured. A marriage ends or a job is lost. A loved one dies or illness alters the course of a life. Children grow up and leave home and suffer troubles we can't ease. Relationships founder, a career that once satisfied loses its luster, a friend is in crisis. Cherished dreams evaporate, old identities fall away, and new ones are slow to materialize. We grow old. After devoting years to busily creating a solid container for our lives, we suddenly find ourselves compelled to stop and take a look at what we've made. Change, in whatever form it takes, demands that we see everything from a new perspective. Peering into these complex structures of our own creation, we wonder just what, exactly, our containers are meant to hold.

I thought I had been laying the groundwork for the day when my sons would be grown. I wrote a book about slowing down and paying attention, about remembering that this time of children and parents all living together under one roof—a time that seems as if it will last forever—isn't the whole story after all; it's just a chapter, one that's over all too soon. "It took a while," I wrote, "but I certainly do know it now—the most wonderful gift I had, the gift I've finally learned to cherish above all else, was the gift of all those perfectly ordinary days." I wrote those words, of course, to remind myself to do what I said, to help me to appreciate the beauty of our life while we were living it, and to prepare myself for changes I knew were just around the corner.

Even so, when the chapter ended, I wasn't ready. And nothing was quite as I thought it would be. Perhaps it's human nature: We want to shield our children from pain, and what we get instead is life and heartache and lessons that bring us to our knees. Sooner or later, we are handed the brute, necessary curriculum of surrender. We have no choice, then, but to bow our heads and learn. We struggle to accept that our children's destinies are not ours to write, their battles not ours to fight, their bruises not ours to bear, nor their victories ours to own or take credit for. We learn humility and how to ask for help. We learn to let go even when every fiber of our being yearns to hold on tighter. We learn that love is necessary, but that love doesn't always save people. We learn that we can't change someone else; we can only change ourselves. We can go down fighting, or we can begin to practice acceptance. Grace comes as we loosen, at last, our white-knuckled grip on what ought to be— but even grace is not always gentle or chosen. Sometimes it arrives disguised as a burden—as loss or hurt or unwanted upheaval.

I began this midlife journey grieving not only the loss of a friend and the end of our family life as we'd always known it, but also my own unexpected sense of helplessness and failure. For a long time, I couldn't bear to be at the grocery store at three in the afternoon when the high schoolers came pouring into town; it hurt too much to think of what "should" have been and wasn't. I couldn't read the sports section of the local newspaper; it saddened me to see Jack's old teammates' names there and not his. I had a hard time passing by the door of his empty room, being with my friends' children who were still living at home, looking at the basketball hoop in our driveway, setting the table for two.

I had believed that if I was a certain kind of mother (fully present), and loved my children in a certain kind of way (unconditionally), I could count on a certain kind of outcome (no regrets). I anticipated a graceful, bittersweet passage into the next phase. Healthy, happy young adult children moving seamlessly into happy, healthy young adult lives as I took up new interests and reveled in all my newfound free time.

But real-life stories are more complicated

than that. By the time we delivered Jack to boarding school, I did know it was the right thing. He was excited and nervous and eager for a fresh start, and that was a joy to see. It was a relief, after a year of watching our younger son sink into despondency and lash out at everything and everyone, to be moving forward, even if forward meant apart. But I also felt as if I'd let him down—if I'd only been a better mother, I thought, and had somehow done a better job of loving, he wouldn't have had to struggle so.

It took another mother's story, and her willingness to entrust me with her vulnerability, to set me straight. Barbara and I were an entire generation older than our three younger roommates at Kripalu, and the two of us bonded right away. Her yoga practice was lovely to watch, elegant and quiet, just as she was. Barbara was kind and soft-spoken, petite, with long silvery blond hair and dark chocolate, expressive eyes. Gentle as she was, I sensed in her a coiled, reserved energy. Like me, she itched to get outdoors for fresh air and time alone every day, and she clearly cherished—no, perhaps needed—her long, solitary noontime runs.

"Tell me about your kids," I said to her on our first night, having just showed everyone pictures of mine.

"I have a son," Barbara said softly, almost hesitantly, and for just an instant it crossed my mind that there was something a little odd about that. Hadn't she earlier mentioned two boys?

Conversation moved on though, to the younger women and their boyfriends, and I didn't give it another thought. Barbara was an ideal roommate—during the day. At night, she drove me nuts. I'm a light sleeper, and Barbara was a night-owl insomniac. No sooner would I have finally settled into a hard-won, fragile sleep than she would slip into the room at midnight, or one, or even later, from who knows where. (There is nothing happening at Kripalu after ten p.m.!) I could tell she was doing her best to be quiet as she began getting ready for bed, using the light from her cell phone to see in the darkness. But once awake—and aware that in just a couple of hours my alarm would go off—I could never get back to sleep. Why doesn't she just go to bed at a reasonable hour? I'd fume to myself, pulling the covers up over my face. What on earth is she doing out there? Patrolling the hallways?

One afternoon, midway through the month, I found myself sitting cross-legged on the floor, shoulder to shoulder with Barbara as we faced in opposite directions for a partner exercise.

"Share something you're struggling with," Devarshi instructed. "Partners, you are going to listen carefully, in silence. And then, at the very end, you will reflect back to your partner what you heard them say."

I could feel Barbara's slight shoulder pressed against mine, could sense her drawing in a long, deliberate breath. And then she said, "This is not something I'm going to talk about with anyone else here. But somehow, I have a feeling you can handle it. And I also think I can trust you to hold this as a confidence. I really don't want it to become part of the training, though. I don't want anyone else to know what I'm going to tell you."

It felt oddly stressful and strange, to be part

of a one-sided conversation, so accustomed am I to jumping in with reassurance, to filling up any painful spaces with my own well-intentioned, inadequate words. But my job was to listen, not to respond.

"I don't feel I deserve to be here," Barbara continued in a near-whisper. "I don't actually feel I deserve to be anywhere. Maybe not even on the planet."

She was silent for a moment. Her sadness hung in the air between us, untouchable. And then she said, "Last August my son took his life. He was just a few weeks away from going off to college. And I found him, hanging from a tree, in the woods behind our house. I realized afterward that he'd been out there, wandering around all night, before he finally did it. His brother and I had gone out looking for him, but at first, for hours, we just thought he was with his friends.

"When I found him, he hadn't been dead very long. But I was too late. And all I can think about is, if only I'd gotten to him sooner. Or if I'd had any idea something was wrong.

Or why didn't he talk to me, or to someone? And I just feel like I failed him so completely, by not knowing, and by not saving him."

She paused and we were quiet together for a moment. I could feel my own throat, dry as paper. My hands, starting to shake a little; her body joined shoulder to shoulder with mine; the exquisite, inexplicable *rightness* of our connection, of our separate, unknown lives aligning in the raw intimacy of this moment.

"So it's been very hard for me to be here," my roommate finally went on, "trying to become something, trying to become a teacher. I'm not sure I can do it. It's actually really hard for me to be anywhere. I guess it's just hard to believe I even deserve to be alive myself."

I could not see Barbara's eyes, but tears were running down both our faces, and even so, all I could offer her was my open, unconditional silence. My assignment was not to console or advise, but to listen with the ear of my heart— to hear her story, take it into the depths of my being, and then offer it back to her with love.

"At night," Barbara said, just as Devarshi was

ringing the chime to signal the end, "when I close my eyes and try to go to sleep, all I can see is his poor body, hanging from that tree."

In that moment I knew two things for sure. Barbara did indeed deserve to be here, just as much as any of us deserve to live and love and walk upon this earth. And her story could just as easily have been my story, or any other mother's story. Did I believe that if she had been a different kind of mother, or had somehow done a better job of loving her son, she could have saved him? Not for one second. Could I put myself in her shoes and feel her loss? Absolutely. As sharply and deeply as I have ever felt anything in all my life. Could I love this woman whose shoulder was pressed against mine? Yes. With my whole, heavy, human heart.

It was that simple. And that painful. And that profound. We were connected and her pain was my pain, just as my love for my own sons was her love for hers. "When one tugs on a single thing in nature..."

For the better part of a year I'd berated myself for the fact that my independent, occasionally defiant but well-intentioned son hadn't had the adolescence I'd envisioned for him. Even as he began to navigate through the world by his own lights, I couldn't let go of the feeling that I'd let him, and therefore myself, down. Yet here I was, wanting with every fiber of my being to assure the grieving woman next to me that she had loved her son enough. That her mothering had been enough. That her life, her very human lapses, had not determined his destiny. And that she was worthy of love and belonging and happiness even as she struggled to find a way to live with sorrow as her constant companion. I also knew that, in entrusting me with the full weight of her story, of both her loss and her shame, she had just taken one small but tremendously courageous step back into her life.

I wanted to be worthy of that trust. Which meant it was time for me to be brave, too, and to step into my own story—even the parts that make me sad, and especially the parts that don't quite fit with who I think I should be. In order for my belief in Barbara's worthiness to carry any weight at all, I'd have to believe in my own worthiness as well. This is how souls grow up—side by side, as we move out of our dark, self-imposed prisons of isolation, secrecy, and self-judgment, and into well-lighted places of connection, compassion, and self-acceptance.

When it came time, a few days later, for us to demonstrate our skills in our first practice teaching classes, I happened to be in Barbara's group of "students." And our teacher Devarshi was on hand to observe and critique. Barbara did everything she possibly could to undermine herself as a teacher. She whispered. She got confused and lost her train of thought. She giggled nervously, twirled her hair, muttered to herself, and, finally, gazed down at her feet and just gave up. Every word and gesture she made on her mat conveyed her belief loud and clear: "I don't deserve to be here."

Not surprisingly, based on what he'd just seen, Devarshi agreed. The next day, he called Barbara to his office to suggest that perhaps she wasn't meant to become certified as a yoga teacher.

For twenty-four hours I'd been wrestling

with myself, wanting to save Barbara by leaping to her defense. I wanted to tell someone on the faculty to cut her some slack, or to share what I knew so she would get another chance. But I had made her a promise. She wanted her story held in confidence, and I had to honor her wish. And, as we were often reminded during our teacher training, we were not there to save other people. They must decide to do that for themselves. All I could do was encourage Barbara to reach out and trust someone else.

She thought it over and gathered her courage. And then she confided in one of the teaching assistants, a young man just a couple of years older than her own son. "I'll help you," Stephen promised. And he did. He arranged for Barbara to have an opportunity to repeat her practice teaching test; she did better. And then, every day over the next two weeks, he gave up part of his lunch break to work with her. Barbara's poses were already beautiful. Stephen helped her remember that *she* was beautiful, too, and that she had something valuable to offer: her presence.

They worked on voice and confidence, on

pace and sequencing, on projection. Most of all, though, Stephen encouraged Barbara to be herself, to let her own quiet authenticity shine through. And, by graciously offering her the gift of his time and his faith in her, he gave her the greatest gift of all—he let her know that she mattered to him, and that she did indeed deserve to be there.

Of course, entire books have been written about the devastating shame endured by survivors of suicide. Yet my guess is that every one of us, no matter how competent we seem to others or how ideal our lives may appear on the outside, finds some reason to believe that, deep down, we don't deserve what we have. That we aren't good enough, or really lovable, or truly worthy enough to be here.

There may be nothing any of us ever does that's harder than sharing the bare-naked truth of ourselves—and nothing more healing than the realization that, chipped and cracked and imperfect as we are, we are also worthy and lovable. Knowing Barbara better, I came to love her more. Her story broke my heart but it also enlarged my heart and taught me an invaluable lesson. I knew it could have been me walking in her shoes, or any parent. Never again did my friend's late-night wanderings annoy me or even keep me awake; I just popped in my earplugs, kept an eye pillow close at hand, and sent her all the loving energy I could summon at midnight.

Since that day when Barbara and I sat shoulder to shoulder together, I often remind myself that any moments I spend regretting anything in my sons' lives are moments wasted. Each time I second-guess the choices I've made as their mom, I'm allowing shame to trump love, the past to obliterate the present, regret for what's over to overshadow the beauty and the goodness of what *is*, right now. They made mistakes. I made mistakes. No doubt we'll all make plenty more in the years to come. But we've loved one another. We did the best we could with what we had and with what we knew. And that's enough. Their lives, their fates, their destinies, are beyond my control, a fact that has been as liberating as it was difficult to accept.

Embracing what is—my sons as they are, myself as I am, the mysterious forces at work in all our lives, even my own failings as the simple human shortcomings they are—is a relief. For it turns out that shame can't survive for long in the bright light of day; when it comes face-to-face with compassion and understanding, shame withers right away. It sounds like a paradox: the idea that embracing our own frailties, and revealing our most vulnerable selves to others, makes us stronger. And yet when I take that risk—when I share some of my own story, or when I summon the courage to open the door and invite a trusted friend to join me in my darkest place—I feel both more trusting of the world and more resilient as I face it.

Living with Barbara for a month, becoming her friend, sharing walks and laughs and lunches and books and yoga clothes, turned out to be just as important to me as any other aspect of our teacher training. But my guess is that something similar was true for every one of my classmates: What happened outside our classroom, in the new relationships

we formed with one another and with ourselves, was as transformative as any part of
the proscribed curriculum. For it is in recognizing and embracing our connections with
one another that we're reminded, again and
again, that we are all vulnerable, that we all
struggle, that we all stumble—and that to be
fully alive is to keep on loving and forgiving
and connecting anyway. They say that, when
the student is ready, the teacher appears. What
Barbara taught me, of course, is that, in the
most humbling sense, we are all both teachers
and students. Not masters but apprentices—
indispensable, integral, interconnected parts of
the whole. To be human is to be both receiver
and giver, leader and follower, as we travel
together through the wonders and tragedies of
this ongoing story of life. Barbara leaned into
my shoulder and offered me her trust when I
was finally ready to learn the lesson I'd been
tiptoeing around and just barely avoiding for
years—that I'm just like everyone else: imperfect *and* worthy, damaged *and* lovable, unique
but not special, a perfectly acceptable work in
progress who will never be "finished," yet who

is blessed nonetheless with my own gifts to share.

On our graduation day, I showered my roommate with rose petals as she walked modestly, joyfully, to the front of the processional to receive her certificate. All down the line, our classmates tossed flowers and offered words that captured her special qualities: grace, courage, humility, beauty, strength, empathy, kindness, resilience. After it was all over, just before I carried my packed bags out to the car, I spotted Stephen. "You know," I said, as we hugged good-bye, "what you did for Barbara was amazing. It meant everything to her."

Stephen's eyes filled even as he smiled. "She reminds me a lot of my mom," he said simply. "I would want someone to do the same for her. So, really, it was nothing."

Nothing *and* everything. Perhaps that's what love is.

"When one tugs at a single thing in nature, he finds it attached to the rest of the world." As I look at my life now—and at the rest of the world—with these words in mind, I do see things a little differently. What would happen, I wonder, if I stopped questioning and doubting what I do, stopped judging my own efforts, stopped critiquing the sentences I write, and began instead to simply trust the process—not just the ups and downs of my work, but everything else as well, indeed, the endlessly evolving process of life itself?

Writing has always helped me bring form to formlessness; it began as my private way of teaching myself what I need to learn in order to be at home in my own life—not as I sometimes wish it were, but as it really *is*: beautiful, messy, fleeting, ordinary, *mine*. But I still struggle with the belief that I should be producing something more tangible or useful in the world.

"You should do work that makes a *real* difference," scolds the voice in my head. "Get out of the house. Feed the hungry, save the planet, visit a nursing home." As I sat at my kitchen table four years ago and wrote a book I wasn't sure anyone would read, I worried I was being self-indulgent, spending hour after hour engaged in the slow, halting process of moving from experience to thought to word. What, really, was the point? Why would anyone else care? Why should I?

Now I'm coming to believe that there is room in the world for all our stories, not only the heroic narratives of extraordinary people who inspire us with their accomplishments, but also simple stories of ordinary struggles. I suspect that every mother, no matter what her circumstances, muddles her way through the intricate dance of holding on and letting go; that no parent ever feels they get it exactly right; and that though our stories may look different on the surface, they are in many ways the same— about lives that feel as confusing and exhilarating, as mundane and precious, as imperfect and as blessed as my own. Sharing the truth of who we are and how we grapple with the everyday stuff of life, of what brings us joy and what brings us to our knees, is simply a way of reweaving and reaffirming our connection with one another. Telling a story, or listening to one, we are reminded of the divine that lives in each of us, and of our frailty as well. "All of us hold within us the ultimate design of the universe," suggests the writer and healer Carolyn North, "and your story, like mine, reflects it perfectly."

And so, even as I sense my life moving now in a different direction, I think I've finally got the message: It's not for me to judge the gifts I have to offer the world, but it is up to me to summon the courage to offer them. There are as many ways to be of use and to express our love as there are people on this earth. Some save lives in emergency rooms while others flip pancakes in church basements; some compose symphonies that make our spirits soar while others sing lullabies to sleepy children; some open their wallets to fund a museum wing and some open their hearts to a cat who shows up at the door; some prepare haute cuisine in fancy restaurants and some cut sandwiches into triangles at an old folks home; some prepare court briefs and some prepare garden beds. And there is worthiness and beauty in all these efforts.

Me, I am home again, writing at dawn, washing the floor, making soup for a friend, flinging tennis balls for Gracie to chase, watering the geraniums, calling my sons, doing the supper dishes, spooning up close to my husband, listening to the steady sound of his breath as he sleeps beside me. I am staring up at stars, listening to stillness, reading a poem, sitting cross-legged on my yoga mat, whispering my mantra, watching my breath. I am living my life.

Going away, even for a short time, taught me something about what it means to stay. Settling back into myself and my house and my marriage, talking with my boys about the ups and downs of their days, finding my way back into my writing, I am surprised by a new and deeper gratitude for the way things are. I know now: I will not judge or turn away from any of this—not from my life as it is, not from the people I love, and not from any calling that tugs at my soul, whatever it happens to be.

It seems that an honest answer to "What now?" isn't going to have much to do with my youthful aspirations or definitions of success. It will rise from deep within, as I slowly fill this container I've worked so hard to build with all that it is really meant to hold—work that may be neither ambitious or impressive, but work that suits who I am now, this less critical, more accepting middle-aged me. My real task is not to try to reinvent myself or to transcend my life after all, but to inhabit it more fully, to appreciate it, and to thoughtfully tend what's already here.

Perhaps this is the "privilege" Joseph Campbell refers to: embracing and welcoming the person I actually am and quietly making the contribution I have to offer—whether it's a manuscript page or an e-mail to my old next-door neighbor, a talk delivered from a podium or a kind word with a stranger in the grocery store, a dinner party for ten or Sunday breakfast for my husband. What matters is not the grandness of the gesture, but its source. If I do my work, all of it, with love, then it is worthy.

Learning who we really are, we rediscover our eternal, immutable connection with everything and everyone else in the universe. Living our lives, we help one another to live; loving what is given us to love, we bring more love into the world. And as I allow myself to open to this energy, to the infinite power and possibility of love, I'm also catching a glimpse of my path outward, from the intimate engagement of family life and motherhood into the wider world.

"It's all about love," Margaret tried to tell me. But that was when I was still so busy trying to figure out what I should be *doing* that I couldn't see the truth that had been hiding in plain sight all along: All I really needed to do was focus on who I wanted to *be*. Love was the lesson I went to yoga teacher training to learn, although I didn't know it till I got there. Love was the education my teachers provided, leading by example. Love was what Barbara and I offered to each other, sharing the stories of our lives. Love is what I've brought home with me, although love was already here. And love, I'm beginning to understand, is the gift I've had to offer all along, in all its many different forms. I just didn't ever quite believe that it—or I— was enough.

～ 10 ～

cleaning

*Keeping a home in order is like
keeping a life in order. The process
is continual. It doesn't end.*

—Victoria Moran

*T*he original scheme called for a loft in
Jack's bedroom. He was twelve, and capti-
vated by the idea that we were going to build a
house from scratch, a house with a room that
would be imagined and created just for him.
Given that our plans were pretty simple—post
and beam construction, a second floor tucked
under the eaves, no attic—a small reading loft
with a ladder didn't seem out of the question.

   "By the time you get your house finished and
actually move into it," our builder predicted,

putting a kindly hand on my arm, "your son won't care much about having a loft in his room." He was gentle with this news. A man with grown sons and grandchildren of his own, he knew better than we did that the house we were about to build would not be a home to boys for very long. Hard as it was for any of us to imagine a life other than the one we were in the midst of living, he encouraged me and Steve to look at the big picture, to envision our longer future there as two adults growing old together, rather than as a family of four all under one roof.

We tried. Henry's piano, we agreed, needed a space in the living room; it might be years before he was ready to take it to a permanent home of his own. But the loft Jack sketched out on a piece of graph paper would remain on the drawing board. We nixed the idea of a separate home office for Steve, made all the bedrooms smaller, whittled away at the plan.

Even so, with both boys gone, the cozy, efficient house we'd built and lived in for just a year before Henry went off to college seemed too big after Jack left as well. It was too quiet, too empty, with too many uninhabited spaces. The Ping-Pong table in the basement became the repository for out-of-season vases and boxes of Christmas decorations. The lid on the piano stayed closed. We turned the heat to low in the boys' bedrooms and carried the coats and extra boots they'd left behind down to the closet in the cellar. Our border collie, Gracie, who was always to be found wherever the boys were, took up a permanent post on a rug near the back door, as if her new assignment was to keep watch for homecomings.

Gracie was a puppy when our sons were little boys. The three of them came of age together, amid baseballs sailing through the backyard, tennis balls and Frisbees and badminton birdies in flight. If it could be tossed or caught or hit or chewed, Gracie was there, hunkered down, all sharp ears and eyes and attention as she awaited her moment to leap, her mouth parted just slightly in what we all were certain was a smile of anticipation. From the moment we brought her home as a squirmy two-month-old black-and-white ball of fur, until first one and then the other son aged out of

Little League, she never missed a single game, could be counted on to sit fully engrossed—if pained to be excluded from the action—on the sidelines, jaws snapping shut every time a ball slapped into a glove. On a couple of memorable occasions, she managed to give her collar the slip and take off in a blur of pure border collie velocity, straight out to her customary spot in the outfield, where she'd spin around and crouch into position, ready to make a catch. Games were stopped in order to return Gracie to the bench, but no one ever really minded; she was a vision of athleticism and exuberance. In our own backyard, she was always a starter, an essential part of every team; she knew just how to get herself under the arc of a ball, how to receive it in her teeth and relinquish it with grace to the pitcher. The rules were modified to accommodate her lack of an arm, but not much. Gracie was a serious player; she commanded respect.

Now I see how both Steve and I have come to depend on her to mitigate the silence, to fill the emptiness left in the wake of two absent boys. When our sons were little, Steve was greeted as he walked through the door each night by cries of "Daddeeee's home!" and entreaties for a game of catch in the yard. The balls and gloves would be located, the most urgent news of the day hastily dispensed with, and out they would go. I'm not sure who looked forward to this daily play time more, my husband or his boys, but it was just one of many small rituals that made family life rhythmic, predictable, and good. And Gracie was an essential ingredient in that mix, too.

Thinking of those days now, I see that our dog has simply carried on what our sons, growing up as sons do, could not. Having lived through and absorbed their childhoods into her being, she sees it as her job to continue traditions they outgrew long ago. It's been years, of course, since our sons came running to meet their father at the door, but Gracie still does it, still dances at his feet and begs for a ball game before he's even had time to put down his bag or change his shoes. And Steve, as ever, is happy to oblige. It is good to be loved, to be welcomed, to be needed, whether by boy or dog.

But even this ritual is changing, for much as Gracie wants to do what she's always done, it's the idea and the memory of that sacred routine she holds on to now and acts out with unflagging enthusiasm every evening. At eleven she's too old to chase down an endless stream of balls as she used to do. But still, she and Steve go through the motions. He bends down to greet his girl; she urges him outside; he tosses the ball high and she snags it, expertly and on the fly, as she has done thousands of times before. But once is enough now, maybe twice on a good day—though God forbid they should ever pass on the game altogether.

And suddenly I think I understand why Jack has been campaigning for a puppy, looking at border collies online, and insisting that we need to give Gracie time to train her successor— impossible as it is for any of us to imagine life without her. For Gracie is the bridge between what's over and what is unfolding now. She, unlike the two aging humans in the household, has moved without regret into this new chapter, rejoicing in every son's homecoming and stoically accepting the inevitable farewell nose kisses. When Henry's home, she sleeps in his room and keeps an eye on his suitcase, attuned to the moment when there are more clothes going back into it than coming out. When Jack is here, she will still give everything she has to give in order to play defense under the basketball hoop. He picks up the ball and she's suddenly two again, every bounce an excitement requiring a move, a quick response, even though the price is high: He will have to carry her up the stairs at night.

When her boys are gone, when it's just the two of us here, she acquiesces to less-thrilling entertainments—early morning walks with me and Steve, brief pursuits of the wild turkeys in the yard, digging a hole under the rhododendron. Imprinted for life with the beauty of balls and boys, she hasn't relinquished her passion for either. But like us, she's adjusting to this new life even as she carries all our yesterdays within her and upholds our family ways, embodying for each of us the beauty of continuity and the illusion of permanence.

Joy and love: the contents of a dog's heart. No wonder, upon seeing Gracie, our fully grown sons drop to the floor, face-to-face and nose to nose, and eagerly become their younger, sweeter, sillier selves. And no wonder my husband and I find ourselves talking to her as if she were a child herself, as if in carrying on the traditions born in our sons' childhood years, she is also allowing us to play our old parenting roles for just a little longer. Our sons may be grown and gone, but Gracie, loyal companion of their boyhoods, is still here. Still here and, though decades older than all of us in dog years, still exuberantly herself, reminding us that to live well is to honor both the beauty of routine and the enchantment of the moment that is right now. I'm beginning to think Jack is right: She is a good teacher.

And although I have often been an unwilling student when the subject is change, I think I am finally ready to embrace the assignment. Lately, the weight I've carried all fall and winter has begun to lift. What felt like emptiness just a few months ago now feels more like breathing room. What I first experienced as loneliness is slowly blossoming into an enriching, surprisingly welcome solitude. And even loss, I see now, is nature's way of urging life to take a new form. Life just as it is meant to be—always changing, and always inviting me to adapt and change along with it.

Quiet has many moods. When our sons are home, their energy is palpable. Even when they're upstairs sleeping I can sense them, can feel the house filling with their presence, expanding like a sail billowed with air. I love the dawn stillness of a house full of sleepers, love knowing that within these walls our entire family is contained and safe, reunited, our stable four-sided shape resurrected. But those days are the exception now, not the norm. And at last I am able to also see the beauty of this new configuration, too, of grown children going forth and returning home again, even as Steve and I find our way back to the private intimacy we shared as a unit of two before our children arrived.

Eventually, one of us will live on here alone, a thought that has never really occurred to me until recently. And yet just as I had to remind myself to stop and notice and give thanks for our life as it was while our sons were growing up and away from us, I remind myself that this new chapter in our marriage, too, will one day have its ending, that there are more losses, more changes, to come.

The seemingly solid structure of life, I now know, is a fantasy; things are constantly coming apart and then being rebuilt into new forms, over and over again. Recalling how my own family has swelled and multiplied and shrunk and shifted through the years, I think of all the births and marriages and deaths that have altered the shape of our life together, changing everything from the way the holiday tables are set to the birthday dates scribbled in my calendar. Perhaps this is the overarching lesson to be learned as we marvel at the miracle of new life, mourn at the gravesites of loved ones, or toss fistfuls of rice into the air at weddings: not to regret the passage of time, but to find ways to acknowledge it. To remember that this imperfect, unpredictable life, this day, this opportunity to love and cherish one another, is fleeting, singular, not to be missed.

Spring is here. There is sweetness in the air, an irresistible invitation to soften and open and welcome new growth. And as I carry screens up from the basement and crank open the windows in the kitchen, the damp, seductive smell of greening earth inspires me to action. I want to do more than my weekly pass through the house with duster and vacuum and mop. Instead, a fresh look at things, through fresh eyes. Ever since we moved in and set up house-keeping four and a half years ago, I've been so preoccupied with the daily necessities of life and work and teenagers that I haven't had time to pause and consider what's actually working and what's not.

But things are different now. Instead of organizing my days around the comings and goings of everyone else, I can decide for myself what matters. Instead of making a daily accounting of what we need—juice and eggs; new shoes for one son, a haircut for the other; an oil change for the car—I now find myself wondering what we can do without.

Looking around at these comfortable, clut-tered rooms, I see that even in this short space of time, we've accumulated things that have outlived their usefulness. But instead of cocooning myself in what's familiar, I'm ready to change the way we live here, to pare back and get rid of stuff we don't really use or want, and then to move into those empty spaces. Perhaps we don't need teenagers upstairs playing music that reverberates the floorboards to make this house feel full after all. We can fill it with light and spirit and newfound purpose.

"Simplification of the outer life is not enough," Anne Morrow Lindbergh notes in her classic book of midlife reflection, *Gift from the Sea*, "it is merely the outside." But simplifying the outer life feels exactly like the next step for me right now, a way of physically and emotionally clearing out what we're done with and making some space for what's next.

I start in the small office off the kitchen, with the idea of weeding through all the books. Every single volume comes off the floor-to-ceiling shelves; I figure that by the time Steve gets home from work tonight, things will be back in order. But what begins in the morning as a simple bit of spring cleaning leads me straight into a heart-to-heart dialogue not only with my books, but with my past and present selves. It's not a day's task, after all, this chat, but it's apparently a conversation we need to have. Which books have gone mute? Which ones are speaking up, demanding to be returned to the shelves?

Long gone are the days when I would sit on my bed surrounded by dictionary, thesaurus, bottles of Wite-Out and Post-its and colored pencils, and first and second drafts of book manuscripts marked up by hand. And so the reference books—my old dictionaries, *Roget's Thesaurus*, *Bartlett's Familiar Quotations* (well-thumbed in the pre-Internet age, obsolete now), *The Chicago Manual of Style*, which was my bible during my editing career—all go into a pile by the back door. Remnants of a past I let go of years ago, they have become artifacts. Letting go of them turns out to be easier than I thought.

Paging through the cookbooks, I'm surprised how few I actually use, how often I've been seduced by "maybe someday" photos of exotic dishes I can now admit I'll never take the time to make. When my sons walk through the door these days, they want pancakes, steak

dinners, chicken casserole, my apple cake—
the same sturdy, familiar meals I've always
made and that speak to them of home. And I
am happy to oblige. The rest of the time, my
husband and I are here alone, two growing-
older people watching our weight and trying
to accommodate our slowing metabolisms.
How many risotto recipes do I need? A whole
shelf of cookbooks can go, too.

Since the day in 1989 when, thirty minutes
after reading the results of my pregnancy test,
I raced to the WordsWorth Bookstore in Har-
vard Square to buy a copy of *What to Expect
When You're Expecting*, I've managed to acquire
an entire library of parenting books. From *You
Are Your Child's First Teacher* to *Yes, Your Teen
Is Crazy!* these books have been guideposts at
each step of the way, reminding me I wasn't
the first mother to wonder if it's okay to let the
baby cry or whether a sixteen-year-old is ready
to drive alone or why there's a cigarette butt in
the birdhouse. I'm not sure now why I didn't
trust myself more, but I do know I won't ever
open any of these books again.

I'm not done being a mother, of course, nor

are my sons so grown-up that they don't need parenting. But I'm pretty sure I know what I need to know: take care of our relationships with one another, tell the truth and ask for the truth, solve problems together, love them no matter what. Looking at all these titles, at pages folded over and passages highlighted in pink, I think about how seriously I took on the spiritual and physical work of motherhood. No wonder I felt at a loss when I found myself relieved of the job.

But packing these child-rearing books into a couple of boxes to pass on to another mother feels like a rite of passage I'm ready to embrace—my identity is no longer intertwined with my children, my role no longer defined by their needs.

So much of this last year has been about trying to figure out how to meet this new, unfamiliar responsibility to *me*, trying to decide what my own priorities actually are, now that I'm finally free to choose.

I still don't have all the answers, but now, with the room in complete disarray and my books in piles all over the floor, I have an idea.

Certificate or not, I don't feel quite ready to be a yoga teacher, but I am certainly ready to do something. Why not use the skills I learned during my month of training to teach writing instead? I could begin right where I am, teaching what I continue to learn by doing it myself. I could send an e-mail out to friends, put a press release in the newspaper, and welcome whoever shows up on my doorstep willing to attempt the soul-searching work of transforming the stuff of their lives into narrative. A minute later, I'm standing in the living room, counting possible seats and imagining the room full of women with notebooks and pens.

One new idea has a way of giving birth to the next one. And from the living room, it's only three steps into the adjoining nook that we've never quite figured out what do with. The space had already been drawn into the house plans as a small office for Steve when we decided that was an extra we didn't need. But since this oddly shaped little room had to get built anyway, we figured we'd put a small second television in here. We furnished the narrow space with a loveseat and a table, a couple of chairs, and a TV in the bookshelves. But then, except for Jack, who played video games on the screen, we rarely set foot in there again. I wipe a finger across a shelf, leaving a streak through the dust. The Xbox is long gone, the room yet another lifeless, extraneous place that I barely remember to clean, let alone use.

Until now. In a flash of inspiration I see exactly what it needs to be: a sanctuary for yoga and meditation. And so I begin clearing the shelves in there, too—packing up the kids' old videos and CDs into boxes, carting out all the stuff that's accumulated on the shelves, and filling them instead with the books I'd stacked on the floor of my office, the ones that I suspect are going to guide me on through the next chapter of my own life: books of poetry, nature writing, spiritual explorations, yoga manuals.

"How would you feel about getting rid of the leather loveseat, and that old table and chairs?" I ask Steve as we sit down to a late dinner that night, in the midst of the mess I've created. "We aren't using that little room at all anyway, so I was thinking about just emptying it out, and turning it into a kind of studio space, for yoga and meditating."

To my surprise, he doesn't hesitate. "Let's do it," he says, perhaps as relieved as I am to realize that we can ask our house, and the shape of our lives within these walls, to change as we change.

It feels as if we are turning the lights back on around here, reclaiming and reinvesting in a house that hasn't felt quite as much like a home since both our boys left. And yet there's no need to keep it as a mausoleum, dedicated to the way things were. We had put years of thought and effort into settling here, creating a home and a life for four. But there is also something to be said for unsettling. If we're not growing, not changing, but just existing in our own well-worn grooves, then we're simply putting in time. Now, with the rooms torn apart, books scattered everywhere, and my mind brimming with new ideas, time feels surprisingly expansive again. Suddenly, there's so much I want to do.

I remember Jack, in third grade or so, saying, "Everyone else in the family goes someplace every day. Dad goes to work. Henry and I go to school. But you just stay home all the time." Surprised he would even notice such a thing, I explained how lucky I felt to have a job I could do from our house—and that I actually liked staying home and editing books, so I could be there if he or his brother needed me. Right up through my sons' high school years, I organized my work days around their school days, convinced I had the best of both worlds— engaging work I could do without leaving the house.

If people can be divided between those who itch to travel widely and see much, and those who prefer to stay put, sink their roots, and go deep, I am definitely in the latter camp, a root sinker by nature, happiest puttering in the garden, chopping vegetables in the kitchen, or curled up in an armchair with a book in my hands. Home is the only place I've ever wanted to be; the good life was always the one we created right here, under our own roof.

But finding my own rhythm at home over these last months has proven as strange and difficult as it's been for my husband and me to find a new way to be alone with each other. It's taken me this long to truly feel "at home" again, for my first reaction to our sons' departure was to flee. Being with my friend through her illness gave me a good reason to be home less; being needed was a relief and gave me a sense of purpose.

Eventually, though, I had to stop moving long enough to hear what my heart had been trying to tell me. Sitting on my yoga mat day after day in a silent house, putting my heart up on a block, feeling my feelings and crying my tears, was harder than staying busy or helping someone else. There were many winter days when I wondered what was wrong with me— it felt as if I was mourning for everything: the past that was and the past that wasn't, the loss of my youth, the shortness of life, our empty nest, everyone I'd ever known who was now gone, all the things that hadn't turned out the way I thought they were supposed to be.

I was cowed by that dark current of grief, unsure where it had come from or where it would take me. Now I suspect that allowing myself to sink down into it was an essential

part of moving forward without regret, and
that the gift of that darkness has been worth
the trouble. Learning to be myself *for* myself
has been, and continues to be, a challenge. Yet
more and more, I find myself able to stay with
what is and to attend to what's lurking in the
shadows—the stuff my friend Nancy came to
think of as her compost pile. And then, out of
that black, fecund place, arises a new, more
creative, more authentic response to my life
just as it is.

Deliberately withdrawing from the familiar
obligations and distractions of home in order
to go away on a spiritual retreat—to claim
time and space that's just for *us*—may feel like
an indulgence; it undoubtedly requires some
planning and some sacrifice. But finding the
courage to say "This is what I need right now"
seems to be a crucial step in any intentional
journey into the second half of life—whether
the retreat consists of a pilgrimage in India or
a single Saturday night spent holed up alone
in a bed-and-breakfast scribbling in a journal;
a weekend meditation workshop or a month

living in a dorm room and practicing yoga; or, as in author Joan Anderson's unusual case, an entire year's sabbatical from her marriage in a cottage by the sea. What matters is not the where or the when or even the how long, but the willingness to pause and take stock, to fully experience the full range of our emotions as we honor our own endings and beginnings.

A good life is always partly a matter of luck, but it is also a choice we make for ourselves— a choice of deliberation, attention, creativity, limits. A choice predicated on this belief: I am worthy. And this, too, takes practice. After years of trying to be, as Joan Anderson so aptly puts it, "all things to all people," of caring for children, meeting the demands of our jobs, tending to marriages and colleagues and friends, most of us are so used to putting everyone else's needs before our own that we are hesitant to stake out some quiet territory that's just for us. We are so afraid of wasting time that we are reluctant to take the time— time we desperately need if we are to nurture our inner lives and reconnect with who we are and what we know, deep down.

And yet a journey from what was to what is demands not only faith and patience, but also a willingness to clear out some physical and emotional space in our overstuffed, overscheduled lives, space that allows room for spirit to enter and for guidance to be gleaned. We need a quiet corner in the house, an empty hour in the day, a time and a place in which we can regularly turn away from the noisy world and attune instead to the wisdom of our own bodies, the spaciousness of our own spirits. Alone with ourselves, we touch the essence of who we are and we get a glimpse of who we might yet be. And it is this small beam of light, this glimmer of possibility, that will show us the way forward, for to change within is to change without.

No one can begin to answer the question of "What next?" without first letting go of "what was"—a slow releasing that ought not be rushed, no matter how arduous the process nor how eager we may be to move through it. Perhaps all transformation begins with a wound, some loss or sorrow that must be reckoned with. And then, as our assumptions and identities are shaken, as the old, familiar layers peel away, we begin to meet unknown parts of ourselves—unexpected feelings, new longings, tender vulnerabilities, and even gifts we didn't know were in us. There is nothing pleasurable about molting and shedding, nor should there be. In fact, I'm coming to suspect that the discomfort of release and transformation may be the price we pay for the subtle rewards of the midlife journey—hope, perspective, acceptance, renewed energy, and fresh inspiration.

Now, waking up as I always do to watch the sun rise over the mountains, savoring the day's rich beginnings, the calm and quiet of early morning, it feels as if nothing much has changed—and as if everything has. Of course, all that's really changed is the one thing that matters most—my own perception.

Breathe. Relax. Feel. Watch. Allow. The years from here on in will be what I make of them. Inner harmony can be translated into outer harmony. Why not open myself to even more change, and then see what happens next?

In my new yoga space there is room, barely, for two mats to lie, side by side. I hang a strand

of faded Tibetan prayer flags that I've had in
a box for years across one wall and a smaller
string of them in the window that looks out to
the fields below our house. On the sill: a couple
of crystals, a black heart-shaped rock picked up
on a walk many summers ago, a glass egg that
catches the sunlight, a tiny jade Buddha. My
favorite poets and thinkers keep me company
from their new homes on the bookshelves. A
photo of me and Marie, taken on the beach in
Maine the year before she got sick, is placed so
that I can greet my friend here each day. Photos, too, of our sons, black-and-white yester-
years that hold them in time as the little boys
they used to be. There are a couple of pillows
in a corner, an angel figurine from a friend on
a shelf, a painting by another on the wall.

Most nights now, before Steve gets home
and I begin making dinner, I come into this
small room and take a seat on the floor. I
don't expect miracles. But I have given myself
a sacred space, and now I simply offer myself
the even greater gift of time to use it. Someday,
perhaps, something will happen here. For now,
I love this room, this emptiness, the fading

light, my own quiet company. I am learning, by sitting, to become, in the words of Terry Tempest Williams, "a caretaker of silence, a connoisseur of stillness, a listener of wind."

I come to rest in the quiet house as darkness falls and I welcome that stillness into my being. I picture my sons, each of them far from home, busy with lives of their own making. With my hands cupped before my heart, I offer prayers for their safekeeping and send them my love. Holding them this way, imagining them and silently loving them from afar, is a new kind of caring—mothering by faith, I call it. "May they be happy." I form the words of the Buddhist lovingkindness meditation in my mind. "May they be safe. May they be well. May they be peaceful and at ease." This, too, is a practice.

But I am coming to believe that all practice, done from the heart, changes the world in some small way for the better. And so, from where I am, I affirm my connections with my children, wherever they are. And then— because why stop now?—I cast a wider net, one that includes all children, and all parents, and all beings everywhere. May we be happy. May we be safe. May we be well. May we be peaceful and at ease. Awakening this energy of love, sending it forth into the world, somehow affirms my own small place in the great scheme of things. There are many ways to be a mother, many ways to pray, many ways to serve.

The days have been chilly for May, a long reluctant tease of spring. But this cool evening is perfect for a fire. I have a pot of tea on the stove, mugs on a tray, a candle lit, chairs tucked in around the fireplace—and nine women arriving any minute for the first of six weekly evenings of a memoir-writing workshop.

I've never taught anything to anyone before and never expected I'd have the confidence to try. Lately, though, I find myself recalibrating my expectations—of myself most of all. Loosening up a bit, I no longer feel compelled to tell myself who I should be.

Oddly enough, it seems to be a deepened sense of humility—the midlife liberation of realizing, "Oh, I'm not so special after all"—that's providing a welcome respite from some of my old worries about what other people will think of me and my less-than-perfect efforts. Slowly, I'm getting the message. Age can't be ducked. There's no getting around the fact that I'm different than I was: not as ambitious, not as attractive, no longer ripe with potential. But on the flip side of these diminishments are the perks that come with age—less need to be right and more confidence that what I have to offer is enough. Less worry about the things I can't control anyway, and a more easygoing faith that things will all work out in the end.

For me, the big surprise of growing older is turning out to be this: Fear never actually goes away. But I've had a lot of practice by now in confronting it. And whenever I do take a step into what scares me, even if it's just a tiny step—something as small as being the first one to reach out in a relationship, initiating a hard conversation, doing a headstand two feet away from the wall, or offering a writing class on Monday nights—I feel as if my deficiencies matter less and less. Whenever I get out of my own way, something good is right there waiting for me, ready to meet me where I am.

*   *   *

I doubt there's much I can tell these women
that they don't already know about *how* to
write; I want them to think about *why* we
write, and why our stories, all of them, matter
in the first place. No matter what our work has
been to date, whether as mothers and home-
makers, or as professionals out in the work-
place, or both, midlife requires us to readjust
our focus—age and circumstance conspire to
call us inward, into a deeper conversation with
ourselves.

And where I once thought "teaching" would
mean knowing more than my students, I see
this work differently—simply as an opportunity to create a time and a place for a group of
women to come together and write and speak
their own truths as they discover more about
themselves and one another. If midlife is the
time when we long to stop defining ourselves
by what we do and begin to seek instead a
more complete understanding of who we are,
then writing brings us to the very heart of that
challenging, often surprising symposium with
the self. What I want my students to learn in

this room over the next six weeks is that our own ordinary voices deserve to be honored, our own real-life stories to be drawn forth, honed, shaped, and shared.

The page is a receptive ear for the soul's murmurings. Writing has helped me figure out what I know for sure and, more important, it has given me a way to grapple with those questions that seem to have no answers. At times, it has been a kind of call and response between my doubting, questioning, seeking self and some wiser self whose voice I am still learning to summon and to trust. But sharing what I write is what takes me to my edge, to that place where my own uncertainties and vulnerabilities are brought to light and exposed. And what a relief it is, always, to realize I can survive the glare, and that I'm not alone after all.

Teaching a writing class may not be all that different from teaching a yoga class: create a safe place in which people can come together, set aside the concerns of the day, tune in to their own quiet center, and become acquainted with what's there. Like yoga, writing takes practice. And just as in yoga, you start wherever you are, you flail around awkwardly for a while, and, if you stick with it long enough, if you allow yourself to be more curious than critical, if you put your trust in the process, eventually you get close to something essential, something important, something worth the effort: the essence of who you are.

I look around at this home we've created and that I care for daily, a container now not only for our family life as it was during our sons' teenage years, but also an empty vessel waiting to be filled with new purpose, new life, new memories. Perhaps for a few hours on Monday nights at least, my living room will become a sanctuary, a place where other women may take the first steps of their own magical journeys as they are inspired to go in search of what's already inside, just waiting to be birthed.

I touch a match to the fire, sit down on the wide stone hearth, and wait for the first knock on the door.

~ 11 ~

reunion

And when is there time to sift,
to weigh, to estimate, to total?

—TILLIE OLSEN

I suspect we all wanted to grow up to be Jill Ker Conway. Or to be just like her, our much adored and admired college president. In my memory, I'm one of four hundred impressionable young women listening, rapt, as she stands at a podium and greets the Smith College freshman class of 1980. Perhaps we hoped that just by being there in her bright orbit for four years, we, too, might ascend to greatness, or at least come to possess something of her grace and intellect, her clear sense of mission, her easy elegance, her quiet charisma. Slender, tidy, she was a mite Katharine Hepburn–ish in her trimly tailored tweed suit and understated pearls—though Jill (we all called her Jill, as if she were one of us) seemed kinder and more cheerful, refined but without the slightest bit of an edge.

Arriving on campus in the fall of 1976, a slightly pudgy, shy, intimidated freshman, I was relieved to have escaped my small-town life at last—there would be no going back *there*, of that I was certain!—but painfully aware of how little I knew about the world I'd just entered. I didn't have a clue what to wear, let alone how I was supposed to act or who I wanted to be. I didn't know anyone who read *The New York Times*; had never heard of Virginia Woolf, Madeleine L'Engle, or Sylvia Plath; was not exactly sure what my classmates were talking about when they referred to Choate and Chapin and Dana Hall. I had never listened to jazz, or heard a poem read aloud, or eaten with chopsticks, or had a pizza delivered to the door. There was a lot to learn. The first night, over dinner in Martha Wilson House, as we passed bowls of mashed potatoes and

platters of pot roast smothered in gravy, someone suggested we go around the table and say
whether we were virgins or not; fortunately,
I had relieved myself of that burden over the
course of the summer. "I slept with an actor,"
I said when it was my turn, feigning nonchalance. My Smith education had begun.

I haven't been back for more than twenty
years, and yet as I drive through town, register at a table set up on the sidewalk outside
the Alumni House, and lug my suitcase up
the wide curving staircase to my room on the
third floor of Northrup, the past rushes in like
a tide, overlapping every moment of now with
a memory of then. Even the woman whose
room is next to mine in the dorm is instantly
familiar—I do not have to rack my brain for
her name or try to place her in context; as we
exchange hellos in the hallway, I feel as awkward and ungainly in her presence now as I
did when we were eighteen.

Blair was the type of exquisitely groomed,
casually entitled girl I knew even then that
I would never be. With her thick, straight,
perfectly blond and perfectly blunt-cut hair

and tall athletic build; her off-hand manner; her designer shoes (Pappagallo wedges
then, Manolo Blahnik flats now), visible pedi-
gree, and prelaw path, she seemed imperturbable, destined to glide through her charmed,
well-accessorized life with nary a blemish on
her skin, a run in her stocking, nor a hole on
her résumé. Perhaps I remember her so vividly all these years later, though we were never
friends, simply because she seemed to so thoroughly embody the expectation that ours was
a generation of women who actually could and
would do it all.

That fall of our freshman year, the most
popular garment on campus was a T-shirt
that had been designed for Smith's centennial
the year before. "Smith College 1875–1975,"
it said across the front, and on the back, "100
years of women on top." We all bought them
within days of arriving, in two or three different colors, and wore them without a trace of
irony. There was no mistaking the message of
the times.

So I can't help but wonder, as I walk around
the idyllic campus, stealing looks at name tags

and trying to match fifty-plus-year-old faces with thirty-year-old memories, who are we now? Have our lives matched our expectations? How have we struggled and what have we learned? I want to know every single life story. I want to ask my classmates what they're feeling and thinking as they wander these paths, meet up with old friends, poke their heads into former classrooms, bend low to brush their teeth at the communal sinks, and turn down the narrow single beds in our old dorm rooms, with their high ceilings and well-worn wooden floors.

"When you leave this place, as you will in a couple of hours," writer Ann Patchett told a graduating class at Sarah Lawrence several years ago, "be sure to come back. Coming back is the thing that enables you to see how all the dots in your life are connected, how one decision leads you to another, how one twist of fate, good or bad, brings you to the door that later takes you to another door, which, aided by several detours—long hallways and unforeseen stairwells—eventually puts you in the place you are now. Every choice lays down a trail of bread crumbs, so that when you look behind you there appears to be a very clear path that points straight to the place where you now stand."

She's right, of course; there are bread crumbs at every turn: the theater building, where my boyfriend wooed me with elaborate picnic lunches he would spend the morning assembling; Wright Hall, where I sat in darkness for a semester memorizing hundreds of Art 100 slides, feeling more sophisticated and worldly by the day; Hatfield, where my freshman-year English professor stunned me with the first C I'd ever received, and her note—"see me!"— scrawled at the bottom of the page, struck terror in my heart; Paradise Pond, where my friend Tory and I would drift aimlessly in a rowboat for hours, reclined, faces tipped to the sky, talking about sex; the back stairwell in Martha Wilson, where I sat on a step listening to my friend play "Summertime" on her clarinet, because the acoustics there were so much better than in her room. I remember the dusky, intoxicating smell of old books in the upper, little-used stacks in Neilson Library, the curve in the walkway just here, the maple tree under which I sat reading *Anna Karenina*, Carole King's "Tapestry" drifting through open windows, the sense of life opening before me vast and boundless as a landscape.

What I feel, coming back to this place I once loved and knew so well and where I began, in a true sense, to grow up, is time caving in on itself. Fifty-one? How could that be, when I was just here, choosing an English seminar for second semester? How could it be, when I don't feel like whatever I thought a fifty-plus-year-old woman was supposed to feel like? The truth is, I just feel like, well, myself—as if the ardent, yearning, younger version of me is close enough to reach out and touch, shimmering like a hologram superimposed upon the somewhat more restrained, less naïve, but still yearning middle-aged me. Perhaps the white-haired woman in a navy blue cardigan, sitting on a bench in the quad with her cane propped beside her, is thinking exactly what I'm thinking: "It looks almost the same as it used to, things haven't really changed much; I haven't changed much either."

But, of course, I have. We all have. Things may not change but people do. Life has had its way with us and now, thirty years after our own commencement speaker, poet Maya Angelou, suggested that "the horizon leans forward, offering you space to place new steps of change," I am living the back side of what I once thought of as my future—albeit, a future that's turned out to be as much about bowing to the consequences of the unexpected as about executing the plans I once harbored in my heart.

How could I have known that the freedom that seemed so desirable and elusive in my twenties would come not from escaping myself, but from finally accepting myself? Or that liberation—that word we threw about so earnestly as undergraduates—would turn out not to be about grabbing the brass ring, nailing the dream job, or getting the life I always wanted, but rather about fully experiencing the startling beauty, the pain, the wonder and surprise of the great, winding journey itself?

"I feel as if I'm finally the grown-up I used to try to imagine myself being when I was here," my friend Wendy says as we walk down the hill toward town on our first afternoon. "But what's funny," she continues, "is that nothing in my life has really turned out the way I always thought it would."

Wendy had gone straight to California after graduation, landed a job as an assistant to a famous movie director, and cut her teeth in the film business, first in LA and then in New York. Over the years, she's worked as a producer, a festival artistic director, a film scout, a screenwriter. And yet, despite her heartfelt desire to marry and have children, she didn't get to do it all. The jobs came and went, relationships began and ended, family members needed support, and Wendy stepped off one path and onto another, to do what was asked of her. She took care of a dying aunt, her mother, others who depended on her. The years went by and her interests and prospects shifted along the way.

Now she says, "I spent a lot of years wanting what I didn't have—the home, the husband, the children—and thinking I wouldn't be complete until I was married with a family. But something's changed. I finally realized I *am* complete. And instead of seeing what's missing, I feel grateful for what I have. My life isn't about form anymore, it's about content. It's true that I don't always get to choose the content, but I can decide what to do with it. And I guess I'm just really enjoying the fact that the content is as rich and as gratifying as I make it."

With her wide smile, long, dark, curly hair, and curvaceous figure, Wendy is still beautiful, as dramatic looking as she was when we were both double-majoring in theater and English three decades ago. But she's also seasoned, at once warm and thoughtful, sexy and vivacious. And we fall easily back into our old intimacy, despite the fact that, except for a couple of overlapping years in New York when I was single, our lives since have rarely crossed. While I was reading child-rearing books, she was reading film scripts; during the years that my calendar was determined by kids' schedules and school vacation dates, hers was dictated by annual pilgrimages to Park City and Toronto and Cannes.

And yet by the time we sit down over coffee in Northampton, we've discovered that the questions and struggles of midlife have provided us with far more common ground than not. Perhaps none of us looks age fifty in the eye without pausing to wonder if we're really doing what we're meant to do here. Without reflecting on our life's work and asking, "Is it enough?" Without turning a more attentive ear to the soul's quiet urgings. And without finally catching at least a glimpse of our true calling: the deceptively simple and endlessly challenging task of being the person we're capable of being in any given moment.

Wandering through town, we note that while much of the campus may feel suspended in time, everything around it has been transformed. The first article of clothing I ever bought in college was a white half-slip, purchased the week I arrived, at Ann August, where an elderly saleslady placed my twenty-dollar bill in a pneumatic tube and it was whisked away to some unseen cashier on an upper floor; my change was returned in a capsule, dropping down a chute. It was another world, the last vestiges of another time, already vanishing. Within a year the venerable ladies' department store was gone and the East of Heaven Hot Tub spa had become a favorite Friday night destination. Main Street burst into life and went upscale. By the time I graduated, the town had proclaimed a renaissance, acquired its nickname, NoHo, and remade itself into a bustling hub: upscale, hip, artistic, musical, countercultural, proud of its reputation as the most politically liberal midsized community in the country.

Yet, between the two of us, Wendy and I can still recall the long-gone seventies tenants of nearly every storefront; this was home, each place indelible, our life downtown comprising its own bread-crumb trail: Bart's Ice Cream, Beardsley's Restaurant, Pinch Pottery, Kinney Shoes. To our delight, there's one cherished haunt from then that still thrives now; although the Gunne Sax dresses from our day have been replaced in the window by cream and gray linen from Flax, Country Comfort otherwise looks exactly the same.

We open the door and step inside, erasing

years. The calendar page has been turned over four hundred times since I chose a long red skirt from these racks for a Valentine's Day dinner my sophomore year—and yet the tiny, birdlike woman who greets us now is the same one who advised me so long ago about my look for date night. It's been decades—decades since I owned anything red, since I set foot in this store, or even thought of this petite, kind woman from whom I bought just about every other piece of clothing I adored during my college years. Now, though, the memories come flowing back.

Bit by bit, as it began to sink in that the clothes I chose to wear said something about who I wanted to be, it was Eva who pointed the way, her understated, accessible taste gently shaping and guiding mine. Eva was all about comfort, real life, femininity, and beauty with a dash of flair. Junior and senior year, I had a job in a trendy boutique in town, but the clothes I wanted, the ones I felt like "myself" wearing, were always the ones that Eva had for sale in her little shop across the street.

"I can't believe you're still here!" I exclaim, a

bit weak-kneed from that time-collapsing feeling all over again. "It's been thirty years!"

"I've been here all along," Eva says with a smile, "ever since we opened the doors on Main Street in 1975."

For some reason, it makes my day to find her, to realize that Eva, the feisty, creative, warmhearted fashion advisor of my earliest adulthood, chose this particular spot on the planet more than three decades ago and then just stayed put, building a life around a place that changed around her and a calling that never ceased to satisfy. "Bill left for Mexico years ago," she explains, referring to her ex-husband. "He'd had enough. But I never wanted to be anyplace else. So, we stayed friends, and I stayed here. I still love it."

It's clear she does; the store is still, as it always was, a feast for a woman's senses, stocked with an abundance of colorful imported baskets and scarves and purses, cases stuffed with hundreds of pairs of earrings and necklaces from all over the world. Lovely beaded tops for evening hang near racks full of the kinds of clothes I'd wear every day if I could—flowing linen pants, drapey sweaters, soft, clingy T-shirts in every color. The long, fat brown braid I remember from the seventies is gone; Eva's hair is partly gray and cut shorter now, yet otherwise she is almost exactly the same: a diminutive, five-foot-tall pixie with a ready smile and an infectious enthusiasm that suggests that the bounty of the store is merely an extension of her own closet, and our patronage here a delightful surprise visit between old friends.

"You know," I admit, "I would always come in here and covet all these earrings—you really did have the best in town—which is actually why I finally went and got my ears pierced, back in college. But then I turned out to be too wimpy to handle it. I wanted to wear gypsy hoops, but I couldn't even bear putting earrings in my ears."

Now, here, I'm doubly glad I decided to try again: Spread out before me, all these years later, is a veritable buffet of earrings. "I haven't actually taken these studs out yet," I tell Eva, pointing to one of my tiny fake diamonds from

Claire's, "but I think I'm finally ready to buy my first pair of pierced earrings—and I definitely want to buy them from you! Better late than never."

The selection is overwhelming, though, and our time's running out; we've spent nearly an hour chatting, no time at all shopping. Eva doesn't mind; she takes the long view. "We'll definitely be back!" Wendy and I promise, saying our good-byes. "I'll be here," Eva calls out as the door chimes ring behind us.

As we make our way back up the hill toward campus, the two of us link arms for a moment, just as we used to do. And I realize how glad I am to be here with a friend who knew me way back when. When I think of myself in my twenties, what I see is forward motion—a young woman who wasn't at all sure where she was going, only that she didn't want to look back. The goal, I was pretty certain, was to get as far away as possible from where I'd been and create a life for myself that was bigger and more impressive than the one I'd left behind. But if the geometry of twenty was a long, straight line going in one direction and only one—forward—the shape of now feels more like a spiraling circle.

These days, I want to stop moving so fast and turn around instead—to look back and see where I've been, to retrace some steps, fortify old connections, study the bread crumbs. Instead of running away from the past, I want to assimilate and claim it, to gather up all my past selves—dreamy child, restless teenager, impassioned college student, young mother, early-middle-aged woman—and fold them into the person I am at this moment. I want to reassure myself that all those mes are still there, even though nearly everything around me has changed. To say, "This is my life, all of it, and these are the people and places and experiences that have made me who I am."

"The great thing about getting older," as my fellow Smith alum Madeleine L'Engle observed on her way into her nineties, "is that you don't lose all the other ages you've been." No wonder the impulse is strong at this moment to find whatever vestige of the idealistic twenty-one-year-old English major still lingers here, and to see just how the dots have connected for everyone else.

Being with my old friend grounds me, binds the past into the framework of the present and makes it easier to contemplate the future. Enduring friendships, relationships that entwine and diverge and then circle back to enfold and sustain again—what better reminder could there be that the most beautiful achievement of life is not the self-sufficiency I was once so keen on asserting, but enduring, meaningful connection. Wendy and I share a small piece of common history, a particular time in a particular place that shaped us both. Looking at her now, I see the girl she was. I think it's the same for her: She knows me so well today simply because the two of us inhabited a handful of indelible yesterdays together.

My friend and I agree that what we each recall most vividly from our time at Smith is our sense of both the burden and the privilege conferred by our education. Our way had been paved by the feminists who came before us. And, as we were often reminded, they had

done the heavy lifting so we, the first generation of their daughters to come of age, could
reap the benefits. There was nothing we could
not do, nothing we should not try.

Role models abounded. During our four years,
a parade of remarkable women—poets and poli-
ticians, businesswomen and activists, professionals and philanthropists—visited Smith to tell
us their stories and inspire us to think big as
we went out into the world and began to write
our own. Maya Angelou and Adrienne Rich,
Jane Pauley and Sally Quinn, Cris Williamson and Joan Armatrading—they came, spoke,
read their poetry and sang their songs, and
we crowded into the lecture halls and theaters
to listen, hanging on every word, studying
their self-confidence, memorizing their lyrics,
inspired by their strength. We walked in the
long shadows cast by our most admired alum-
nae. In addition to Madeleine L'Engle there
were Anne Morrow Lindbergh, Julia Child,
Sylvia Plath, Betty Friedan, Gloria Steinem.
I looked up to them all, read their books and
then slipped on white gloves and visited their
manuscripts and first editions in the hush of

the rare-book room, deeply proud to be a part of this lineage. Anything seemed possible. "Anything is," each of these women assured us, whether in person or by example.

Now, for this May weekend, the class of '80 is back, more than 150 of us returned in the hope of somehow connecting our variously complicated "now"s to a fleeting yet identity-forging "then." Someone notes that most of us are the same age Jill Ker Conway was when she took off her pearls and "retired" from the Smith presidency in order to roll up her shirt-sleeves and go make the world a better place for underprivileged women.

"I was always aware," she says in a much-anticipated address to our class on Saturday afternoon, "that while I was busy raising money for this entitled institution, there were women who could not afford to feed their children, who had no access to health care, who were abused by their employers. The longer I stayed, the bigger my debt to those women became. And so, as I entered my fifties, I knew it was time for me to figure out how I could make a difference for them."

Now approaching eighty, this wise, energetic woman is still pursuing that calling. She stands before us without so much as a note, smiling warmly, as trim and articulate and lovely as ever, as she recounts her groundbreaking work as the first woman on the board at Nike. She recalls her years of travel throughout the third world, visiting factories, bringing nutrition and fair wages and improved working conditions to underprivileged women from Cambodia to China. These days, she tells us, she is slowing down a bit, working on a book about aging and the needs and rights of the elderly—and yet, in the next breath, Jill acknowledges that she also contributes time to various environmental initiatives and continues to serve on the boards of Nike and Colgate-Palmolive, in the belief that changing corporate culture from the inside out is a powerful way to make everyday life better for women everywhere. Widowed, childless, accepting the physical limitations of age, our beloved role model is also, it seems clear, truly happy in her life, as engaged with dear friends and good causes in her own small town as she is with the larger vision that still guides her.

The room is stuffy, our luncheon has long since been cleared away, the questions and answers go on for an hour, and yet at the end of Jill's talk the standing ovation is immediate and lengthy and heartfelt, just as it always was—and is—for our cherished mentor. Clearly, she still represents what we aspire to become.

Unfortunately, I am next on the afternoon agenda. I'd agreed months ago to host a discussion at our reunion, using my book about motherhood and the adolescent years as a pathway into a general conversation about where we are and what's on our minds. But I leave the campus center after Jill's galvanizing address wishing we could all just call it a day. We've been fed, inspired, and filled up to the brim; surely others will feel as I do: It was enough.

And I'm pretty sure I have nothing to offer that can begin to compare with the shot-in-the-arm dose of motivation we've just received. Will anyone show up for yet one more indoor event on this exquisite, world-in-full-bloom May afternoon?

The answer, it turns out, is yes. My class-mates arrive, crowding into the room, sitting on the floor, leaning against the doors, squeez-ing onto the extra chairs we drag in as more and more women find their way in. Suddenly, I find myself with a serious case of nerves; there's no way I can pull out my little stack of handwritten file cards after Jill's flawlessly spontaneous performance.

"You never speak without notes!" warns the voice in my head that always has to be right. But for once I ignore it. I look around at the faces in the room, at these women who gradu-ated with me in the pouring rain thirty years ago, threw their soaked caps into the air, and then went forth and met the challenges and joys and heartbreaks of their lives. I remind myself that every single one of them has known self-doubt, that every one of them has struggled, and that, no matter what paths our lives have taken since we left here, deep down we are all more alike than different. And then, for the first time in my life, I leave my notes in the bag at my feet and simply begin to talk about what's been on my mind for months.

How strange it feels to be more than halfway through my life and still trying to figure things out. How naïve I was at twenty to imagine I could snap the parts of my life together as if they were pieces in a jigsaw puzzle—marriage, children, career, home—in the belief that once I had all the pieces in place, I would feel accomplished and fulfilled and live happily ever after. How hard it's been to let go of so much that's over, without having something concrete to reach out and grab on to. And how, in its own surprising way, the back side of midlife is turning out to be as intense and emotionally confusing a time as my early twenties were— a time of asking, "Now what?" without any signposts around to say, "This way."

"I wish we had sat around like this thirty years ago and talked about how scared we really were," I say, "and how baffling it was to want so much for our lives—and yet to not really have any idea who we were or what we were capable of.

"And I wish some older, wiser women had been willing to clue us in back then, not just about how to go out and make it in a man's world, but also about the fact that 'making it' wouldn't actually be the thing that would bring us happiness.

"I'm not sure we would have listened, but we might have. And what a radical message that would have been for a bunch of women about to graduate from college and take the world by storm: the idea that in the end it really wasn't going to matter much how impressive we might appear to everyone else, or how much money we made, or how nice a house we lived in, or whether we ever ran a company or wrote a play or did brain surgery. That our future happiness would not actually have much to do with our job titles or what colleges our kids went to, or even how much we accomplished during our years on the planet. And that what feels important now, as we come back here thirty years later, is not what we've done, but who we are. Whether our lives reflect our values. How we feel about the person we are inside. How well we love. How much we are loved in return. And how gracefully we are learning to let go."

These, it seems, are the topics on everyone else's mind, too—the endings and lessons and transformations that have led us to
this moment, and the sense of urgency with
which each of us yearns now to find our own
true path and follow it, to become who we are
really meant to be.

Blair, my next-door dorm neighbor, is leaning up against the door frame, half in, half
out, as if debating whether to stay or to run
for her life. I look over at this woman who
used to intimidate me just by breathing, and
am startled to see her eyes wet with tears. And
then I look down at the wooden mala beads I
wear wound around my wrist, and remember
my lesson from Kripalu, the one I've translated
for myself in the months since leaving there
into a pared-down, nonnegotiable precept for
living—when in doubt, do the loving thing.
And so I try simply to send a silent message
her way, a look I hope she can read as both an
invitation and acknowledgment, not of what
separates us but of all we share. She meets my
eyes, takes a step in, comes closer.

"I'm fifty-one years old," she says, her voice full of emotion, "and I'm still not sure who I am."

I can feel the atmosphere change in the room, nerves settle, as if everyone has just exhaled at exactly the same moment. In fact, what happens next feels almost like magic: an invisible, breathtaking shift from watching, judging, and comparing to trusting, accepting, and listening—intently.

"I'm not ever going to be Jill Ker Conway," someone says. "But I guess it's time to let that go anyway." We laugh, nodding our heads, grateful to be relieved at last from the task of filling those refined one-and-a-half-inch heels.

"We're not all meant for boardrooms," someone else affirms, "but I think I can finally say that's okay, that my life doesn't matter any less for that."

A slight, elegant Asian woman stands up, nodding her agreement even as she struggles to speak through her tears. "I bought the whole story," she says. "All I did was work. And push my children to work harder. But now, I look back and feel as if I missed it, I missed my own life. I missed everything that mattered. For years, I just kept working and pushing and trying too hard to get ahead, thinking that's what I was supposed to do. I'm not close to my kids at all. I'm divorced. I have a house, and a career, and no real relationships with anyone. I feel as if I don't know who I am, either. But I'm afraid it's too late for me."

The conversation takes flight from there, dipping, soaring, punctuated by laughter and tears and nods of recognition. And if my class-mates' uncensored, no-holds-barred tales of midlife reckonings and second journeys, of love lost and found, of doubts and struggles, of sickness and health, of children growing up and moving out, of dreams realized and dreams revised and dreams released, tell me anything, it's this: It is absolutely not too late. Not for any of us. No matter what long hallways and unforeseen stairwells we've wandered down, no matter whether our bread-crumb trails led to the place we always thought we wanted to be or brought us to the edge of a precipice we never could have anticipated, it is not too late. Not too late to question, to reflect, to change course, to choose love over fear, to embrace life.

On the contrary. In fact, the empathy and understanding and encouragement so freely offered and gratefully received by the women gathered here seem to confirm something I've been suspecting for a while now: Once we soften our grip on what's over, accept time's passing, and open ourselves to what's next, there is something tremendously liberating about being exactly where we are.

Looking around the room, absorbing all these wildly varied yet thematically congruous stories, it occurs to me that as we move into our fifties, my classmates and I have more in common with one another than ever before. There is not a woman among us—childless or not, single or married, gay or straight—who isn't confronting the physiological, emotional, and situational changes wrought by age. So many of the old, divisive issues have faded away with time. Career versus child-raising isn't a dilemma anymore. The search for men or mates has been largely supplanted by a search for meaning. Released from some of our youthful agendas and ambitions, we've learned that what matters most is not the size or the scope of the work we do, but the intention behind it, the love that fuels it, the satisfaction of doing it.

We are mothers and ministers, research scientists and social workers, artists and bakers, business owners and church volunteers, world travelers and cabin dwellers—a cross section of smart, vulnerable, thoughtful women bound by our deep engagement with the sorrows, joys, and mysteries of the second half of life. Pangs and regrets and fears seem to go with the territory. We have come up short in some areas, exceeded our own expectations in others, endured endings and beginnings. And yet as we learn to accept the aspects of aging that can't be changed, we also seem to be discovering a new, unexpected freedom—a sense that the moment has arrived, at long last, for us to live life on our own terms.

The sun is sinking, sending shafts of golden, late-afternoon light through the long, faded drapes, but no one is in a hurry to leave. It amazes me how easily we've shed our public faces and revealed the truths of our lives—not as we once thought they would be or as we want others to perceive them, but as they really are right now. This, it seems, is the conversation we were all longing to have as we arrived here yesterday with our old yearbooks and memories and hopes. A conversation we probably couldn't have risked thirty years ago, when any crack in the facade or shadow of vulnerability seemed too treacherous. But a conversation that, once begun, moved directly into matters of the heart—matters that are, of course, the ones of greatest significance now that the burning question is no longer "What should I do?" but rather "Who do I aspire to be?"

Someone asks me to read the last chapter of my book aloud. I turn to the end, in search of the passage I want, but my eye falls instead on a quote by Buddhist teacher Jack Kornfield: "To live is to die to how we wanted it to be, and to open more to truth. To love is to accept. It is the most extraordinary power."

"To live is to die to how we wanted it to be." The words resonated when I wrote them down four years ago, as I watched my sons growing up too fast, as I anticipated the moment the older one would leave home for college, as I worried through too many sleepless nights that my younger one was losing his way, as I anticipated with dread the moment when they would both be gone.

But today, here, reading them aloud to this group of women, they assume even greater depth. For surely this is the work we are all engaged in now, this continuous process of death and transfiguration as we learn to let go of our old illusions of youth and independence and control, and to embrace our lives as they are. No one told us, thirty years ago, we couldn't have it all. But life itself has taught us how foolish we were to ever assume we could. Time and experience have shown that accomplishment and power do not guarantee success, that being busy is not the same as feeling alive, that happiness is not an achievement but a choice. There are no easy paths, and it turns out that the only given in this life is its uncertainty.

And yet what a relief it is, to be seen at last as we really are. There's not a soul here who can claim foolproof solutions to life's troubles or a game plan for the rest of the journey. But we can be present for one another. We can offer encouragement and companionship along the way, as we turn our older, softer faces to the wind and tune our ears to the solicitations of the soul, calling us now toward a deeper, more nuanced understanding of our own true natures.

The night ends late, with quite a few members of the class of 1980 lingering in the living room of Northrup House. We've long since changed out of dinner clothes, into jeans and T-shirts, cranked up the music, and set up an impromptu bar. The mood is relaxed, intimate, festive, and there's not a husband left in sight. I was too much of an introvert in college, too worried about belonging and fitting in, to ever be comfortable in a scene like this. So it surprises me to realize how ridiculously happy and at home I feel now—barefoot, drinking wine from a plastic cup, squeezed onto a sofa with a couple of women who could easily have been friends thirty years ago, but who I somehow missed during my four years on campus. No matter. It is easy enough to connect and catch up, as we pore over the old black-and-white yearbooks spread across the coffee table, piecing together histories, remembering those who have died, those who are missing, those whose lives have carried them to distant shores.

Someone has clearly put a great deal of thought into the playlist, and finally it's just too hard to resist; everyone is on their feet, twirling, swaying, boogying, singing along to the Commodores' "Brick House." What would I have thought on the eve of my graduation, if someone could have flashed me forward thirty years to this mild spring midnight, this room full of exuberant fifty-plus-year-old women dropping their butts to the party anthem of our era? Could I have possibly grasped then what it's taken me the three decades since to learn? That such joy arises not because life has turned out perfectly or as planned, but because it hasn't, not at all—and yet, because we are human and ever hopeful, we are moved to dance and sing our hearts out anyway.

This joy, this ease, this is what I want to

carry home with me in the morning and into the next years of my life—the joy of being part of a dance so much larger and more intricate than my own fumbling steps, and the ease that comes of knowing that my task going forward is pretty simple after all: to be present for everything and to live each moment with my arms spread wide, open to all of it. Change is part of being human, but it's not the enemy. Hard as it's been to see at times, I realize now that the losses of these last two years have created as many opportunities for growth as they've foreclosed paths I once took for granted. The question that's haunted me for months now—"What am I going to do with the rest of my life?"—has come to feel a little less urgent, a little less complicated. Slowly, almost imperceptibly, it has begun to answer itself. The next step is simply the one that's right in front of me. And perhaps the wisdom I've been searching for isn't really knowledge after all, but something more achievable, something right at hand, something closer to surrender.

～ 12 ～

present

These are our few life seasons.
Let us live them as purely as we
can, in the present.

—ANNIE DILLARD

The spot on my left temple was barely notice-able at first, a vague shadow that darkened and thickened so gradually I wasn't quite sure when it appeared, more like a raised freckle than an age spot. I barely noticed it and then, one day, I did. At first, it didn't bother me and then, one day, it did. I dabbed on a bit of concealer and forgot about the spot until the next morn-ing, when I covered it up again. All winter long and through the spring, I patted on a scrim of makeup and pretended the dime-size crusty area was nothing, until one day it occurred to me that pretending and denial were probably the same thing. When I finally called my dermatologist, a man so tightly booked that he schedules appointments a year in advance, he told me to come in the next afternoon.

My dad was fifty when he had the first basal cell carcinoma removed from his forehead. Since then, he's endured more skin surgeries than he can count, some minor, some so deep they've laid him up for weeks—legs, back, arms, shoulders, face, scalp, a third of an ear. He's undergone skin grafts, flaps, reconstructions, and thousands of tiny stitches to fuse his fragile, ravaged skin back together. Given how many times he's returned from the hospital looking like Frankenstein's monster— chemically peeled, bruised and battered, sliced open and sewn back up again—he's had a remarkably sanguine attitude, accepting without complaint the funny hats, the 100 SPF sunscreens, the cocoon sunglasses, long sleeves and long pants on the hottest of days. He has learned to cover up, to move beyond vanity, to value his life more than his looks. And yet, still, the spots keep coming, the biopsies are positive, the surgeries and plum-colored scars accumulate.

My grandmother always said we had peaches 'n' cream complexions—fair, pink cheeks that pop freckles after twenty minutes in the sun. Skin that is never marred by acne in adolescence, that glows with health at age twenty, but that—unless you stay indoors and take lifelong care as my grandmother did—doesn't wear well over time. We blush, we wrinkle deeply, we blotch, we flake and crack in winter, we burn in summer, and we get skin cancer in old age. When I call my dad to tell him my own biopsy has confirmed an infiltrative basal cell and that I'll need a second surgery to remove the rest of it, he suggests it might be time for me to meet his plastic surgeon. Every Christmas I slip a jar of my favorite shea butter cream into my dad's stocking; now, in return, he's giving me Dr. Bryan.

My father, who still works a fifty-hour week in his dental office at age seventy-five, managed years ago to find a doctor willing to see him at six a.m. Since he's due for a follow-up from his most recent surgery, he arranges for me to come along for a pre-op consultation for mine, which is how I happen to be riding alongside my dad through the thinning darkness of a predawn June morning to a hospital in Massachusetts. It is one of the most unexpected and most comforting surprises of middle age—the fact that when called upon, my parents are still willing and able to parent *me*. I don't often turn to them for advice or help, but I'm aware always that the safety net I've taken for granted since birth remains intact even now; if I should fall, I know my mom and dad are right there, arms spread wide, ready to swoop in and catch me before I hit the ground. And yet it also feels these days as if the gap between us is narrowing, the boundaries between generations blurring, as my own children turn into adults, as I grow old myself, as my parents approach their eighties, as time flows on like a river, carrying all of us onward.

So many of my friends have lost parents by now that I often hesitate before mentioning mine, still alive and well. But I'm also trying to prepare myself for the next phase of our life together, when my brother and I will become the safety net, when we'll be the ones calling doctors, offering advice, caring for them.

I remember saying good-bye to my mother and father right after sophomore year of college, before heading off for a summer of camping in Europe with my boyfriend. Looking at them standing there in the driveway, arm in arm, it suddenly struck me, at the ripe old age of nineteen, how grayed and frail they seemed, as if they'd shrunk while I'd been away at school into two smaller and more vulnerable versions of the looming authority figures of my childhood. For a moment, I actually considered bailing out of the trip—What if they needed me? What if one of them died while I was gone? Of course, when I do the math now, I have to laugh. My "elderly" parents were all of forty-two and forty-three at the time; not only did they manage to survive without me that summer, they are going strong more than three decades later. Even so, there's no denying we are in another season now, one that compels us all to renegotiate our relationships with time.

My dad has brought coffees for the two of us, and we are out on the road a full hour before the first traffic. These early summer days are still lengthening; although it's not yet five, the brightening sky is streaked with pink. One day, I think to myself, I'll remember this drive, the poignancy of our dawn mission and all that is unspoken between us—love that has moved at last beyond judgment, awareness that life has become for both of us a kind of balancing act between loss and renewal, routine and change, disintegration and healing.

I may be a woman with two grown children of my own, but the truth is, I'm grateful that, for a few hours at least, I can still be the child again, with my dad in the driver's seat taking me to see the doctor. And although he wouldn't wish the saga of his own skin on anyone, I'm pretty certain my father is as glad to have my company this morning as I am for his; glad, too, that he can be of use. We've had our struggles with each other over the years, but they are history now, fading with each passing year.

The father of my childhood was unpredictable, quick to anger, impatient, unyielding. I'm not sure when, exactly, his edges began to soften; when the old wariness between us eased into this new, more complex and affectionate caring. I always knew my father loved me; what's changed, I think, is that now I feel his love. Compassion has cleared the air between us. And so I try to memorize my father as the dear being he is right now, not the intimidating, larger-than-life disciplinarian of childhood memory but the small, elderly, white-haired grandfather he has become.

I note the way his mottled hands hold the wheel, the familiar hunch of his shoulders, the way he hikes up against the car door, eyes intent on the road. His face is crisscrossed with scars and tiny puckers, creased, pale but for the smattering of coffee-colored age spots across his forehead. It looks as if someone has nipped a chunk out of his ear, its fiercely pink rim sharp as a broken shell. His thinning hair lifts from his scalp in wisps, light and dry as dandelion fluff. And yet, so powerful has his presence been in my life that even now I have to remind myself he's not invincible, that someday I will travel through this world without him. For now, though, we are speeding into the day, our unspoken love for each other tangible and clear as the dawn light. And I inscribe these fleeting moments of rare togetherness across my heart, moments I didn't ask for, couldn't have anticipated, and that will never come again.

It is apparent, as we arrive for our six a.m. father-daughter appointment, that my dad is adored in the plastic surgery wing. He is, it seems, their most resolute frequent flier, well-known to the receptionist and nurses on the early shift as the good-natured dentist who drives down from New Hampshire for the predawn time slot. He introduces me with pride, of course, but a bit of rue as well—I am here, after all, thanks to his genes, a second-generation skin cancer patient. And yet I do take comfort in the fact that he's well-versed in this territory, advising and reassuring me as I try to figure out what "normal" is going to mean for me from now on. Straw hats and sunscreen, certainly, but what about thinking twice before sitting down at noon in the lawn chair by the garden? Will I grow accustomed, as my father has, to the daily deliberations between cautious and carefree, sun and shade, indoors and out?

My father's fair skin has provided him an opportunity to practice dying a little every day. With every surgery, he's reminded that no matter how early he gets up in the morning, no matter how hard he works or how long he's able to ignore the stiffness in his shoulders or his weariness at day's end, he is mortal after all. And yet it seems to me that in becoming more humbly human he has also become more fully alive. Perhaps with each return visit to the operating room where bits and pieces of his body are meticulously carved away, his heart has grown larger, as if the resignation to pain and forbearance itself has scooped out more space for kindness, for patience, for gentleness. The soul, it seems, learns more from its losses than its gains. Forced to let down our defenses, to acknowledge our vulnerabilities after all, we find that what flows in and fills up the empty spaces is not more fear, but more love. We grow older, we learn to live with our own frailties, and paradoxically, we find ourselves not sliding down hill, but moving instead into a more generous, unencumbered existence.

"The incision will go from here," Dr. Bryan says, touching the corner of my left eye with a gloved finger, "to here." He draws an invisible four-inch line over to the edge of my scalp. "Then I'll just tug the skin from your cheek upward, and stitch it right along this natural laugh line," he says, gently adjusting my face into its future shape. "I'll do everything I can to minimize scarring. It'll be kind of like a mini face-lift. On one side."

The walk is my friend Carol's idea. For years she and Marie walked together in fund-raisers, logging a few hundred miles and raising thousands of dollars between them—for the three-day Avon Walk for Breast Cancer, the Walk for Hunger, the Boston Marathon Jimmy Fund Walk. Just the month before our friend died last fall, on the same Saturday I was delivering Jack to school, Carol had limped through the final miles of the Jimmy Fund Walk, cell phone in hand so she could receive the funny, encouraging texts Marie was sending from home, urging her old partner on to the finish line. What Carol learned during that long, hot, lonely day was that walking twenty-six miles at age fifty without any training is a terrible idea. And that walking without her friend at her side was almost more than she could bear. She did it, though, because she knew that if Marie had had her way, she would have been out there too, laughing and chatting, easing Blister Block over her heels, and raising money for the cause she'd come to care about above all others.

There were lots of things, in the end, that Marie didn't have time to do. After managing to keep her disease at bay for three years, she wasn't quite prepared for how swiftly and inexorably it swept in and claimed her body in her final weeks of life. Still, she rallied to take a drive with her husband one early autumn afternoon to choose a site in the cemetery for her ashes. She browsed poetry collections and selected the readings and hymns for her service. She listened to music, found herself returning again and again to Barber's Adagio for

Strings, one of her favorite pieces, and decided she wanted that played, too.

"I feel like a character in a movie," she admitted, shaking her head. "It's so weird to be doing this, planning a funeral for myself." She paused, the way she often did, as if to deliberately switch gears and summon her resolve. "But I guess this is part of it," she continued. "And poor Bruce is going to have enough to deal with as it is." She considered writing out a to-do list for Thanksgiving, so her husband and children would know how to get her traditional dinner on the table. And then she decided to let that one go. "They'll figure it out," she said, "and do it their own way."

Instead, she applied her remaining strength to making a difference for the women who would come after her. She wrote her obituary, meticulously and with clear intention— to make sure anyone who wanted to honor her memory would know exactly what to do. Marie had worked tirelessly and given generously to many good causes over the years, but in the end, there was only one that really mattered to her, and that was to fund research into finding a cure for the disease that had cut her life short. If her efforts could help someone else, she felt, then perhaps her suffering would not be in vain.

So I'm not at all surprised when my friend Carol sits me down at her kitchen table one June morning and says, "I have an idea. And I hope you don't have plans for September sixteenth, because that's the day of the Jimmy Fund Walk. I think we should walk for Marie."

She's already looked into the possibility of cutting through some institutional red tape at Dana-Farber Cancer Institute, so that all the money we raise can go directly to Marie's oncologist, who runs a cutting-edge ovarian cancer research department. If we're willing to commit to a large enough sum, she's been told, it can be done. We both remember our friend saying, as she considered her treatment options, "I don't want to end up with my name on some T-shirt!" But we're also pretty certain she'd like the idea of the old neighborhood walkers regrouping and lacing up their sneakers alongside some new recruits, this time for a cause. And so it is that Team Marie is born.

Carol puts out a call to Marie's friends around town, the two of us spend an afternoon in her kitchen making lasagna and salad and cake, and by the end of our kick-off party that evening eleven women have committed to walk from Hopkinton to Boston in September. A group of others say they're willing to go at least partway, someone's volunteered to design stationery for our fund-raising letters, and, after much discussion, there's a plan to create a T-shirt with Marie's name on it. We even have a team motto, the words she left me with last October: "There is so much goodness in the world."

Is it what she would have wanted, given the way things turned out? There's no way to know for sure. But it does feel as if our friend handed us some marching orders. And for those of us who have spent months missing her, it is a comfort now to think that, together, we can carry on the work she began with such resolve. Raising money for Marie's cause, training, walking, joining forces with thousands of others three months hence—suddenly it feels as if there is a beam of light shining into the darkness, the hole in all our lives filling now with a new certainty of purpose.

We will walk for our friend, for her doctor's research, for all the other women battling for their lives, but for ourselves as well. For, when it comes right down to it, the needs of the living inevitably conspire with the desires of the dead. We want to keep their memories alive, to carry our loved ones with us and within us, to enlarge ourselves for their sake, but also for our own. And so it is that loss and grief give birth to practical determination. How else to absorb life's blows other than by availing ourselves of the transforming power of love?

Softening our wounded hearts, we find unexpected solace in service. And each time we reach beyond ourselves with some small gesture of compassion, we, too, are comforted. It may not seem like much—a letter mailed, a check written, a phone call made, or even some miles walked with numbers pinned on our backs. We may doubt our efforts, fearing that our small deeds of activism fail to measure up to the heroic efforts of others who do more. Indeed, we may dismiss our own humble contributions as paltry offerings. Yet this is the way healing begins; in fact, it is the only way. One by one, we rouse ourselves. We view the world through gentler eyes. We show up and do what we can, when we can. And so it is that our own small circles of caring begin to grow, and loneliness and grief are transformed into hope, direction, and community.

In college I carried my books in a green canvas tote bag with white lettering on it, a quote from theologian Howard Thurman. "Don't ask yourself what the world needs," it read, "ask yourself what makes you come alive, and then go do that. Because what the world needs is people who have come alive." Back then, I wondered what great calling would make me come alive, what passion would inspire me to offer up the best of myself to some worthy cause. Now, in my fifties, I no longer have an entire lifetime stretching before me nor do I expect either salvation or inspiration to arrive like a lightning bolt. What I see, instead, is that the world changes as I do—one day and one small gesture at a time. Accepting that, relinquishing my grand schemes and youthful plans in favor of a more modest and intuitive approach, I find myself aspiring instead to simple kindness. And I think I do finally understand the message on that canvas tote bag.

For thirty years the challenges and satisfactions of love and marriage, career and homemaking, motherhood and friendship have made up the weave and texture of my life, each strand in the fabric inseparable from the next. It is not this or that, but all of it together that's made me feel alive and connected. I am a mother, a cook, a writer, a gardener, a wife, a daughter, a woman offering a shoulder to a friend. Meaning has come not from assigning more importance to one kind of work than another, but from learning to approach all these roles and tasks with care and attention.

Yet there's no denying there's been a shift over this last year, as subtle as it is significant. Perhaps there is always a time of loss and letdown when a great endeavor comes to an end: the book is written, the house is built, the children are raised, the harvest is in. And then, as busyness and ambition give way to rest and completion, the "What next?" question arises.

I used to answer that question with a new to-do list. Now I find myself less inclined to rush forward, but waiting and listening instead. My desire to make a difference hasn't waned; what's changed, I think, is my discernment. I'm learning to trust that the next right thing will present itself; that moment to moment, I do know where to place my feet and in which direction I ought to go.

So it is with this walk. What will motivate me to spend the summer training, logging miles alone on the country roads around my house? A desire to honor my friend by carrying her legacy forward, certainly. But something else, too, something that's really just for me: the opportunity to rise to a challenge. I want to age not only with acceptance but with contentment. To do so, I suspect, demands both action and stillness, energy and surrender, a willingness to stretch in new directions even as I make my peace with what is. I am learning when to say a quiet "no" to things I don't really want to do anymore. At the same time, I am making a promise to myself: to say "yes" to both work and pleasures that truly matter to me, whatever they turn out to be. Not surprisingly perhaps, when I approach life this way, work and pleasure often go hand in hand.

In the back of my awareness, I also know this: The day will come when I shall have to recall the luxuriant splendor of long, solitary walks, rather than take them. I will have to learn to reconcile my longings—to move and dance and make love and stretch and run—with the reality of my own aging body. I will have to become an apprentice all over again in the art of acceptance and the lessons of letting go. And so for as long as I'm able, I aim to drink deeply, to immerse myself in the world at my feet and experience its riches, to revel in this magnificent, wild, physical body I am blessed to inhabit. I will appreciate myself as I am right now, before the creep of time and age and dissolution encroach any further on possibility. Before this life I cherish vanishes into nothingness, like all the ones preceding it.

My surgery is scheduled for seven a.m., the morning after our Team Marie party. Since I have to arrive by six, Steve drives down from

New Hampshire the night before, to spend the night with me at a friend's house in our old neighborhood, a few minutes' drive away from the hospital. But, of course, I don't sleep. I lay swaddled in darkness, marking the hours till five, when I can finally slip out of bed and take a shower. According to the instructions, I must skip the rest of my usual routine: No deodorant, hair gel, body cream, moisturizer, or makeup of any kind are allowed. No coffee, no water, no breakfast. It is no big deal, this little nip and tuck, and yet anxiety has lodged in my chest like a brick. The sight of my wan, bare face unnerves me. I want to be on the other side of this day, back to normalcy.

Steve walks me as far as the registration desk. "Give a call when you're done," he says. He kisses me good-bye and heads off in search of food, coffee, a newspaper, the routine comforts of morning.

Half-reclined on the bed in the tiny operating cubicle, separated only by curtains from the morning's other surgical patients, I'm naked but for a gaping blue hospital johnnie. It is freezing. An old woman on the other side

of the curtain moans again and again; someone asks her to breathe deeply. A nurse arrives
to take my vitals. She scribbles on a chart,
drops my wedding rings, watch, and earrings
into a plastic bag, along with my purse and all
my clothes, writes my name on it, and slides
the bag onto a rack under the bed. Tidy. Efficient. Hundreds of outpatient surgeries are
performed each day in this vast, windowless,
subterranean operating basement; clearly, they
have their systems worked out.

Another nurse describes the risks of anesthe-
sia and surgery, the possible complications of
recovery. "Can you read this okay?" she asks,
handing me the first of many forms.

I squint at the blur of squirming black lines. I
can't read it. Not really, not quite. She patiently
retrieves the bag, and, embarrassed by my failing eyesight—couldn't I have read these lines
just a month ago? last week?—I rummage
around in my purse for my latest pair of drug-
store glasses; apparently she is going to stand
at my side and make certain I actually comprehend every word of fine print in this stack
of paper before allowing me to put my name

to the forms. Have I had anything to eat or drink since midnight? I must sign a document swearing that I have not.

A surgical nurse steps in to wash my face with antibacterial soap. With a Magic Marker, she draws a black circle around the place on my temple. I watch as yet another RN ties a bit of tubing around my arm, slides a needle into a raised blue vein, and hooks up an IV. Dr. Bryan pops in, buoyantly cheerful, dressed head to toe in blue scrubs, smiling as if he's genuinely glad to see me, as if I am an old friend who's just happened by. The anesthesiologist comes next, proffering reassurance, oblivion, a good morning. And it occurs to me that lying here on this bed is as good a time and place as any other to practice surrender. What else can I do, after all, but let go? What is any illness, any physical condition, any kind of surgery, no matter how minor, but an opportunity to die a little, to give up the illusion of control and give in to what is? The stream of pre-op visitors continues. A fresh-faced resident, tall, square-jawed, and dazzlingly handsome, arrives and introduces himself as Dr. Bryan's assistant. He draws up a stool, glances at my chart, and then asks, leaning in close, as if he is speaking to a very small child, "So, Mrs. Lewers, do you understand why you're here today?"

I tell him I do. "Well, good, good," he says, as if I've just aced a test. "Why don't you explain to me, in your own words, as you understand it, the nature of the procedure you're having today."

I am defenseless before this friendly, harried, attractive man who is young enough to be my son. With my limp hair; my parched, naked face; the thin, flapping johnnie, I feel exposed, featureless as a plucked chicken, stripped clean of everything that makes me me. And suddenly, it seems exceedingly important that I let him know that yes, I do at least have my wits about me, if nothing else. This, I think, is what it will be like to grow old, slipping toward death, invisible.

What a brief, vast distance it is, from the easy defenses and comforting landmarks of my familiar workaday world, to this foreign, unsought place, the bustling, overpopulated country of illness, affliction, and surgical repair.

How swiftly a person is transformed here into a patient, an individual into a name on a chart, a block on the OR schedule, a time slot in a doctor's overscheduled day. I consider my pale arms, ghostly white under the fluorescent lights, stippled with gooseflesh, a blue plastic ID bracelet circling one wrist, the stout silver needle taped to the other, something now flowing into my body from a bag on a pole. It is as if I have stepped out and left myself behind, so abruptly detached am I from the poor shivering body laid out on the bed. Some part of my physical consciousness reports that my feet are freezing. Despite the warm blankets a nurse continues to pile on top of me, I can't stop shaking.

Meanwhile, my mind floats away. I try to imagine all the days and nights my friend spent over the years in hospital rooms and transfusion rooms and doctors' offices. I am just a day visitor here, a casual tourist, briefly passing through for a quick tune-up before I'm on my way back home again. But a glimpse of these foreign shores is enough to give me at least a cursory education in the culture, the slightest inkling of what Marie must have endured without complaint for years. What an extraordinary act of will it took for her to accept what she could not change, and with what tenacity she fought to improve the odds where she could. How little she pitied herself. How determined she was to be more than another statistic. How she made it a point to connect with her doctors, to befriend her reserved oncologist, to come to know and care about her nurses and the rotating members of her medical team. And how, just by being herself, she made certain that they all came to know and care about her, too. I wonder if, in her shoes, I would have such fortitude.

The first nurse returns with two more heated blankets; she tucks them in snug around my feet, gives my leg a little squeeze. "We're going to get you warm yet, sweetheart," she says and pads silently away in her soft sneakers. Tears prick my eyes and gratitude washes over me like a wave. Such a small kindness, yet with it I feel my own humanity handed back to me. When I look up, there is Dr. Bryan, his blue eyes peering down at me, and I am glad once

again to be my father's daughter, to have followed this man's work up close for years. I am
in safe hands.

"But," I tell him now, "I don't think the anes-
thesia is working yet, because I'm still awake."

"Oh, it worked, all right," he answers. "We're
all done. You rest now." And he's gone.

It isn't much of a day for celebrating, this gray,
muggy Wednesday. In years past we've marked
my husband's summer solstice birthday with
lobster dinners in Maine, or hiking with our
boys and our friends on Monhegan Island.
There have been epic poems written, surprise
parties thrown, memorable gatherings around
our porch table, cards and presents and cakes
and people. But today I can offer none of these
things.

I have a swollen, bandaged temple from yesterday's surgery, stitches, pain that ripples up
and down the side of my face whenever I smile
or frown. It is raining. Our sons are both away
at their summer jobs—Henry playing piano
at a resort in Maine, Jack in Boston, staying
with our old next-door neighbors during the

week and commuting by train into the city for an internship. So it'll be just the two of us tonight, alone; given how tired and sore I feel, it's really more like one and a half. How to create a birthday out of this?

We think about going out to dinner, but I look awful and Steve says he'd rather eat at home. And so I muster the energy to shop for food, then stand in the rain in the parking lot at the grocery store, trying in vain to keep my face bandage dry while shoving my key into a car door that refuses to open. Of course it doesn't—after a few seconds of fruitless key-jamming, it dawns on me that I am trying to force my way into someone else's car. I have no idea where I left my own. I wander around for a while, pushing my cart, getting wetter and wetter, till I finally spot my old silver Acura with its faded Red Sox Nation bumper sticker, not far from the entrance. I have no memory whatsoever of parking it. No wonder the doctor told me not to drive for a day.

Home at last, I haul in the grocery bags, swallow a couple of extra-strength Tylenol, put the entire Van Morrison play list on the stereo, and spend the afternoon roasting vegetables and making pasta sauce, salad, and a chocolate cake with chocolate frosting. Outside, the rain comes down in sheets. I am singing "Days Like This," belting out the song. The kitchen fills with good smells.

For twenty-five years I've written birthday cards to the man I married, and it suddenly occurs to me that the only thing either of us really wants right now is a decent shot at twenty-five or so more. We are at an age, and at a stage in our lives, where every day offers up its reminder that we would be fools to take any moment of any of this for granted. "Life is a gift," reads the plaque a friend gave me recently, "that's why they call it the present." And for today, anyway, we hold that gift, luminously intact, in the palms of our hands—our health, our togetherness, our children, our love, our future.

Now that I'm home again, with a cake in the oven and up to my elbows in dishwater, I am even thankful for yesterday—one day in the hospital has made me absurdly, giddily aware of just how wonderful any day *not* spent in the hospital really is. Nothing like a minor health condition to make me appreciate every working body part. Nothing like a little excision and a few obliterated hours to bring me to my knees, kissing the solid ground of my own messy, mundane, incredibly lovely life. Nothing like checking out of the world for a day to make me euphoric at the simple fact that I've been allowed, this time, to check right back in.

When Steve arrived in my post-op cubicle yesterday afternoon, I was just coming round, making a long, slow landing back into myself—so intent on the absorbing task of returning to my own body that I didn't even notice he was there. The nurse had phoned him, told him I'd be ready soon, but that she wanted him to hear my discharge instructions, too. Good call.

"Hey, there," my husband said, bending down close. He smiled when he saw me and kissed my head, never letting on for a second that he was shocked by my sagging cheek, my paralyzed brow, my eye drooping shut like a stroke victim's. He had no idea, at that moment, whether or not this weird, new lopsided version of my face was permanent, but I will forever give him credit for not registering one iota of dismay at the sorry, crooked sight of me. It wasn't until I got a look in a mirror myself, an hour later, that I actually appreciated what he'd just done for me, that I fully comprehended the grace and fortitude of that smile.

This, I'm pretty sure, is what weathered, well-seasoned love is all about: being able to produce a heartfelt, adoring gaze even as you watch the integrity of your beloved's body eroding in increments. Taking infirmity in stride with a smile, even when your wife looks like hell, even when she can't stand up to put on her own pants, even when you're pushing her down the hall in a wheelchair, even when you don't know for certain if she is destined to look forevermore like a bad Cubist painting. There's no doubt now; indeed, I know for certain: I can grow old alongside this man.

Darkness is falling early tonight, despite the fact that it's the second longest day of the year. The mountains disappear slowly under a thickening cloud cover, night descending upon us like a blanket. The cool breeze whishing through the window screens carries the lush, leafy scents of early summer, the breath of the wild mingling with the homey essence of indoors—rain and green grass, peonies, pungent garlic and onion, hot bread, chocolate. I light candles, open a bottle of champagne, and we sit down to our dinner in the kitchen. I have picked a bouquet for the table: pink bleeding hearts, wispy wild ferns, ebony tulips. I've written a love letter and tucked it inside a card. My husband is sixty-two.

I remember the year my own dad turned sixty, the late August surprise party my mother threw in their backyard, the scrapbook she made, the sense we all had that this birthday, in particular, meant something, that it signified my father's passage into the late afternoon of his life. While my own young children ran around outside, I chatted with my parents' friends, men and women I remembered from my childhood but hadn't seen in decades. Each conversation began with a moment of shock and dawning recognition: Everyone was old! Now, I can't help but marvel at how quickly we've ended up here ourselves, with so many years suddenly piled up behind us and not quite so many left ahead. Only yesterday I was drenched in the demands and sensations of young motherhood, my sons' soft, sturdy, familiar bodies as much a part of me as my own. Later tonight, if they remember, they will each call home; they'll wish their dad a happy birthday and ask me how I'm feeling. They'll call to please us, to let us know they care. But already their lives have lifted them up and set them down elsewhere, while ours shift and settle and grow more deeply rooted here.

This morning, I filled the bathtub with hot water, climbed in, and then, realizing my dilemma, summoned Steve into the bathroom. While my husband kneeled beside me and held a towel over my bandage, I washed my hair. Another humbling first. What else, I wonder, will we be asked to do for each other as age exacts its toll?

This, I suspect, is the territory that lies just ahead and around the curve of today. A place where loss grows more familiar, where joy is harmonized by sorrow, where endings outnumber beginnings, and where kindness becomes a sacrament. I stepped into my marriage nearly twenty-five years ago convinced that passion would sustain us; now, I know better. We will endure by the grace of acquiescence, cooperation, patience, and the small daily rituals that keep us close even as change transforms the landscape of our lives.

I have a way of gathering up the bits and pieces of my life—collecting ideas, books, people, news, things, even poems I love and profound experiences I want to remember forever—without really allowing myself the time and space to fully absorb and appreciate any of them. But this, too, is changing. The decision I made months ago to take time in every day to sit still has slowly but surely transformed the way I live inside my life.

It is such a small thing on the face of it, and yet in this world of speed and distraction, choosing to be less busy feels almost countercultural; slowing down, eccentric. Perhaps it is, for there's no denying the expansive, time-bending effects of awareness. Sometimes, I do call it meditation: I sit cross-legged on a cushion in my yoga room; I set a timer and focus on my breath, bringing my attention to bear on the elusive, invisible third eye in the center of my brow point. These sittings are humbling: My mind sneaks away, I chase it down, lead it back, tie it again and again to my breath. Eventually, if I'm not in a rush to get on to the next thing, a small, silent space clears. I savor the taste of quiet, roll it around on my tongue, feel the day's contours softening and opening around me.

Other times, with less organization and intention, I just begin where I am; I drop in place. Either way, the effect is pretty much the same: a respite from noise and and distraction and effort; a sense of my own presence that emanates from a place deep inside. The more patiently I sit and wait, the easier I am to find. I settle onto the granite step outside the kitchen door, lean my back against the sun-warmed wood, and watch the swallows sheering loop-de-loops over the field. A robin alights on the stone wall, trailing a ribbon of dry grass from its beak. I close my eyes, breathing in the sharp, spicy scent of pine needles, mulched in a thick carpet around the blueberry bushes. I feel myself slipping into the flow of time without purpose, each moment connected to the next, droplets of well-being. The wind blows right through me; I listen, and breezes from another world begin to whisper. Down I go. I can feel my heart cupped in my chest, its solid beating; the clouds sailing through the sky, the silhouette of mountains etched across the back of my eyelids, the soft currents of the day, the energy of the universe, of my own sources. My mind grows still. And into the silence comes a pulse, a subtle knowing, light as a feather. *The world simply exists. Journey and destination, they are one and the same.*

~ 13 ~

summer

When all your desires are distilled
you will cast just two votes: to love
more and be happy.

—HAFIZ

For the last few years my friend Maude has been saying we should go to her little cabin in the north woods of Maine. Somehow, although we talk about it every summer, we've never set aside time to make the trip. Even with Henry gone, and Jack away during the week, and no pressing work deadline, I still find it hard to justify time away that's just for me—especially a road trip that doesn't serve some useful goal, time that's taken for no good reason other than friendship and freedom and fun.

Leaving to go anywhere complicates things. It means asking a friend to water the garden and take care of the dog; it means dealing with unfinished bits and pieces, tidying up my desk, answering all the e-mails, making sure there's food in the refrigerator for Steve, and then walking away from everything I could and should be doing at home. I feel a little guilty, leaving my husband to work while I go play. Easier to murmur, "someday, maybe," and put the adventure off for another year. But as the gentle Chinese philosopher Lin Yutang suggests, "Besides the noble art of getting things done, there is the noble art of leaving things undone."

This time, when Maude asks, I say yes.

"There's no plumbing," she warns. "But we have an outhouse, and a shower outside. And there's no cell phone service. But there's a sauna." We drive for five hours, listening to Eliza Gilkyson CDs, snacking on rice chips and hummus as the landscape rolls by, a journey from the thick density of civilization to remote wilderness—one world disappearing behind us; another, much larger and emptier one, unfolding before us as the miles roll by and the road goes from highway to two-lane to winding country to dirt.

We are rattling along slowly, in a cloud of dust, when Maude hits the brakes. A young moose stands just a few yards away, in a grassy clearing at the side of the road. We roll down the windows, grab our cameras, snap off picture after picture. Even Maude's excitable dog, Digby, is quiet, quivering, as if he, too, senses we've just blundered our way into a moment deserving of reverence. The moose is placid, unperturbed, mildly curious about us but more interested in finishing his dinner. We drive slowly on, in awed silence now, leaving him there, chewing.

The rich, woodsy air fills the car. It is almost sunset when we pause again, on the top of a mountain ridge high above the convolution of lakes and forest below. The unframed sky goes on forever, backdrop to a slow-moving fleet of clouds, all aglow in rose and gold, as serene and majestic as sailing ships; in their billowy hulls they carry cargoes of sunlight. Although I've lived all my life in New England and thought I knew it well, I had no idea my home contained vistas like this—such vast, majestic mountains, this string of unpopulated lakes, so much untamed nature.

Standing here, breathing in the quiet of this place, confronted with a glimpse of infinity, I feel both expanded and humbled. It as if the drama unfolding in the sky before us is meant to remind us of our true size: that we are but tiny specks in a limitless panorama, a mute human audience of two, poised here on the edge of everything, just in time to witness the silent spectacle of a summer day's end. The mountains rise up on every side, for as far as our eyes can see, disappearing miles away into the azure, sunlit sea of air. Below, the lakes darken by slow degrees, dissolving in mist and shadow. This is wilderness in its glory. We haven't seen another car, another person, for miles. I think of a line I love by Annie Dillard: "Beauty and grace are performed whether or not we will or sense them. The least we can do is try to be there." Tonight, we are.

It's still light when we arrive at the cottage far below that ridge, nestled into its secluded clearing and cast in early-evening shadow. Lugging our bags and cooler down the narrow sandy path, I can sense my friend's excitement at sharing her favorite, most sacred place with me at last. Maude's cabin is tiny and rough, a cozy wooden shell fashioned of love and sweat and ingenuity. What's here is what it's been possible for two pairs of human hands to create, a modest vision realized over time, through painstaking steady labor and countless summer days. Maude and her husband bought the densely wooded lot years ago, and then dedicated themselves to the arduous task of clearing trees, erecting first a primitive shelter from wood they'd cut, and finally, in time, the two-room cabin with its low-ceilinged sleeping loft.

There's not an inch of extra space and, other than a hand-carved wooden black bear standing guard by the door, not a bit of extra stuff. Everything has been built and chosen and placed in the name of efficiency and simplicity. The only amenities: a tiny refrigerator, a Coleman stove, a faucet outdoors for washing dishes. The secluded outhouse—a sloping, fiberglass roof balanced on four stilts above a

wooden toilet seat set atop a hole in a bench—
is a short walk away, out of sight in the deeper
woods. There is a hammock near the water,
strung up between two trees. A shower nozzle
high on an outside wall, behind a superfluous
door that's rarely closed; privacy is a given. A
long, narrow dock that fingers out into the
water. A stone fireplace under the pines for
cooking. Silence, but for the occasional call of
a loon. Seclusion, but for the chattering company of squirrels, the protestations of blue jays,
Digby splashing happily in the clear, shallow
water. I love it.

We put on sweaters and carry cold beer and
plates of leftover pasta and salad I've brought
from home, down to the two canvas chairs set by
the lake. The last streaks of pink and gold fade
from the sky, the dusk bringing cooler air, the
first stars. For a long year and a half my friend
has been sick. What began as a touch of the
flu one winter afternoon after a snowshoe walk
with our dogs evolved through the months into
a chronic, mysterious, debilitating illness that
thoroughly rearranged her life. I still remember
Maude's call on that February morning.

"Are you okay?" she asked me then. "I was wondering, because I've been throwing up since I got home from our walk yesterday."

"I'm fine," I answered, sympathetic but not terribly concerned, never imagining for a moment that our long, invigorating trek through the woods the day before might turn out to be our last. Sometimes, parts of your life are snatched away right in front of your eyes, but you don't even realize they're gone for good until much later, when what's normal now is so different from what it was before that you can barely remember the old ways, or the easy routines you once assumed would go on forever. I kept thinking, "Any day now, my friend is going to feel better." Instead, as the weeks rolled by, she got worse.

By the time Lyme disease was finally diagnosed, Maude had been sick for months, losing weight and strength, in pain, unable to sleep or focus or work. A year ago, a trip like this would have been out of the question for her; there were times she could barely leave the house. As it is, she has with her a small canvas bag full of nothing but medications and supplements; managing the Lyme, two persistent co-infections, and an ever-changing mosaic of symptoms requires a staggering regime of medications. But, slowly, she is getting well. This summer, there have been some good days. She is weak still; she tires easily. But she's here.

I reach out and give my friend's hand a squeeze. "I can't even tell you how glad I am we finally did this," I say. "And how glad I am that you're better. It sounds selfish to say, but I missed you. I feel as if I finally got my playmate back." As night settles around us, our own voices grow quieter, hushed by the chittering of invisible insects, the measureless sky, the eternal silence of stars.

"I knew you would like it here," Maude says, and I can tell by her voice in the darkness that she's smiling, too.

When I wake in the middle of the night, it's to the steady, insistent slap of water meeting shore; a wind has kicked up and the lake is rough. I'm curled up on a futon on the floor in the loft, just inches away from the open window into which, for the moment, a nearly full orange moon has settled itself, as if its only reason for existing is to shine here, to come to rest like a halo upon my head. I have no interest in more sleep, would rather lie awake instead, warm and cozy under the covers with the sharp breeze on my cheeks, the moon for company, the music of wind and water lulling me into a trance of contentment.

The mingled scents of scoured air, balsam, and metallic lake water create a passageway back in time, returning me to all the pitched tents and rough pine cabins of my childhood and stirring all my romantic fantasies of the good life—simple and sensual and free. We have two nights to spend here and I want to savor every fleeting, wild moment. Soon enough, I'll be home again, to the insulating comforts of running water, indoor toilets, and Internet connections. But tucked into this small cabin, with none of home's easy luxuries at hand, I sense a different kind of wholeness. Or holiness. The quiet breaks and spreads within me, opening like a bud. I wonder if I am sometimes so desperate to learn *how* to be that I forget the simple practice of being, so eager to find the answers to my questions that I lose touch with my own untamed soul, so hungry for certainty that my inner, intuitive voice falls on deaf ears. Here in the darkness, deep in the woods, with the wind ruffling my hair and the music of waves soothing me in and out of sleep, I recognize a familiar person, someone not terribly special, someone you would surely walk right by on the street, but someone I'm actually glad to be. Me.

A colorless morning dawns: molten sky, choppy black lake, no trace of warmth in the wind. But I pull on my bathing suit anyway and make my way down the loft ladder in bare feet, trying not to make a sound. I don't want to wake my friend in the other room, and I'm a little nervous about swimming in the rough water, but the lake exerts a pull. I want to feel that cold smack.

There is not another human being in this empty, untouched world, no sound but the sigh of wind, my cupped palms sluicing through water, and my own breath, ragged at first, but slowly settling, deepening. Never a strong

swimmer, I've always loved the idea of swimming more than the exhausting, bone-chilling
fact of it. I tire quickly, tend to panic easily,
and trust neither my endurance nor my ability
to gauge real distances out in the water. And
yet as I swim out farther and farther beneath
the lowering sky, I find a rhythm. I'm surprised
by a breath more powerful than I expected,
by my ease in the water, by a newfound sense
of strength and power. There is no place on
earth I'd rather be at this moment; nothing I'd
rather be doing than a solitary breast stroke in
this cold, deep, dark lake in Maine; nothing
I'd rather feel than this simple, uncluttered
happiness.

The biggest shift in my life over the last year
has been an invisible one. The effects of menopause, the adjustment to a suddenly empty
house, the slow alterations in my marriage,
a firsthand experience of death and the loss
of my friend—all of these changes have also
changed me, from the inside out. For so long,
things were repeated, our routines and habits as regular and predictable as sunrise—our
family grace, the same since our boys were in

kindergarten; pancakes and classical music on Saturday morning; private jokes and funny sound effects and pet names for everyone; Red Sox games in the summer and the Celtics on snowy winter nights; piles of socks to match and fold and tuck into dresser drawers; someone asking, always, "Are we out of milk *again*?"

As my sons grew up, I tried to pay attention to every moment, more absorbed in their continuous processes of learning and becoming than in my own predictable and less interesting ups and downs. But although my intellect could understand the concept of mortality, my mind never quite bought into it. Even as our children moved into adolescence, I still thought that our family—like the jumble of shoes by the back door, the Red Sox banners hung on the walls of Henry's bedroom, the collection of carved hippos parading across Jack's bookshelf, the faded baseball caps on their hooks in the hall, the smell of Old Spice lingering in the upstairs bathroom— was fixed, like a house in which the furniture never changed. Time, I wanted to believe, was an inexhaustible commodity, and tomorrow would be like today, only better.

Realizing that family life, like everything else, is fragile, fleeting, temporal as a flower garden, has meant beginning to cultivate equanimity in the moment at hand. It has meant letting go of regret—for all that's over as well as for all that we won't ever get to do. It has meant confronting the fact that although time *is* infinite, I am not. My own time will run out.

I recently read about an elderly man who, in an attempt to remind himself to live more consciously, filled a bowl with tiny stones that he counted out to represent the number of days he imagined he might still have left to live. In good health at seventy-three, he thought if his luck held fast, he could perhaps reach ninety; to expect more years than that didn't seem realistic. And so he multiplied 17 by 365, and placed 6,375 small pieces of gravel in the bowl. Each evening before bed, he carries one of the stones outside and drops it in his driveway, pausing a moment to consider the truth of his mortality, the fact that his days are numbered—although, of course, the actual number left to him remains a mystery. Sometimes, returning his stone to the ground at his feet, he mourns the slow, steady subtraction of days; other evenings, he sifts the remaining stones through his fingers and is suffused with gratitude for all that are still left. But either way, he is aware: Each day is precious, singular, and irretrievable. And one of them will be his last. One night, the man's wife confessed that every once in a while, she picks up a stone from the driveway and returns it to his bowl, giving him back a day. The ritual has made them both more conscious—of all that we can never know, and also of the one and only thing we know for sure: This life passes away.

I'm still a novice in this work of losing and letting go. Sometimes, all I want is to hold on tight to everything—this sharp northern summer morning; my own strong body slicing through these dark waves; the eerie, urgent call of a distant loon; the cheerful cabin perched at the water's edge, tidy and snug as a doll's house. Yet moments flow, one into another. The world turns, its heart is never still. All I can do is listen for the pulse, live my life, inhale and exhale. A rumble of thunder rolls down from the mountains, echoes back on itself, its dark reverberation somber as a warning. I take a breath, dive down deep, kick hard, and head for shore.

Maude and I have our breakfast under the covers, sitting side by side, propped up on pillows in her tall bed. Her husband, John, built the tiny room last summer after she got sick, so she wouldn't have to climb the ladder anymore, extending the cabin's square footage from four hundred to five hundred. And then he bought a mildewed old headboard from a local log-home builder, sanded and bleached it and crafted a frame so that the finished bed would be the perfect height for gazing out at the lake. There is no closet, no dresser, just a few wooden pegs for hanging clothes, a shelf stacked with books, the framed view of water and woods and wilderness. We are like two little girls playing house in the deep pines, cozied up with our mugs of mint tea, our bowls of granola and yogurt and berries, the empty day stretching out before us.

By the time we've eaten, and washed the dishes in a bucket outside, and swept the pine needles off the porch, the sun has broken through. A mild breeze has cleared the sky of clouds. We change out of fleeces and sweats into shorts and sneakers, and head out into the morning on foot.

Although they can't be seen from the water, there are a few other cabins scattered around the lake, hidden away in their isolated clearings, accessible from a long strip of dirt road that runs through the woods from one end of the lake to the other. Walking, talking, we peel back layers of ourselves.

A friendship forged in midlife is different from the spontaneous, intense connections of youth and early adulthood. Some of my closest, most cherished friends are those with whom I've shared the long, winding journey of motherhood—an intimate, common history of scraped knees and potluck dinners, impromptu snowball fights and puppet shows and backyard birthdays, meandering late-night conversations after the children are asleep, last-minute scrambles for a ride for a stranded teenager, and private, tearful heart-to-hearts when the news is bad, when a child is in trouble, when a marriage is foundering, when life is just too much to handle all alone. The families in our old neighborhood, the parents of our sons' classmates through elementary school—these are the people whose daily lives have been intertwined with ours for years, and we are bound together still. I will forever love the women whose back doors were always open for my sons, the other moms who loved my children unconditionally and forgave their coming-of-age mistakes as if they were their own flesh and blood, and who are right there even now, to commiserate through the hard times and to celebrate every small victory and accomplishment.

If I were to spend my dotage in the good company of these women, that would be enough in the way of friendship. And yet even this terrain changes and is transformed by time. There is an empty seat at my table, one that no one else can fill. At the same time, I realize that even as I've mourned the loss of one beloved friend,

other friendships have blossomed, ripened, and
become more dear.

Growing older, it seems, we also grow more
adept at recognizing kindred spirits—and perhaps more willing to share the unvarnished
truth of ourselves. By midlife, it is not physical proximity or parenting dilemmas or car-
pools and bake sale duties that draw us into
close relationships, but a sense of shared consciousness, a willingness to invest more of ourselves in return for another's authenticity and
trust, and the belief that supporting and being
present for our friends is both our gift and our
responsibility toward one another. Small talk
and aimless socializing become less tolerable,
as unappetizing to the soul as junk food is to
the body; meanwhile, our need for meaningful, nourishing connection deepens.

There is, I'm discovering, a new, unexpected
freedom in my fifties, one blessedly shorn of
social frills. As time goes on, I find myself caring less about "fitting in" and more about nurturing those relationships that fit who I truly
am. I worry less about what others might think

of me, yet expect more from my most intimate friendships—and am willing to give and risk more of myself in return. Loving my friends, and finding ways to express that love through offerings of more time and more attention and more intimacy, is one of the great satisfactions of coming to the end of the child-raising season. My sons, these days, appreciate a little distance and benign neglect; my friends, on the other hand, welcome me into their lives, and into their hearts, with open arms.

Perhaps this is another unheralded dispensation of age: As the view up ahead grows darker, as loss casts its long shadow across the road, we become better fellow travelers, less intent on getting ahead and more committed instead to keeping one another well, making one another stronger, being good, steady companions on the path.

Making a new soul friend is risky business at any age, but the older I get the more willing I am to cut to the chase when I experience that "click" that tells me: This person is someone special, someone who is meant to be in my life. Maude was the first friend I made when we moved into our new house in New Hampshire. I had called her for advice on my garden, but even before our hour-long consultation was up, we had moved on to talk of books and writing, art and life. We loved the same authors, had read the same novels, but sensed right away that we share more than a literary sensibility or even an outlook on life. Perhaps what we have in common is a particular kind of sensitivity; we are both quiet, reflective, introverted, observant. In the delicate dance of new friendship, we stepped cautiously at first. But I already knew: Here was someone else who thinks and feels deeply; who often doubts the worthiness of her efforts yet continues to strive toward beauty and truth and kindness anyway; who finds it easier to put her thoughts into words on a page than to speak them aloud in front of a group; who might prefer being alone to socializing, but who sometimes feels as raw and solitary in this fast-paced, sharp-edged world as I do. Someone who might turn out to be a forever friend.

Maude is small, slight of build, thin after nearly two years of illness that took both her energy and appetite away. She is quick to tears; my first impulse, often, is to protect her gentle heart. And yet, what I admire most in my friend is her strength and courage. She lives in alignment with deep, unerring values. She quietly holds her ground. Her physical frailty is offset by a rare toughness of spirit; I'm convinced there is nothing she cannot do. And indeed, whether she is painting the kitchen walls, hauling compost in her backyard, or designing a garden for a client, she gives each task her all, gives all she has to give, and sometimes pays the price of having given too much. Struck down by illness, unable to continue her gardening business at full speed, she's confronted this most recent loss in her life by finding other ways to sing her song, other mediums through which to bring more beauty into the world.

In the spring, Maude overcame her reticence and joined my writer's group; she began a memoir, transforming the heartbreaking childhood she'd spent a lifetime working to accept and forgive into something astonishingly, quietly beautiful. Her writing is spare and brave and compelling. Each week, as the pages accumulated, she summoned her courage and sat in my living room and read out loud, sharing searing stories of pain and betrayal. What shone through was not self-pity, but a story of extraordinary richness and nuance and compassion. In remembering, and in writing her own way toward forgiveness and understanding, she gave each of us privileged enough to hear her work the courage to more fully face our own hurt, our own possibility of redemption, our own yearning for love and acceptance and grace.

Now, walking along side by side as we used to do, it feels as if there is no story or struggle we cannot share with each other, nothing we dare not venture. A circle of trust requires only one voice speaking its truth and one open heart willing to listen without judgment. This is a woman who will guard my secrets, who has given me the great honor of receiving hers. And what we find, as we walk and talk on this spectacular summer day, is that our conversation—even as we confess our fears and recount our worst disasters—is increasingly punctuated by laughter. Life *is* crazy, and yet here we are. There are burdens to be sure, but sharing the load lightens our hearts. What better way to navigate the twists in the road, to survive the bumps and bruises of the journey, than by keeping each other company for the ride, finding humor even in the mishaps and missteps along the way?

It is the farthest Maude's walked since she got sick, nearly seven miles; but somehow, without saying so, we decide to go the whole way, to the very tip of the lake, in order to stand on the wooden footbridge and take it all in—a sky that seems released, like a cerulean scarf let loose to billow and dry in the breeze; the silvery green mountains, softened by sunlight; the long blue stretch of empty lake. This is what we came for—to bask in the simple pleasure of being alive and being here. We stand gazing west for a long time, feasting our eyes on the longest view, the most expansive perspective to be had on this day.

By the time we've retraced our steps to the cabin, we're hot and hungry and tired, ready for sandwiches by the water, a swim, a rest.

We are easy together, wanting the same things from the afternoon—time to be quiet, to read and daydream and write. I lie in the hammock, surrounded by pillows and swaddled in a quilt, dozing in the dappled light, lulled by the constancy of water lapping rock, the breeze sighing through the trees. Maude sits in a canvas sling-back chair, low to the ground, with her head bent over her book; she looks up now and then to throw a plastic ring out into the water for Digby to fetch. We don't care what time it is, have no impulse to organize the afternoon.

In the scattered busyness of everyday life, it's easy to lose touch with deep peace; so much so that experiencing it here, with one empty hour unfurling after another, is almost unsettling. It has been a long time since I felt such prolonged calm, such a profound sense of belonging in the world, such pure "beingness." Time expands, the sun makes its way to the west, and then, for the first time since we arrived, the wind abruptly ceases altogether. The sudden stillness is startling, as if the world has slipped into its own silent reverie while I was sleeping. I open my eyes and look out to the water, glassy and smooth, shimmering in the sunshine like a mirror scattered with diamonds. My blue lined notebook is here somewhere, lost among the pillows. I find it, turn to a blank page, and write the first words that come to mind: *If you fear change, you will miss the abundance of your life.*

Later, we roll out yoga mats, side by side, on the dock. Four months after becoming certified as a yoga teacher, I have yet to actually teach a class; in fact, my palms are a little sweaty at the thought of leading a single soul through a yoga practice. But if ever there was a moment to begin, it is now, here, standing on this quiet shore with a friend, as the sun slides down toward the western mountains and this tranquil afternoon comes to an end.

"Yoga," writes the teacher Michael Stone, "is the restoration of intimacy through body, mind, and heart." This, surely, is what I love most about my own practice, whether I'm home alone doing sun salutations to a Tracy Chapman CD or taking a gentle morning class in the sun-drenched studio over the bookstore downtown: the opportunity to get out of my thinking, analytical, judging self and to fully experience the here-and-now immediacy of my own breath, my own body moving through space, my connection with something bigger than me.

Seeking flexibility in my hip joints, what I find is something even better—greater flexibility in my mind and spirit, too. Practice doesn't only bring more ease to a forward bend, it makes it a little easier to adjust to whatever's going on in life as well. Difficult as it is for me to accept some of the inexorable truths of aging, from neck wrinkles to hot flashes, yoga helps me to at least find a more balanced response. Perhaps I can bow gracefully to the inevitability of growing older and, at the same time, delay the stiffness and soreness and weakness that I can actually do something about—surely reason enough to keep showing up on my mat.

No sooner have we stretched out on our backs than Digby is there with us, ecstatically licking our faces as if he's been waiting all day for this most wonderful opportunity. His boundless enthusiasm is the reminder I need: Our yoga doesn't have to be fancy, it just has to be. We laugh, splash our dog-kissed faces with water, and I begin to speak for the first time as a yoga teacher—to Maude, to myself, but also to this wild landscape, allowing myself to be guided by it, carried along by instinct and breath like a leaf on the wind.

Gazing across the lake to the mountains, shaded now in hues of late afternoon violet, we stand still in mountain pose. The tall pines inspire us to balance on one leg in tree pose, sole of foot pressed to inner thigh, palms pressed together above our heads. Folding, arching, twisting, bending—I don't have to stop and plan what to say, or think about what we should do next; instead, I just lead the way and my friend follows easily along, as we flow from one posture to another, quietly absorbed in the hypnotic beauty of water, mountain, and sky, our human offerings folded into the great fabric of oneness. I can feel my thoughts begin to fly away, like birds that have been released. What's left is something words can barely accommodate or describe. Perhaps it is simply consciousness, a self that is both at home in the world and an observer of the world; at once witness to life and a fully engaged participant in life, both dancer and dance.

Coming to stillness finally, in shavasana, my friend lies down on her mat, and I sit next to her, inviting her to close her eyes, to let go, to relax into deep rest. I lift her head gently, cradling it in both my hands, drawing it ever so slightly back and holding it there for a few long breaths. Then I move down and take her feet, cupping her heels in my palms, lengthening her legs, her spine, with slow, easy tugs. My hands know what to do. In fact, I realize, my hands have always known what to do—just as I have long known, somewhere deep inside, that human presence and loving touch are in and of themselves a song, one that I am meant to sing.

My hands sang love songs to my children through all the years of their growing up, songs in the form of back rubs and foot rubs and arm rubs and hugs. I applied Band-Aids to skinned elbows, placed cool palms on feverish foreheads, danced fingers up and down restless spines, walked hand in hand with my sons for as long as they were willing to reach out and lace their fingers into mine. Now, when they're home, touch is still our first pathway back to one another, our means of being close. Sitting on the couch to watch a movie, Henry will reach out and give my feet a massage; it's his way to say, "Love you, Mom," without uttering a word. Jack was the cuddly one, the rough and tumble kid who would nevertheless sidle up and seek comfort in my lap almost to the day he became bigger and heavier than me. He's guarded now, a six-foot-tall young man who most certainly does not want to be fussed over. But he has never refused a back rub. Kneading my fingers into his shoulders, I can feel his whole body relax, the defenses drop, replaced by a sweet vestige of the affectionate little boy he used to be.

Touch is love made manifest, a way to connect not only human to human and skin to skin, but also with our universal life force, with that eternal, all-encompassing energy that unites us, that infuses us with life, that reminds us that we are indeed all one and that the world is a hospitable place to be. "The goal of life," Joseph Campbell writes, "is to make your heartbeat match the beat of the universe, to match your nature with Nature." I can't help but think that we match our heartbeats through our hands. Touching one another is what we humans do. Touch is what we need from one another and touch is what we have to give. It's what keeps us hopeful and what keeps us going, what keeps our hearts opening and softening and trusting.

I close my own eyes now, clasping Maude's small bare feet in my hands. Everything is silent and peaceful and good. I sit like this, in stillness, for a long while, listening with my whole being for the sound of Nature's heartbeat. What I hear is my life, telling me who I am.

∼ 14 ∼

flow

I am rooted, but I flow.
—VIRGINIA WOOLF

*F*or some reason, glad as we are to be married to each other, my husband and I have never been very good about remembering our wedding anniversary. There was always so much going on in those early weeks of September—school starting up again for the boys, new routines to learn, new, conflicting schedules replacing the open-ended days of summer. Usually the day, or the weekend, coincided with some regional booksellers convention that Steve was required to attend. Sometimes we'd plan to celebrate later, with a restaurant dinner; more often than not, those dinners didn't actually happen. The weeks would go by, October would come, we'd let it pass.

My husband has had his hair cut by the same woman in Cambridge for years. We still laugh about the time he came home after getting a trim from Kelly and said, "So I was sitting there in the chair and she said, 'Don't you guys have a wedding anniversary coming up?' And I realized my *hairdresser* is better at remembering our anniversary than we are." It was true. Our anniversary had been the week before. We'd both forgotten it.

That changed with September 11. On that day, I picked our boys up from school at eleven. I'd been watching the news on TV alone all morning, and had talked with Steve just after nine. He'd spent the night with a friend in Yonkers; when I reached him on his friend's cell phone, they were driving into the city, oblivious. "Turn around," I said. "Something's going on. You don't want to go into New York." They did. Steve called back later to say he was on his way home, not to worry, that he'd figure out a way to get back to Boston. Meanwhile, the boys and I headed to a neighbor's house, where the children were already putting together a baseball game in the backyard. It was almost two in the morning when my husband finally let himself in the back door; he'd managed to get on the last train that ran that day and, with a few strokes of luck, had been able to move through a world in which almost everything else had stopped moving.

The next day, September 12, was our wedding anniversary. Even though our quiet Boston suburb was no more or less safe a place to be than anywhere else on that day of stunned, bewildered mourning, I had a strong impulse to pack up the car and leave, as if going someplace more remote might somehow make us feel more secure. We'd been married exactly fourteen years ago on the small island in Maine where my parents spend their summers. The last of three rocky islands jutting out into Casco Bay, Bailey Island is connected to the other two, and to the mainland itself, by a series of bridges; nevertheless, this quiet, windswept island—a community of fewer than four hundred people, soaring gulls, and lobster boats bobbing in the cove—feels a long way from civilization.

It was just after sunset when we finally drove over the final bridge, rolled down the windows, and inhaled the smell of the sea. There is no town on the island, no real center, the closest thing to a public gathering place being the cluster of buildings hunkered near the head of the cove: a library where Carl Jung once lectured, the general store, the tiny post office, one seasonal restaurant. As we approached, Steve slowed the car. Tiny lights flared in the darkness up ahead. Coming closer, as more and more lights appeared all around us, we realized we were driving into the midst of a vigil.

We stopped the car, climbed out, and, without saying a word, joined the group. Someone stepped out of the shadows and silently handed each of us a candle; someone else lit them. Around us, a solemn gathering of women, children, teenagers, old folks, and weather-bitten lobstermen; many faces wet with silent tears. Above, the first stars pricking the severe black roof of the world. I looked down at my sons who, at eight and eleven, knew only that something terribly sad had happened the day before. Now, their dark eyes wide and full of knowing beyond understanding, they stood quietly between us, cupping their own tiny flames with their palms.

What we were doing here, hundreds of miles away from the devastation in New York City, was nothing in the face of such incomprehensible tragedy. And, too, it was everything that could be done in that moment, in that place— a hundred or so heartbroken humans standing together, offering the only thing there was to offer—faith in our interconnectedness, prayers for our healing, tears of compassion. We held our small, hopeful lights in communal silence for what seemed a long time, listening to emptiness. There was no wind; it was a mild evening. The flames burned strong and steady, illuminating sorrow.

Someone, a man, began to sing "Amazing Grace," low and certain and strong. Others joined him, a ragged chorus of voices floating up into the night. And then it was over. One by one, the candles winked out. Low murmurs, people walking away, heads bent, the sounds of car engines starting up, driving away.

We walked into the restaurant, holding our sons' hands, for our anniversary dinner.

It has been twenty-four years now since Steve and I stood in front of fifty of our closest friends and family members and spoke our vows in the small white church on Bailey Island; ten years since the planes flew into the Twin Towers and we observed our wedding anniversary by driving to Maine, holding candles in the darkness, and allowing the waitress to pour our young sons two glasses of Mountain Dew on the house. We don't always celebrate it, but we haven't forgotten our anniversary in the last ten years either. The day before always reminds us to wake up, to pay attention, to be grateful for the luxury of our lives and for each other.

This year, Steve will be attending a board meeting for the weekend of September 11, and I am waiting for a sign, something that will nudge me toward whatever it is I'm meant to do next. It's still new to me, this way of living by opening, trusting that something like grace is already at work in my life. But I'm beginning to believe it. After a lifetime spent trying to figure out what's expected of me and then trying to live up to those expectations, to orchestrate outcomes and anticipate what might go wrong, I am coming to trust that the path I'm meant to be on is simply the one that appears at my feet.

On my way out of the bookstore one afternoon, I spot a yellow flier for something called the Reiki Healing Connection. I've walked past it, tacked up here by the door, countless times before; in fact the logo, a simple line drawing of a hand with a heart in the center, is so familiar to me it seems as if it's been imprinted on my brain forever. Today, though, I stop and read the words. I already know Reiki has something to do with healing, that it's done with the hands, and that one of the country's preeminent Reiki teachers lives in the next town over; I've been hearing of Libby Barnett ever since we moved to New Hampshire seven years ago, though we've never met.

"Reiki means Universal Life Force," the flier says, "the healing energy of the universe." Back home, I sit down at my computer and Google Libby's name.

Reiki, I learn on her website, is an ancient healing technique for stress reduction, relaxation, and healing. Drawing upon the energy found in and around all living things, it uses gentle touch to heal and balance all levels of being—physical, mental, emotional, and spiritual—as well as to enhance the body's natural power to heal itself. Both a practitioner and a teacher, Libby offers two weekends of Reiki training at her house each year, a house that happens to be twenty minutes away from mine. I click a link to check the schedule. The next workshop is this weekend. Of course.

The first thing I see upon walking into Libby's light-filled, cheerful kitchen is what must surely be the most ecstatically happy, robustly rampant house plant in the universe. It takes me a while to find and identify the modest pot of origin, so all-pervasive is this vigorous vine of vibrant green climbing up the walls, across the cabinet tops, around the windows, and on, it seems, into infinity. If ever a plant could stand as a testament to health and happiness in a home, this one could. Libby welcomes me with a broad smile, a hug, as if she's known all along that it was only a matter of time before I showed up on her doorstep, as if this were meant to be, as if we are already friends.

The decor—in fact, the whole house, it seems—is devoted to hands and hearts and healing. Hand- and heart-shaped magnets, plaques, and tapestries adorn the walls. Hands and hearts are featured in paintings, in photographs, in quilted wall hangings, in sculpture. Hand-shaped earrings dangle from Libby's ears; a hand-shaped brooch is pinned to her sweater, and her necklace features a silver palm, fingers spread wide.

The living room, where I join a group of fifteen or so men and women on this Saturday morning, is serene, with pale pink walls, comfortable sectional furniture, windows open to the unseasonably warm September day. A stack of antique Bibles sits on the fireplace mantel next to faded black-and-white photos of the early Japanese Reiki masters. On every surface are Buddha statues, dancing deities, and crystals of all shapes and sizes—enormous, deep purple amethysts, said to deepen intuition, aqua aura clusters for channeling creative energy and connecting with the higher spirits, selenite for angelic inspiration, glittery spirit quartz to promote healing. The stones are compelling and beautiful, charged with mystery and with life. I feel as if I've stepped into a house of hands, a tabernacle of touch, a home infused with spirit, where work and love and life are inextricably woven together.

We go around the circle, introducing ourselves with a few words about who we are and why we came. There are nurses, a doctor, a massage therapist, yoga teachers, and psychologists; hands-on healing is already what they do, and Reiki, they say, appeals to them as a way to strengthen the flow. There is a retired airline pilot, a truck driver, an artist, a dog walker, each drawn by impulses they aren't sure they can explain. "My hands are vibrating," says the burly trucker, holding his palms up to the group, as if baffled himself. "Dogs just come and lean up against me," says the pet sitter. "They feel the energy."

And there are sick people. A woman with bone cancer is taking the workshop between hospital stays; on Monday she will return for further treatment, but armed, she hopes, with a way to bring healing to herself. Someone else has Lyme disease; a former runner suffers undiagnosed neuropathy and swelling in her leg; a recent college graduate is struggling with anxiety and depression. One beautiful young mother speaks of the months she spent in the hospital being treated for stomach cancer. "What I craved more than anything," she says, "was for someone to touch me." Now, in remission, she is gathering her courage to go back to the ward where her life hung in the balance, with an intention of offering hope and healing to those facing their own uncertain prognoses.

"I've been an editor for years, and then a writer," I say when it's my turn, "and a mother at home. But recently, I've felt my life slowly shifting in a new direction. A year ago, spending time with a sick friend, I found myself wishing I had something more than words of comfort to offer. And that feeling hasn't gone away. I think I may be done, for a while at least, with sitting alone in a room, trying to reach out and touch some distant reader with words. I'd rather reach out with my hands and touch someone who's sitting right next to me, instead."

It's true, although until this moment I've never said it, or even fully articulated the idea to myself. But suddenly, having grappled all these months with my "Who am I?" and "What now?" questions, I do know this: The path I've been on is leading me not only down into the center of myself, but back out into the world as well. Perhaps this was the lesson I had to learn down in the dark and loamy soil of the fertile void—not to question my longing for connection, but to trust it; not to dismiss my gifts as unworthy, but to allow them to change and transform just as I myself have changed.

Libby talks to us about her own Reiki journey, beginning when, as a young mother herself, she juggled raising children with a thriving psychotherapy practice. A friend invited her to a presentation about Reiki and, happy to get out of the house for a Saturday, she went along. The concept of placing quiet hands on willing bodies seemed too simple; and yet, given that it *was* so simple, she figured, there was nothing to lose by trying it. Having received the "attunement" in a brief ceremony whereby the ability to access and share the universal healing energy is passed on from one practitioner to another, she began to practice Reiki on her husband and children, the family pets, herself. The effects were subtle, yet significant enough to inspire her to continue: Reiki made people feel better, and that made her feel good, too.

Eventually, she began offering to place her hands on her patients; in time, and somewhat to her surprise, more and more of those patients professed a preference for the silent healing over the talk therapy she'd been trained to do. One day, a woman who had been stuck in therapy for years simply said, "Let's not talk anymore. Just do the hands instead." Weeks went by, things shifted, and Libby's chronically depressed patient one day declared that, while nothing dramatic or visible in her life had changed, she no longer felt discouraged; in fact, the contrary. Things were fine, she said; *she* was fine. And Libby knew she had found her calling.

Now she offers to do Reiki on volunteers from the group as she continues to talk to us. When the chair in front of her is empty, I slip into it. Without pausing in her discussion of Reiki's Buddhist and Christian origins in Japan, our teacher places her hands on my shoulders. The heat is immediate, intense, and wonderful; what surprises me, though, is that it doesn't feel subtle at all—more as if I've just been plugged into a socket and had my lights switched on. I wonder if I'm imagining things, or if everyone else Libby touches warms up like a human space heater. When she lifts her hands away, the heat lingers, seeping downward into my core. It feels as if some last, small, dark rift in the center of my being has been lovingly, gently closed. The word that suddenly lands and settles in my heart, like a bird returning to its nest, is so unexpected I don't even try to hide my smile as I return to my seat on the floor. *Ready*.

The tenth anniversary of September 11 is a day much like the one we all remember—a mild, early-autumn treasure of incandescent beauty;

of endless, benevolent blue sky, bright stillness, disbelief that anything could shatter the calm. By late on Sunday afternoon, the end of our second day, we have learned the secret Reiki symbols and the words that accompany each one. Stepping back into our lives, Libby suggests, we can use these blessings intuitively, reflexively, constantly, empowering people, plants, and animals. The Reiki path is ours to create, in harmony with our own spiritual beliefs; as Libby explains it, once we have Reiki, it is always "on," flowing as we go about our work in the world.

It makes sense: The more willing we are to align ourselves with light and love, the more freely these enlivened forces will work in our lives, and the more we will find ourselves putting our faith in that little inner voice that says "go here" or "do that." Letting go of outcomes, trusting in a higher power or intelligence, we can invite blessings on the food we cook, infusing it with love, and the cars we drive, envisioning safe travels. We can send absent Reiki healing to loved ones far away and we can bring that positive vibration to bear upon the challenges right in front of us. We can call upon the highest healing good to bring love and light into difficult conversations, tricky situations, household projects and artistic endeavors, doctor visits and meetings at work. In a world rife with distraction and disconnection and disease, Reiki offers a way to awaken our own energies of love and healing. It is simple, practical, hands-on, nothing more or less than a sensible, immediately accessible response to fear and suffering.

Having received attunements for the first two levels, we spend our final hours in groups, practicing Reiki on one another. It is yet another form of surrender, to lie upon a table with my eyes closed, as six strangers surround my body, placing their hands on me from head to toe. The touch is light, gentle, unconditional. And, as one after another we take our turns, we discover something else: Reiki flows both ways; to give is to receive and vice versa.

The point, as Libby explains to us, is not so much to *do* Reiki, but to allow it. "Hands on, Reiki's on," she says, reminding us that Reiki happens with every touch, and that we are not healers so much as instruments of healing. Our job is not to will anything to happen, but rather to invite in the best of what is meant to be, not directing the flow of energy but participating in it. And, in fact, not much does happen. Except that, with very little conversation, a group of strangers comes to know one another in an intimate, physical and spiritual way. We entrust our imperfect bodies and our vulnerable souls into the care of one another, and then, instead of talking through our troubles, we simply close our eyes, and place our hands, and allow goodness and the grace of God to rain down upon us all. There are, it seems, an infinite number of ways to tap into the mystery of life.

The crystals catch the late-afternoon sunlight streaming into the room and fling color back into the air. A prismatic shimmer dances across the walls, as fragments of rainbows appear and vanish with the blink of an eye. We have folded up the Reiki tables and put them away and are gathered back into a group, to end the weekend with a silent homage to all the losses endured on this day ten years ago.

Having spent two intensive days tenderly caring for ourselves and one another, it feels natural now to turn our focus outward, to address the wounds of the world with our own prayers of healing and remembrance.

In the years since my family and I stood in quiet vigil as night fell upon a small island in Maine, nearly every external detail of my life has changed. My children have gone from being little boys in my arms to fully grown young men with lives of their own. We live in a different house in a different community in a different state. I have lost a job, written a book, found a new way to earn a living. Dear friends and family members have departed this world and beloved new little beings have been born and welcomed into our midst. Relationships have shifted; new friends have crossed the threshold and taken up residence in my life, cherished old ones have departed. I have even begun to experience the passing of time in a different context, in the way of an older person, aware of the seasons turning faster and faster, the years flashing by.

And yet, amid all this flux and change, I

know now that there has also been some deep constancy. Over the last year, I've finally begun to sense those dark, silent roots and to touch the small, essential part of me that doesn't change after all, that just is and always has been. The part of me that has yearned, for as long as I can remember, to love deeply and well and to be loved in return. Now it seems that what I have been seeking all this time has also been seeking me, as if all my longings and questions have given rise to this one answer, the answer my own ordinary, everyday life seems to offer me over and over again: love itself.

My memories rise up through the shifting sands of recollection to meet this moment, here, now, in which another apparently random group of human souls has come together in an age-old ritual of silent communion. Knee to knee we sit, crowded together in the living room of an old farmhouse in the countryside, many years and many miles from the tragic events that inspire us to pray. And yet for reasons beyond understanding each of us has been called here today, has been given precisely this opportunity to honor our interconnectedness, to affirm our places in the great stream of life, and to envision peace—peace that begins in our own ever-hopeful hearts and extends outward from here, body to body, soul to soul, backward and forward through all time and to all living things.

I knew, on that August morning just over a year ago, that it would probably be my last walk with my friend. I suppose we both knew that, although we didn't say as much. What Marie did instead was apologize for slowing me down. We had always prided ourselves on our ability to cover a lot of ground fast, striding purposefully uphill, talking intently, giving our jaws and our legs a good workout at the same time.

"It's beautiful outside," I said. "We'll take our time."

It was, and we did. What I remember most vividly about our slow stroll that August morning is this: As we made our way carefully down the hill, back toward her house with the sun warm on our backs, we both watched our two elongated shadows, flung side by side at our feet and moving companionably along in front of us. They were like a second pair of friends, us and yet not us. I couldn't take my eyes away from that silent, attenuated pair, their bright darkness somehow symbolic of both our pleasure in being together in the moment and the unspoken sorrow that lay between us—sorrow for all that had already been taken away and sorrow for the final loss yet to come.

Soon, we both knew, I would walk alone. Even then, I was certain that when I thought about that morning later, it would be the shadows I'd recall, the quality of the light, the way our long silhouettes on the pavement seemed so jaunty and carefree, at once solid and ephemeral, almost as if they were more real, more of the world, than we were.

Last summer, vulnerable and afraid, I saw only endings—things coming apart, dissolving and failing, emptying and dying. I could not imagine a life on the other side of grief, or sadness making way for happiness, or passion and desire returning to my marriage, or an existence without children at home ever being as satisfying as the intimacy and engagement of motherhood. Haunted by questions, what I hit up against instead was the simple fact of endless change. Making sense of my life has meant, in part, releasing my desire for permanence.

Now, day after day and week after week, as I walk the roads and trails around my house, as late summer turns to fall, as the ferns by the roadside fade and crumple and the first spikes of goldenrod appear, what I notice is not endings but transformation, the poignancy of process. And what I feel is not so much fear of all the heartache in my future, though I will surely have my share, but rather a new, quiet steadiness, a sense of wholeness and strength inside me.

I suspect now that growing up—or rather, growing up a soul—must always involve a time of falling apart. How naïve I was, to ever think wisdom could come without loss, or understanding without experience. Perhaps this is what Jung meant when he wrote, "One cannot live the afternoon of life according to the program of life's morning, for what was great in the morning will be of little importance in the evening." What I left behind in my own life's morning was layer after layer of my beliefs and attitudes, judgments and fears. These were the defenses I thought I needed in order to become a better version of me, a person strong and competent enough not only to cope with life, but to excel at it. No wonder it was so hard to let them go—all those carefully constructed ideas about what it means to be a good mother, a good wife, a good person who leaps out of bed each morning to go forth and do worthy work in the world.

The great surprise of growing older, it turns out, is not greater certainty about these things, but less. Humility is, without doubt, the first lesson of life's afternoon. For it seems that only when conviction has been stripped away, and the brittle, secret invincibility of youth lies shattered at our feet, are we ready at last to face the truth: Life hurts. Shaken then, brought to our knees, we can choose to turn away and try to avoid the pain of being alive. Or we can grieve our loss of innocence, weep for all that can never be, give thanks for things as they are, and then turn our faces into the wind and

begin the long, slow journey toward acceptance. No wonder it's been said that gratitude
and grief walk hand in hand, for both illuminate the beauty of what is ephemeral and given
us by grace.

Next week, after months of planning and
fund-raising and training, a group of women,
united by their love for one extraordinary
friend, will come together to walk in her memory and in her honor. Everyone who knew
Marie has their own unique story of a special friendship, singular memories of a private, irreplaceable connection, for that was the
kind of friend she was. As her husband noted
in his eulogy, Marie had lots of friends, and
she seemed to have had more *best* friends than
anyone on the planet. Finding our way to one
another now that she's gone has not always
been easy, for what she created within every
one of her relationships was a sense of pri-
mary, specific intimacy—exclusive, intensely
personal, rare. Close as she and I were, I also
know I am hardly alone; among Marie's many
gifts was her ability to sustain and nurture
meaningful relationships with those she loved

across decades and great distances, from her most cherished childhood chum to her grad school classmates to the many neighbors and colleagues and other mothers whose lives she touched during a lifetime of full engagement with the world.

Walking on the country roads around my house this summer, adding up the miles and toughening the soles of my feet to go the distance come September, I've been alone but rarely lonely. I've loved knowing that I'm walking for a reason, and that with every strengthening mile, I'm carrying out, in some small way, my friend's wishes. There's not a day that I slather on my sunscreen, put on my sneakers, and hit the trail that I don't think of her. But I also realize that my own sadness at losing her has settled, finally, into a kind of ongoing, even comforting, conversation with the ineffable part of her I carry now inside me.

What she learned, among other things, during four years of illness was that life is not something to be controlled, but yielded to, one moment at a time. That is a lesson I began to absorb at her side, one I continue to wrestle with to this day, as I muddle back and forth between resistance and acceptance, good days and bad days, fear and faith. I try to remind myself: My task is not to choose between the light and the dark, but to develop and cultivate a quality of attention that allows me to embrace all of it, the full spectrum of experience.

When I'm uncertain or afraid, I call on her. Conversations that used to take place over the phone or via e-mail, if not face-to-face, occur now on some other, ineffable frequency, but still I lay my troubles at her feet. I hear her practical, no-nonsense voice, the unsentimental one that could cut right through to the essence of things. I hear how much she loves me, how utterly and absolutely she wishes me well. Whatever guidance I'm seeking comes from that place of goodness—wherever it is, wherever she is. And knowing that, I feel my own heart open once more and become expansive. It is in this way now that I carry on, trusting that, in some essential, immeasurable way, my friend is with me still.

*   *   *

Driving out to Hopkinton in the dark, it's hard to believe we can possibly walk all this way back into Boston in one day. Hard to imagine that our fifty-plus-year-old bodies will carry us the distance we've all promised to go, and impossible to know how any of us will feel at the end of twenty-six long miles on foot. But it's easy to remember why we're here. It's partly about the money, of course, the thousands of dollars we've each spent the summer raising for Marie's cause. But it's more than that. If our friend's illness had taken a different course, we know she would have been up at four thirty this morning herself, handing us coffees to go and her own freshly baked scones, tying a fleece around her waist, hustling us out the door. We walk today because she can't.

When we arrive at the starting point, thousands of walkers are already here, stretching hamstrings, talking and hugging, gathering into teams on the village green, lining up at registration tables in the school auditorium, picking up numbers, T-shirts, caps. The sheer size and scope of this event we've signed on for is overwhelming. And suddenly it hits me: Everyone has lost someone.

When Henry was in the third grade, a young father of one of his classmates was dying. One day, not long after he'd learned that the cancer he'd hoped to beat had returned, I brought a pot of soup to the door. Richard invited me in, and we talked for a while. A week later, his wife called me.

"Richard is going to need someone," she said. "He says he feels comfortable with you. And so we are wondering if you would be willing to come over when you can, to spend time with him."

In my surprise, it didn't occur to me to hesitate, or to tell her the truth, which was, "I have no idea how to do this, either."

I spent many winter afternoons sitting with Richard. Another friend and I taped him as he talked about his childhood in Poland, his memories of his boyhood, his struggles to find a calling and create a new life in America. Someday, he hoped, his young sons would want to know all this; someday, he believed, they would want to hear their father's voice again.

As spring came, and Richard grew weaker and had to stay in bed upstairs, I began to read to him. There was just one book he wanted to hear: *The Tibetan Book of Living and Dying*. And one parable, in particular, that made a deep impression on him, the story of a wealthy woman who cannot accept the death of her infant son. Crazed with grief, she wanders through the town, carrying his body in her arms and begging for his life to be restored. Finally, someone sends her to see the Buddha. The Buddha tells her, yes, he can prepare a cure to bring her child back to life, but first she must bring him a mustard seed. Not just any mustard seed, but one from a family that has not known death. For two days, the desperate woman goes from door to door in the village; at each house, the reply is the same: "No, we cannot help you. Death has been here." One after another, she hears the stories: "my father passed," "we lost our child," "my husband drowned," "my wife died in labor," "our son took his own life," "my mother died with fever." Finally, she returns to the Buddha, having realized that there is no house, no family, no person anywhere, who is not touched by death.

Accepting mortality at last, she is ready to hear the Buddha's teaching and takes her first step on the path toward enlightenment. Richard found deep comfort in this tale, and we talked about it again and again. Conceding gracefully to death, he came to believe, was not defeat, but rather the appropriate conclusion to an enormous effort. Recognizing his own part in the eternal, universal dance of life and death allowed him to shift focus, from trying to hold on to life to facing the fact of his death with a sense of completion and peace.

I think of the mustard seed story now, as the last members of Team Marie emerge from the row of Porta-Potties; as our captain, Carol, counts heads for a final time and calls out, "Let's go!" and we fall into place, joining the great tide of humanity already streaming toward Boston. Old and young, fast and slow, male and female, healthy and infirm, cancer survivors and those whose lives cancer has touched—stretching out before us and in back of us is a seemingly endless sea of people, an

astonishingly varied cross section of dedicated
walkers. My eyes fill with sudden tears at the
sight of all this caring, all this determination,
all this love translated directly into action. For,
of course, what has felt so wrenching and singular to the eleven of us wearing white Team
Marie T-shirts this morning has also been
lived and suffered and survived, in one way
or another, by every other person on the road
today.

There is no one among us who could offer
up a mustard seed from a house untouched by
death. Yet the human impulse to ease another's
way is strong; it is this empathy, perhaps, that
makes us human. And so we show up where
we can and we give what we *do* have to offer:
ourselves. We do what's possible. And, shoulder to shoulder, in the presence of one another,
we learn to be less afraid.

It is an exhilaratingly perfect morning in an
imperfect world. The September sun is bright
and balmy, gentle on the skin. Enormous white
bundles of clouds drift overhead, drawing the
heat out of the day, sparing us that challenge.
There is an infectious, irrepressible spirit in the

air, a combination of hope and resolution and joy. We feel it in the texts we're all receiving from family and friends, urging us on. And we see it in the crowds who gather to cheer from the sidelines; in the elderly couple who stand at a card table in their driveway, offering orange slices to every person who walks by; in the teenagers handing out water and snacks at the rest stations; in the music blaring from speakers along the route and in the waves and honks of encouragement from passing cars.

I turn around to look for Carol, who's somewhere behind me in the crowd, with her fourteen-year-old daughter and sixteen-year-old son, both of whom have jumped in at the last minute to make the walk with their mom. When I catch sight of my friend, I wait for her to come close and then fall into step beside her, slipping my arm through hers. We walk this way, arm in arm, hips bumping, for a while before either of us speaks. I know what this day means to her. How difficult it is for her to return to this route without her old partner, and also how hard she's worked over the months to anticipate every detail, to inspire our fund-raising efforts and our training, and then to bring us all together here at last, for this long-awaited twenty-six-mile pilgrimage.

"So," I finally say, "is it just as you'd hoped? Just as you've been picturing it all these months?"

She nods. "Better." And then she waves her arm, as if to take in everything—the sunshine, the scenery, the throng of walkers, the well-wishers, our own straggling, stalwart group of eleven. "She was right, you know," Carol says, looking skyward, her voice full of emotion. "There is so much goodness in the world."

It is Monday afternoon, a few weeks later, and I am driving Jack back to school after a short break. He's been home for a couple of days, visiting colleges in Boston, certain after working for two summers in the city that he wants to be there next year as well.

"We've made this trip together so many times," he says as we head south, back to the boarding school he's come to love, his home away from home. He's quiet for a minute, then he says, "I'm going to miss this drive."

"Me, too," I answer, not sure if he means he'll miss the scenery along the way, or the time in the car with me, or the sense of anticipation he feels now, as he heads back to his life at school—his friends and classmates, pickup games of basketball and pizza late at night in the dorm, trips to town on the weekends and Sunday brunch at noon, other things that I probably don't want to know about and that he's wise enough not to share. Somehow, I suspect that for him, it's all of the latter. But I know what I'll miss next year: these hours on the highway with my younger son. I'll miss having him play DJ for me, searching through his iPod to find music he likes that he thinks might appeal to me, too—the Cat Empire and Joshua Redman and Joe Jackson, a little bit of Eminem, for spice; and I'll miss these three-hour interludes, our best opportunity now to catch up with each other. We always stop for lunch on the way, talk about whatever comes to mind, take our time.

"It feels like so long ago that we drove down here that first time," he muses. "But I knew that day I'd be coming back; that this was the place." It's about as much reflection as I can expect to get from him, yet I'm not surprised he's already feeling a touch of longing in advance. Next year, he'll be starting all over again in a new school, making new friends and creating a new life elsewhere, on his own. He'll have to learn to make his own uneasy peace with beginnings and endings, how to say good-bye to a place he loves and how to make a new place feel like home. He'll have to learn for himself not to regret the passing of time. Already I feel for him, this boy who once, at age twelve, said to me, "I don't ever want to get old; I *already* feel too nostalgic for everything in the past!"

We make a stop to buy food for the mini fridge in his room, packages of cheddar cheese and boxes of crackers, a bag of carrots, a tub of hummus, twenty protein bars. For Jack, the hardest part—perhaps the *only* hard part— about not living at home is trying to survive on dining hall rations; he's hungry all the time. And so I make up for not cooking him dinner every night by indulging him every month or so at the grocery store. A year ago, he would have filled the cart with Pop-Tarts and Fig Newtons, bags of chips and bottles of Gatorade. Now he puts apples in a plastic bag, picks up a box of oranges, and asks me how long he can keep them at room temperature.

At the dorm, my son runs his duffel bag and groceries inside, then comes back out to the car say good-bye. He bends down to give me a quick hug, a kiss. He smells of wintergreen gum, aftershave, himself. "Thanks, Mom," he says. "See ya." He waves, sprints for the door, and is gone.

I sit in the car for just a minute more, eyes closed, sketching invisible absent Reiki symbols in the air and offering up the same prayer for my son that I say every day of my life: "May he be supported and guided. May he be happy, may he be well, may he be safe, may he be peaceful and at ease."

I'm in no real hurry to get home, and as always after saying good-bye to one of my boys, I, too, feel a touch of nostalgia for everything that's over. I suppose it shall always be so. But I also know now that it's okay to feel it, to allow my heart its fullness for what's gone as well as its gratitude for all that is good. On this soft October day, the Berkshire Hills are scarfed in mist beneath a pale, watery sky. Driving north, I watch the scraps of cloud shift imperceptibly, softening the colors, blending dark pine with flashes of red maple, diffusing yellow birch, dissolving the autumn landscape into a hushed, foggy sea.

On a whim, I swing off the highway onto the exit for Northampton. I've been wanting to go back; today, I have time to wander, stop in and see Eva, have a cup of coffee, look for a pair of winter boots. Walking up Main Street to Country Comfort, I know immediately that something is wrong. The store windows are empty but for huge paper signs proclaiming, 70% OFF! STORE CLOSING! Inside, the racks have been stripped clean. What's left is almost nothing—a pile of old baskets, some display shelving for sale, a glass case heaped with tangled jewelry. A shock of bleak desolation, the way the living room looks the morning after a long, good party, when all the guests have gone home and all that remains are the lipstick-stained glasses on the coffee table, empty bottles and crumpled napkins on the floor, the tattered remains of revelry. A young woman with long blond hair sits behind the cash register, reading a book.

"What happened?" I ask her. "Where's Eva?"

"Eva died," she says, just as I am beginning to take in the news on the wall behind her, covered with handwritten notes of sympathy, obituaries from local newspapers, photos of Eva and the store. "She had a kidney transplant ten years ago, and over the summer it started to fail. She knew it was coming. But still, the end was a shock for everyone. She was sixty-five, but she seemed so much younger. And she was still right here at the store the week before she died."

I stand there trying to take it in, at a loss, not quite able to believe that after all these years she could just vanish, her legacy disappearing right behind her. It seems that others feel the same way, that the entire town of Northampton has been in mourning for two weeks. There are vases of flowers, mostly wilted and drooping now, scattered across the countertops, and more cards and notes in piles everywhere. The

Edward Gorey calendar on the wall is still on the September page, a macabre scene from *The Deranged Cousins*—the kind of off-beat detail Eva would have appreciated.

I stumble through my own Eva story: my memories of coming to my fashion senses in the seventies under Eva's tutelage, my delight in returning last spring after thirty years and finding Country Comfort, and Eva herself, unchanged; my intention to come in today and finally buy some earrings, my shock at hearing that she's gone. It's clear the young woman has listened to countless variations on this theme by now; nothing I say surprises her, but she is kind, a good listener, sympathetic to my sadness and disbelief.

"Everyone loved her," she says. "It's really been overwhelming. People had such a strong connection with Eva and with the store, and no one can quite accept she's really gone or imagine downtown Northampton without her here."

She points to the case in the center of the floor. "But you can still get your earrings. That's about all that's left; Eva always bought so much jewelry. She took a lot of pride in it, and she picked out every single piece herself. There's still some really beautiful stuff here. All seventy percent off, too."

I spend a long time sorting through earrings. "Try them on if you like," the clerk says. "Tomorrow will be the last day, I think, so you should take what you want." Finally I choose two, a pair of dramatic silver drops and a pair of intricately carved sterling studs from India that I decide to wear right now, and then I select four more pairs to give away. The young woman wraps my purchases carefully in tissue paper and slides them into a plain brown paper bag stamped with the words *Country Comfort* in red. I pick up one of Eva's business cards and tuck it into my pocket and then I say good-bye.

Nothing lasts. But perhaps nothing really ends, either. I do not know how I'm connected to everything else in the universe, nor can I ever really hope to know. But what I'm finally learning is simply to listen here, at the edge of this not knowing, and to embrace life as the fathomless mystery it is. There would be no chance for any of us to get to know death if it happened only once. Instead, we are offered an infinite number of opportunities to recognize the truth: that we are both living and dying all the time. Being related at every level, utterly dependent on one another and intimately interconnected, means that each of us participates, in every moment and with every breath, in the great, universal dance of change and transformation, birth and death, love and loss, shadow and light.

Each time I watch a cascade of autumn leaves drifting toward the ground, or hear the harsh calls of wild geese overhead at dusk, or see how much my young nephew has grown since his last visit, I taste the bittersweet truth of impermanence. These changes are both life's eternal heartbeat and death's steady pulses, reminding me to let go of all the things I cling to. "By daily dying," as Theodore Roethke wrote, "I have come to be."

Driving home through the pale, transparent light of this October afternoon, I feel a quiet grief at Eva's passing, but, as so often happens these days, my sadness is intertwined with

gratitude. I realize that her legacy isn't vanishing after all; that although the store itself is
gone, Eva's gift lives on in every other estab-
lishment in a town that came into its own only
after she envisioned what was possible. She
endures in the planters full of flowers in front
of storefronts, in the swept sidewalks and art-
ful shop windows, and in the spirit of cama-
raderie between the merchants who, thanks
to her generous disposition, came to see one
another as friends and colleagues rather than
as competitors.

Perhaps our paths crossed randomly, but
somehow I think not, choosing to believe
instead that there is invisible magic at work in
all our lives, magic that sets us down on the
routes we're meant to walk, magic that leads
us to one another, magic fueling every journey undertaken in the name of mystery and
love and faith in the ultimate rightness of
things. Surely it was my soul's own compass
guiding me back to Eva's door today, so that
I might brush against her earthly spirit a final
time. Brief as our connection was, I count
Eva among my guides, for what is a spiritual

teacher if not one who reminds us by example that to live and work well on this earth is not nearly as complicated as we make it out to be?

Eva's life on Main Street stands, for me, as a testament to the fact that meaning and purpose come not from accomplishing great things in the world, but simply from loving those who are right in front of you, doing all you can with what you have, in the time you have, in the place where you are. It's not the doing that makes it special, it's the loving.

A year ago, I yearned to undertake an exploration that might lead to some new sense of purpose for the second half of my life. I wondered who I should be and what I should do, now that I was no longer needed as a mother of children at home. Aware of time running out, I wanted to make sure I didn't waste any of the days left me. Now I see that the journey was never meant to lead to some new and improved version of me; that it has always been about coming home to who I already am. It is about learning to dance along the edge between what I know and all that is unknowable. Learning how to wake up and be a beginner again every morning, even as the face I meet in the mirror reveals the lessons etched by time and age. Learning how to be at ease in the shadows of uncertainty and trusting the path to reveal itself.

Perhaps the central work of aging has to do with starting to realize that each of us must learn how to die, that falling apart happens continually, and that our own experience of being alive is never simply either/or, never black or white, good or bad, but both—both and more. Not life or death, but life *and* death, darkness *and* light, empty *and* full. Two currents sometimes running side by side, yet often as not entwining into one, our feelings and emotions not separate and discrete but instead streaming together into a flow that contains everything together and in constant flux—all our love and loss, all our happiness and heartache, all our hope and our hopelessness as well.

And just as the sun can shine through raindrops and send a rainbow arcing across the sky, my own heart is growing spacious enough to accommodate both joy and sadness at once, making this voyage toward old age not one of destination and arrival after all, but of continuous transfiguration. As I loosen my grip on the past, as I keep taking one small step after another in the direction I want to go, I discover I'm being supported and guided after all, and that as soon as I'm willing to embrace change, something or someone comes along and shows me how. Magic wasn't something I had to go in search of; it was here, within me, all the time. When hearts are open, when love is flowing, magic happens.

A letter arrives, addressed to me. The handwriting is familiar, but it takes me a minute to recognize it. My own. And then I remember. During our final week of teacher training at Kripalu, we spent an entire day in silence. Not only did we not speak, we did not make eye contact with others, or read, or use our computers, or even write in our journals. It was a day set aside just for being intimate with ourselves. A day to attend to sunlight and shadow, to the steady beating of our own hearts, to the interplay of feelings and emotions, to the spaces between thoughts, to the time between moments. Late that afternoon, as we sat on the floor, our teachers handed out paper and envelopes.

"Write a letter to yourself, from the you whom you found and befriended today, to the you who will walk to the mailbox months from now and need to be reminded," Devarshi instructed. "We will hold these letters for you. And someday, we'll mail them. I think I can tell you this: Your letter will arrive at the right moment."

I carry the envelope out to the garden with trembling hands. I have no idea what I wrote all those months ago, had completely forgotten even writing at all. I wait for a minute, looking out at the mountains, their familiar, comforting shape etched into the clean blue air. And then I slit the seal and begin to read:

What I want to say to you, my dear, is this: Just for today, live the passionate truth of who you are. Stop looking at what is undone, what you haven't achieved, where you've fallen short. Look, instead, into your own full heart. If your journey brings you to a choice between love and fear, choose love. Vulnerability is its own grace and its own gift. Offer it. Be brave enough to be vulnerable. Allow yourself to be seen—dancing, and falling, and failing, and trying again. You are loved, and all that you have to offer is deeply needed. Your own presence is a force for healing. Be present. There is more going on than you know, more guidance and support surrounding you than you can even begin to imagine. Trust it. Your own strong roots are in place—in your own body, in the earth, in the ongoing story of your life, just as it is. Put your faith in those roots, and allow yourself to go with the flow. Let go and breathe into the goodness that you already are. Move with the current, not against it. Resist nothing. Let life carry you. You have work to do. Begin it.

afterword &
acknowledgments

He was elderly, a little shaky on his feet, uneasy about the knee replacement he was to have early the next morning. His name was Dwayne, and he was the first stranger I ever laid my hands on. "I do Reiki healing," I told him, with more confidence than I felt. "It may help you feel a bit more relaxed about tomorrow."

I never know, when I arrive to volunteer at the local hospital, who will be waiting for Reiki, but usually there are a few people willing to sit and receive some hands-on energy. My job is simply to participate in the mystery of human connection, to be a channel for whatever love and light and healing is available to those who are in need.

I sat quietly with Dwayne for thirty minutes or so on my first day at the hospital clinic, resting my hands lightly on his shoulders, his thigh, the knee that was to be operated on.

"Well, that was interesting," he said when we were finished. "I felt something happen. I'm glad I came."

"Me, too," I said, meaning it. "I'm glad we were here for each other."

It is what we humans do, after all, when we're being our best selves: We show up for one another, and we ask, "How can I be helpful here?"

It is July as I write these words, a bittersweet summer twilight. Already the season is turning, the events in these pages receding into memory. But what does feel fresh and vivid in my mind, even now, is my gratitude to those who have shown up for me and for my winding journey with this book. Friends, guides, teachers—you appeared, often unbidden, just when I needed you.

Special thanks to Randall Dwenger, Ann Patchett, and Dani Shapiro for listening early on, with both ears and hearts, and encouraging me to sit down and write the questions;

Daphne Kempner and Joel Meyerson for twice offering me your Internet-free cottage where silence reigns supreme; Carol Cashion for love and truthfulness, for reading every draft, for the vault, and for always, always being there; Maude Odgers for the multifaceted gift of deep friendship in all its guises; Tracy Tobias for being my ideal reader; Margaret Gurney for saying "go"; my teachers Rolf Gates, Pam Gaither, Hari Kirin Kaur Khalsa, Alexandra Teague, Devarshi Steven Hartman, Jurian Hughes, and Libby Barnett for showing me so many ways to stretch and so many ways to love; the women of Verve for tireless cheerleading and for being such eager first-responders; my parents, John and Marilyn Kenison, for your lifelong faith; Priscilla Warner for arriving in my life like a fairy godmother, just in time to walk me across the finish line; my dearest, oldest colleague in publishing, Jamie Raab, for grace and wisdom and for so effortlessly melding business and friendship over all these years; and the rest of the team at Grand Central Publishing, especially my editor and fellow empty-nester, Karen Murgolo, who inspired me to write in the first place, publicity director Matthew Ballast, art director Diane Luger, subsidiary rights directors Peggy Holm and Nicole Bond, and managing editor Carolyn Kurek.

A hug-in-print to my neighbor Debbie Day: This book would never have been written if not for you, urging me on and then showing up day after day to do every chore with which I might otherwise have distracted myself. You embody the mystery of connection and inspire me to be better than I am.

Margaret Roach, I had no idea, when you first hailed me across a stack of bound galleys and offered me a place to stay in the Berkshires, that we would become soul sisters and writing partners. Six a.m. would be lonely indeed if you weren't on the other end of my Skype connection. You have given new meaning to the words "I'm here."

And finally my love and gratitude to my guys: Henry and Jack for challenging me, always, to grow right along with you; and Steven Lewers, for being my partner in everything. I'm so glad we are here for each other.

about the author

KATRINA KENISON is the author of *The Gift of an Ordinary Day: A Mother's Memoir* and *Mitten Strings for God: Reflections for Mothers in a Hurry*, and the co-author, with Rolf Gates, of *Meditations from the Mat: Daily Reflections on the Path of Yoga*. Her essays have appeared in *O: The Oprah Magazine*, *Real Simple*, *Family Circle*, *Redbook*, *Woman's Day*, *Health*, and other publications. From 1990 until 2006, Kenison was the series editor of The Best American Short Stories and she co-edited, with John Updike, *The Best American Short Stories of the Century*. She lives with her family in rural New Hampshire. Visit her website: www.katrinakenison.com.

1-13